A word from the Lithuanian publisher, Povilas Masilionis.

You Can't Build a State on a Foundation of Lies

When Politika publishing translated Russian journalist Galina Sapozhnikova's book into Lithuanian, the Lithuanian title was *The Price of Betrayal*. The publisher Foreword included, as a shield against our political hawks, who see "Russian propaganda" everywhere, mention of Article 10 of the European Convention on Human Rights, which was ratified by the Lithuanian Republic Seimas (Parliament) on 27 April 1995, which states: "Everyone has the right to freedom of expression. This right shall include freedom to hold opinions and to receive and impart information and ideas without interference by public authority and regardless of frontiers…"

Sadly, this failed to protect me. On 8 March 2017, a squad of 11 armed and unarmed Lithuanian "servants of justice" barged into our office, seizing the book, the company computer, and all related its files as well as other publishing documents. I, as the publisher, was taken to the 3rd Police Department of Vilnius and interrogated as a special witness.

I was interrogated in accordance with the first part of Article 170/2 of the Lithuanian Criminal Code, which was "shoved in" 7 years ago in the Lithuanian Seimas – "On USSR's crimes against the Lithuanian Republic or denying or grossly belittling it." – even though in the testimonies in Galina Sapozhnikova's book on the events of 13 January 1991 and the Medininkai murders of the same year, there is no "denial" nor "gross belittling." Rather, the book brings some clarity to these tangled cases of days past. The author's opinion is clear: the state was not intending to objectively investigate the January 1991 events or the 31 July murders in Medininkai, with documents not fitting the official version disappearing from the casefiles. After Article 170/2 which criminalized denying Soviet occupation, it became problematic to talk about these issues. But we must talk about them, because you can't build a free democratic state on a foundation of lies.

That interrogation began my "procession to Calvary" as a special witness which has yet to end.

The computer confiscated by the officers had not only the software needed for the company's work, but also the manuscripts of a few other unpublished books and photos, jeopardizing the functioning of the company.

I handed out part of *The Price of Betrayal*'s print run to friends and acquaintances for free, because the stores we talked to were scared to sell them. The manager of one of the stores let it slip why they won't have the book: the police have started checking book stores for suspicious books and a few books had been taken off the shelves.

That is the kind of democracy that is now practiced in the restored Lithuanian independence…

Povilas Masilionis
March 15, 2018

THE LITHUANIAN CONSPIRACY and the SOVIET COLLAPSE

Investigation into a Political Demolition

by

GALINA SAPOZHNIKOVA

CLARITY PRESS, INC.

© 2018 Galina Spozhnikova
ISBN: 978-0-9986947-1-9
EBOOK ISBN: 978-0-9986947-2-6

In-house editor: Diana G. Collier

Cover design: Valdas Anelauskas / R. Jordan P. Santos
Cover photo: permission from Almay Stock Photos

ALL RIGHTS RESERVED: Except for purposes of review, this book may not be copied, or stored in any information retrieval system, in whole or in part, without permission in writing from the publisher.

Library of Congress Cataloging-in-Publication Data

Clarity Press, Inc.
2625 Piedmont Rd. NE, Ste. 56
Atlanta, GA. 30324 , USA
http://www.claritypress.com

TABLE OF CONTENTS

Introduction
-9-

Chapter One
Operation Discreditation
-13-

Chapter Two
The Lithuanian Syndrome 25 Years Later
-41-

Chapter Three
And Then They Called for Ded Moroz...
-71-

Chapter Four
The Great Lithuanian Witch Hunt
-93-

Chapter Five
Romantics vs. Traitors
-122-

Chapter Six
The Lithuanian Underground
-153-

Chapter Seven
Homeland or Death?
-192-

Chapter Eight
And If You Run Out of Enemies
-226-

Chapter Nine
Without a Homeland
-261-

Chapter Ten
The Consequences of One Event
-292-

Glossary of Names
-358-

Endnotes
-367-

Index
-372-

Dedicated to the "Red Professors" —
the brave Lithuanian old men who stayed true to
themselves and taught me to never back down.

ACKNOWLEDGEMENTS

I would like to thank my family—the parents who are no longer with us, my sister and my husband—who supported me through the years and this long investigation and never doubted me.

INTRODUCTION

...As I remember all the events in the Baltics now, they can seem comical. But back then, for the first time, it was scary.

Autumn of 1991, Tallinn, Estonia. The events that brought about the new-fangled independence of the Baltic republics, Latvia, Estonia and Lithuania, were an unexpected present from the failed August Coup against Gorbachev in Moscow by hardline members of the Communist Party.[1] Here in Tallinn, there was a whirlwind of hopes and events, visions of a whole new future ahead, which would no doubt be clear and bright. There was no Lenin monument on the square in front of the Estonian Communist Party Central Committee but the Bronze Soldier from that era would stand for another 16 years. And in August 1991, there were no worries, no pain, no long lines to get a residence permit from the citizenship[2] and migration department. In Latvia and Estonia, those lines would be made up of people of Russian descent, those with whom they used to break bread, with whom they had been friends, married and started families. The Baltics' third republic – Lithuania – seems like a shining example of propriety when compared to Estonia. Lithuanians resisted the urge to humiliate those who had lived alongside them for decades, and gave rights and citizenship to all of its residents, former Russians, too.

But that was still a ways off during the first days of the restored Baltic independence. As much as I would like to call them "days filled with joy", I just can't. There are a few moments which stopped me from sharing the joy of the titular nation. This worry had been lingering since January 1991's tragic events in Vilnius, Lithuania, where it was understood that a Lithuanian protest had been attacked by Russian tanks. Estonians set up barricades from heavy boulders in Tallinn's Toompea (Cathedral Hill), dragging them there in case the Soviet tanks came, but they never did. Instead the "beacon of democracy," Boris Yeltsin, came to Tallinn, mainly to show that he wasn't like Gorbachev. To show that he was above all the other soviet-mentality people – those Estonian workers from the important factories of Soviet Union times, who demanded rights guarantees for themselves and for some reason didn't signg along with the choir of smiling Baltics relishing independence. Having signed everything asked of him by the Baltics and meeting with the Russian-speaking deputies for exactly 3 minutes, the future president of Russia fled. How else could one call the debacle with the President's secret car ride to St. Petersburg avoiding the Tallinn airport where he was expected by his compatriots, the members of the Russian minority?

Yeltsin's plan to increase his power paid off: 7 months later, the whole world was applauding Yeltsin as he stood on the tank during the August coup. And Estonia gained its first political prisoner – the Director of the Tallinn Hans Pegelman Electronic and Technological Factory, Igor Shepelevich. The official statement said that he was taken into the bullpen for supporting the State Committee of the State of Emergency (GKChP), i.e. for allegiance to the Soviet Union In actuality, he was arrested for his wise prediction: he knew how badly this whole independence story would turn out for the Baltic Russians.

And we, as official Russian journalists in Estonia, started trying to get Shepelevich out of prison even though it was highly dangerous – getting into the losing camp could have ended your career, professionally and socially, because those who defended the USSR were shunned like they had the plague. Articles were published anonymously in the *Komsomolskaya Pravda* where I then was a correspondent., There was no Russian embassy in Estonia at the time; the hastily appointed *chargé d'affaires* was a full-on "democrat", so we couldn't expect any help from him. The local newspapers were writing that all those who disagreed with the new democratic – post-Soviet, post-communist – order would soon be deported.

The "reporting people to the authorities" practice, once such a lamentable feature of the Soviet period, came back so fast, you could think it had never left. Neighbors wrote petitions, saying that they didn't need a Moscow correspondent in an Estonian house. You could hear someone's steps in the long corridor leading to the Tallinn press correspondence post and the door handle kept moving. After the things that happened to me in the next 20 years – multiple blacklisting as an "enemy of the people" in all three Baltic countries by their secret services, a few searches on the border, and one official deportation – that fear of the turning door handle seems silly. But back then it didn't seem silly, because along with other Russian residents of the Baltics, I was in the "losing" camp.

I assume that the "victors" have kept different memories from those days. Memory is selective: for example, I remember the response to the August Coup[3] in Tallinn by visions of the flabbergasted fledgling tank boys on armored cars that kept breaking down, who were being given apples and pies by Estonian old ladies. And the American embassy in Tallinn recalled the Estonian rebels' heroic defense and even found bullet marks in the Tallinn TV tower, which were left by non-existant bullets…

By the new year, we managed to get Shepelevich out of prison. And in my personal file, that was the story that started a series of my personal professional victories – the fact that we stopped events in Estonia from devolving into a "witch hunt".

…Which made it all the more surprising when I found out that in Lithuania, which was basking in its own romanticized feeling of generosity post the arrival of democracy there, the machine of political injustice never stopped for a day. Tens of thousands of people were convicted on political charges, hundreds of people lost their homeland forever, thousands of those fled their country due to the sticky atmosphere, which slowly became the only breathable air – this is what was revealed when five years ago Algirdas Paleckis, recalling the tragic events in Vilnius of 13 January 1991, made his famous remark, "As it now turns out, our people were shooting our people." This phrase cost him a few years of legal trials, the revoking of his state awards, harassment from the media and a considerable monetary fine. Lithuanian justice wasn't satisfied with that – there were separate punishments for the witnesses who supported Paleckis and told the court what they had witnessed with their own eyes... But the repression machine is insatiable and always demands more.

The trial of people in absentia for the events of 13 January 1991, which Vilnius tried to make a second Nuremberg trial, was only part of the whole picture called "Lithuania" and its new image as Europe's political prison, which I write about here with genuine sadness.

Let me advise readers: this is not just a set of interviews documenting whatever happened to the people engaged in the Lithuanian "pro-democracy" revolution, but an arduous piecing together of a conspiracy that, domino-like, would play a catalytic role in bringing the entire USSR down, and shed light on the dubious roles of some of the major players, including Gorbachev and Yeltsin themselves...

This book unites the voices of people whom the Lithuanian Republic persecuted and stripped of their homeland and good name, only because they didn't cast aside their beliefs. For not becoming turncoats as the Lithuanian Communist Party did against the CPSU platform secretaries Mykolas Burokevičius and Juozas Jermalavičius, for writing honest books like Valery Ivanov and Juozas Kuolelis did, for dying like lieutenant Viktor Shatskikh and General-Major Stanislav Tsaplin did, and those who have stood up for all of these years – like many other heroes on these pages you are about to read.

Read their stories, which no one has wanted to hear for 25 years.

For they contain the true story of contemporary Lithuania and the Baltics. Without the varnish.

| Chapter One |

OPERATION DISCREDITATION

A Short History of the Issue.

"Stop it! Stop the murder!" repeated Vytautas Landsbergis weakly, his hands shaking. But everything had already happened: TV anchor Tatiana Mitkova had refused to read the official version of the events in the Lithuanian capital, TVs were instead showing tanks and dead bodies, the world was shocked when it heard of another Soviet aggression, and Boris Yeltsin made an immediate visit to the Baltics in order to sign treaties on behalf of Russia, distancing Russia from the USSR. The leader of the Lithuanian pro-democracy Sąjūdis movement, Vytautas Landsbergis, phoned his signature in, but was in Tallinn by morning.

Vytautas Landsbergis is considered to be one of the main orchestrators of the Vilnius tragedy in January 1991 (photo from a TV screen)

And I approached him for an interview.

I was ashamed to hear his words – at the time it felt awkward to even be on the Soviet side. Prepared by the exposures of the *Ogonek* magazine[1] and taught to be repentant, Russians automatically felt guilty of any death on the planet. (Twenty-five years after that publication, it was clear that we had consciously been led to that belief.) So we, the Moscow journalists, almost broke down in tears as we genuinely felt sorry for the Lithuanians whom the Russian tanks had harmed. And in 1991, it seemed clear who were the victims and who were the killers even without anyone saying a word.

The Soviet Union was on its deathbed. Mikhail Gorbachev, so it seemed, made one last attempt to preserve it: the order to the Pskov airborne troops and KGB taskforce Alpha Group on the night of 13 January 1991 to take over Lithuanian telecommunications and stop the broadcasts of the freedom-loving "voices". Once he found out about the casualties, the last president of the USSR denounced all of his orders and said his famous, "I have never sent Alpha to Lithuania!" And Alpha Group, who had never had a failed mission until then, returned to Moscow in deep confusion...

For twenty years, no one in Russia recalled this story, not until 2010 when the former commander of Alpha, Mikhail Golovatov, was detained in a Viennese Airport on Lithuania's request. That is when it turned out that Lithuania had quietly made a whole list of people responsible for the events of January 1991.

But why, though, some twenty years later? First, the Lithuanians are not quite pleased with the new society they have built – people are migrating from the country on a massive scale. Their national spirit needed uplifting. Second, facts contradicting the well-polished legend were poking out from all of the holes – now there are books saying that it wasn't Soviet soldiers who fired on the crowd, but unidentified snipers from a roof; another book mentions their American instructors. Shades of much later events – among others, the rooftop snipers in Ukraine's Euromaidan.[2]

"Landsbergis and Audrius Butkevičius [at the time, the Director of the Department of National Defense – G.S.] have the blood of those thirteen who died on their hands. It was by their will that a few dozen of dressed-up border guards were stationed in the Vilnius TV tower. They shot live rounds at the crowd from above. I have seen it with my own eyes, the bullets hitting the asphalt and ricocheting near my feet. A few affected border guards have also told me how it happened. They tried to get the truth out through the press, but they couldn't prove anything, because they were erased from the defender lists," wrote Vytautas Petkevičius in his 2004 book *Ship of Fools*. He had been one of the founders and leaders of Sąjūdis, but was ultimately greatly disappointed with the movement. It is curious that after Petkevičius died, Vytautas Landsbergis sued his three children demanding that they publicly admit that their father slandered him. Lithuania's Supreme Court found that the children bore responsibility for their father's words…

But former Alpha commander Mikhail Golovatov didn't know anything about that, because nobody in Russia is really interested in Lithuania. His arrest warrant said: "Suspected of, while being a member of the CPSU, intentionally executing the policy of another state (USSR), while intending to illegally change Lithuania's constitutional order." It is impossible not to see the contradictions: in January 1991, the USSR was a sovereign state, of which Lithuania was officially a part, and the law he was accused of breaching was adopted in 2002, 11 years after the events, by a new state which did not exist as such in 1991.

But no: there are no limitations for conviction of this crime, said the Lithuanian prosecutors, having requalified it as "a crime against humanity".

And then Lithuania started to seek out the "formers" all over the world. They managed to catch only one of the tank crew, Yuri Mel, who is expected to take the fall for everybody. The list of designated enemies went unpublished until the last moment – it had to be assembled bit by bit.

So what if the USSR Prosecutor-General, Nikolai Trubin, back in May 1991 had written in his information letter to the Supreme Council that the Lithuanian side had provided no proof that the 13 civilians died at the hands of the Soviet soldiers, that at least 6 of the deceased were killed from above and in the back, with a minimum of two run over by cars, not tanks, and another had had a heart attack. In another instance there were 7 shots made into a dead body. The body of Ignas Šimulionis? The investigation wasn't continued, because the USSR was falling apart; all 37 original volumes of the case were given to Lithuania by Russia as a gesture of eternal friendship. If not for the words of Algirdas Paleckis and the witnesses he brought to court, the truth about the events at the Vilnius TV Tower would forever be buried under the debris left by the USSR, with new institutions of political repression built upon its ruins.

"Why did you remain silent for so many years?"

I asked the same question to everyone I met in Lithuania, court witnesses, tank crews and market sellers. All of the people, who knew of the snipers and the rooftops for all these years.

"Because we wanted independence," they all said on record.

"Why did you start talking now?"

"Because independence turned out to be worse than the Russian yoke," they all added, off the record...

What did they mean?

Over the 20 years since its independence Lithuania's population has dropped by a little over a million![3] This drop is even seen on the streets – they are empty. All of the giant industrial factories built during Soviet times are destroyed. There is no manufacturing. Out of the world of once-known Lithuanian brands only the Vilnius TV Tower remains – as a symbol of the struggle for freedom. If you take that symbol away, Lithuania will have nothing left, no struggle, no freedom.

***

MIKHAIL GOLOVATOV:
Former commander of the Alpha taskforce

"I have fought in wars and I know how bullets whistle by"

Colonel Golovatov was arrested in the Vienna airport twenty years after the Vilnius events

"Michael, have you ever been to Lithuania?" the Vienna airport border guard asks, looking at the passport owner with visible interest.

"Yes, I have," said the reserve colonel and former commander of the Alpha taskforce.

He had nothing to hide. Nor any desire to hide it: Vilnius would always remain in his memory, no matter how hard he tried to forget. At the least, because that is where a fighter died, and not just any fighter, a friend's son...

Unlike in Lithuania, the Austrian officials were competent and quickly understood that the man in front of them was no "terrorist" as he was described in the official papers by the Lithuanian law enforcers, so they let him go to be safe. That is how Mikhail Golovatov, and the whole world with him, found out that Vilnius was planning a grandiose court trial where he was one of the main criminals.

Why Has the Law Been Made Retroactive in Lithuania?

Sapozhnikova: *How can it be possible? For 20 years Lithuania hadn't accused you of anything and then suddenly they add you to an international wanted list...*

Golovatov: No, they hadn't accused me of anything. In the 90s, Alexander Korzhakob, who was in charge of Boris Yeltsin's security at the time, frequently told me: "Every time Boris Yeltsin meets with Landsbergis he tells him: 'Why is Golovatov still the commander of Alpha, even though he was part of the Vilnius events?' and demands my resignation." And I replied: "What does Landsbergis have to do with Russia? I was an officer in the Soviet Union and now in the Russian Federation and fulfilled my duty with honesty." The shifts began immediately in March 1991 and quite honestly, I can't understand why Boris Yeltsin took the stance that he did – that we supposedly did some violent actions against democracy. I was given an order and that order coincided with the actions I did, along with the other fighters. In November 1992, I retired and continued work – I was a director of joint companies with the Brits and the Americans. I was sent to London more than 80 times and around 30 times to America and never considered myself someone who had committed a crime.

And then in July 2010, I am detained at the passport control in Vienna and shown an arrest warrant signed by a Lithuanian prosecutor. And what is the charge? That I, as a communist, fought Lithuanian independence! May I remind you, this was in January 1991. And Lithuania left the Soviet Union in September. So who is being dishonest here? Why does the law have a retroactive effect in Lithuania? Laws adopted in 2002 are supposed to detain people a whole 11 years after the events in Vilnius.

Sapozhnikova: *That old story returned not just with your arrest warrant. They also started a trial of Algirdas Paleckis, who doubted the official version of the events.*

Golovatov: The witness testimonies in court only confirm his words. They included the law enforcement who did surveillance as well as common women who say it and confirm: yes, they saw the tank crews hide inside when they were being shot at from the roof. Did Russia prepare all of them? Or did I personally ask them to testify like that? No. And the charge sheet was 700 pages retelling my alleged actions during the three days I spent with my taskforce in Lithuania. You could do that much only in five years, I reckon... They accuse us of secretly pilfering from weapons warehouses and raiding hunting stores. As if we didn't have our own weaponry? How does this even fit in with the Lithuanian prosecution's accusations of crimes against humanity?

We Were in Our Own Country and Weren't Even Thinking About Using Our Weapons

Sapozhnikova: *What mission were you given in 1991?*

Golovatov: To go to Vilnius to conduct reconnaissance on sites with the aim of liberating them from their takeover. On 6 January we set out for Vilnius with two other operatives. By 8 January we coordinated our assigned goals. It was initially discussed to block eight sites: Department of National Defense, Ministry of Print, the Supreme Council, etc. But the main mission given to me was to liberate the TV center in order to organize broadcasts in Russian on all of the Baltic republics, because it was broadcasting Landsbergis' blatant propaganda. The same went for the TV Tower. The best day for this would be 11 January, because it was the day of the nation-wide strike and the majority of the protestors would be in front of the Supreme Council building. I requested around 60 armed men, who were to be divided between two sites, and we did just that. The HQ operation included Deputy USSR Defense Minister Vladislav Achalov, Deputy Interior Minister of the Soviet Union Oswaldas Pikauskas, the Deputy Commander of the Airborne Troops, Lithuania's party leaders and Deputy Chairman of the KGB Stanislav Tsaplin. The HQ was situated in the military garrison Severny Gorodok, headed by division commander Vladimir Uskhopchik. The operatives arrived on 11 January on two planes and were stationed in the conscript training center. We selected the sites which needed liberation in order to organize Russian language broadcasts and the time of operation – the night from the 12 to the 13 January – and reported it to Central Command. I think it was reported personally to Gorbachev.

From 1 am to 2 am, the first crew went out and then we moved out to our liberation objectives. We had pulled in support from the army units, Pskov airborne divisions and convoy troops, to whom we would hand the sites over for protection. There were no other mission goals such as arrests. We were tasked only with liberating the buildings from the extremists that had taken them over and retaining control of the transmitting center, so they couldn't shut it down. I divided the operatives into two groups, myself remaining in the TV Tower, because I considered it a hard-to-reach target – you had to scale up to the 32nd floor or the like, where the transmission stations were. There were around five thousand people around the tower...

Sapozhnikova: *Were the Landsbergis supporters armed?*

Golovatov: It is a fact that everything around was barricaded and that the protestors surrounded the building in a tight ring, around the TV Center and the TV Tower. General Achalov was supposed to provide access to it with four tanks. It was a deterrence factor – if the tanks start moving, then the smart people should stand aside.

Sapozhnikova: *And how did you get to the TV Tower?*

Golovatov: A closed 131 model ZIL truck. It was a tactical element, which allowed us to slip inside. Neither the tank squad nor the troopers could get to the tower. Avoiding the crowd, we advanced from the back. There were no crowds there and we could deploy. We were radio-equipped and control was handled through individual radio stations built into the helmets. We breached the windows and entered, and were met with physical resistance.

We fought in Afghanistan and were considered well-prepared, but we weren't even thinking about using weapons in our own country. Fighting hand-to-hand, we pushed the people occupying the tower out of the first floor. They activated the fire extinguishers and inert gas. We were well-equipped so we put on gas masks, but they couldn't remain there anymore. According to firefighter regulations, you must reach the 32nd floor in 39 minutes; our operatives reported that everything was under control in 15 minutes.

Neither the Pskov unit soldiers nor the operatives of Alpha Group used weapons. That is impossible. They are useless during mass riots – they will only anger the crowd.

Minus One

Sapozhnikova: *Were you aware of what was happening around the TV Center at that moment?*

Golovatov: Around 3 am I received a report on everything on the second site and I hear: minus one – which means that one of us was wounded. It was lieutenant Viktor Shatskikh. He was in the rear guard and a bullet from a Kalashnikov assault rifle hit him in the back through the bulletproof vest. If you ask me now, after 20 years, who shot him and whether it was an accidental shot – I can't say... We didn't have an opportunity to evacuate him to the hospital: the crowd surrounded the TV Center so tightly that an ambulance couldn't get through for 40 minutes. When he arrived at the city hospital, he died of blood loss...

Sapozhnikova: *And what was he shot with?*

Golovatov: A Kalashnikov assault rifle. A 5.45 caliber round. We had our standard gear: I, as the leader, had a Makarov pistol, the operatives were armed with either sniper rifles or AKs chambered to 5.45 mm AK rounds. But Viktor Shatskikh was in the closing part, the last one, and not in the assault vanguard. None of our men were behind him, so he couldn't have died from friendly fire. After the report about Shatskikh (who was near the TV center), the events that are now known as "our people shot our own" commenced at the TV tower. There were reports from the blockade leader, where the convoy troops were, that there were shots coming from the nearby houses and that there are wounded among the civilians. The armored car and tank crews who were in close proximity to the TV Tower repowered to HQ, and HQ reported to me that shots had been fired at the armored vehicles. The crews locked the hatches and sealed themselves inside. I finished my task, reported to HQ that I had secured the site and handed it over to the convoy troops and was returning to the military base where I was stationed.

Sapozhnikova: *Could there have been a third side in this? Some kind of die-hard Soviet patriots?*

Golovatov: Impossible. And I say this with confidence – I have been part of all the preparation and meetings on the USSR side!

Sapozhnikova: *What weapons were they using?*

Golovatov: Not army ones, that was evident by the sounds. It wasn't automatic fire, but single shots. I have fought in wars for 20 years before this and I know how bullets whistle by, and how a shot from a smoothbore weapon differs from a rifle round. And the shots coming from the roofs were smooth-bore. It was later revealed that Mosin-Nagant rifles were there, because the ballistic experiments were conducted immediately, when Lithuania was still part of the Soviet Union. Then it unfolded like this: I reported that we had handed the site over and that we were returning to base. I said that we would only ride in armored vehicles, because I saw the flashes on the roofs myself. Three APCs arrived, we got into the troop section and at 4:30 am we moved out to the division HQ. In four different places, they threw rocks off from bridges at us. Can you imagine what would have happened if we were in UAZ trucks under a tarp sheet? It wouldn't kill anyone, but could cripple the men. So my demand to exfiltrate only in armor paid off twice.

Returning to base at around 5 am, I spent two hours trying to get Viktor Shatskikh's body from the city hospital morgue, because they were refusing to hand it over. We managed to retrieve it only with the help of Vilnius military prosecutors.

"It is not a Wedding, it is a Funeral"

Sapozhnikova: *And how old was Viktor Shatskikh? How did he get into Alpha?*

Golovatov: Twenty one. It turned out that hostage situations at pretrial detention facilities were so common in that period that the Internal Affairs Ministry couldn't handle it. And then they started coming to us. We had to go there and conduct command HQ and tactical training, aimed at dealing with hostage rescues on aircraft and railway transport or public places, all over the Soviet Union.

During the courses in Vitebsk as part of the paratrooper division, I met with Viktor Alexeevich Shatskikh, Viktor's father. He was from the border troops and his son graduated from the Golitsyno Military and Political Academy, where we routinely draft new operatives. A capable, prepared officer – he also wrote poetry and sang. He came to us in August and died in January, having served only six months. He wasn't married and is survived by his parents and sister...

15 January we returned to Moscow on the same planes that we arrived in. Alpha commander Viktor Karpukhin and Viktor Shatskikh's father met us at the Vnukovo airport. That was a sign for me – usually when returning from an operation we would be met by one of the men from our department or a man from the KGB central office – then this time we stood on the airfield for forty minutes, we unloaded the coffin and the only ones there were Karpukhin and the father of the dead lieutenant. We buried Shatskikh on the 17 January.

In January 1980, during the funerals of operatives who died in Afghanistan, the procession would go on for 8-10 kilometers, but here I got an order to make sure there were as few people as possible. But I told them that it wasn't a wedding, it was funeral. Whoever will come, will come... If we usually were there, where trouble was – in the Union republics – well this time, the trouble was in Moscow itself. It was January 1991.

Gorbachev Outplayed Everyone

Sapozhnikova: *Right during the days when Mikhail Gorbachev said that he never sent Alpha to Lithuania?*

Golovatov: In the morning of 7 January, a delegation of Lithuanian representatives flew on to Vnukovo on the very same airplane that we came in and they were supposed to meet the president. But Gorbachev outplayed everyone. He delegated this to the president of the Council of Nationalities, Rafiq Nishonov, and the Lithuanian representatives, having had the door slammed in their face, returned home having not met Gorbachev. And later he said that it was his first time hearing of this.

But I had other information. They were going to institute presidential control in Lithuania. That was the aim of it all – to provide the opportunity to broadcast Gorbachev's address all over Lithuania....[4] And then Gorbachev declared that it was "the first time I have heard of this"...

But the HQ talked to him on the night of 13 January! I still have my memory and it hasn't been 50 years, just 20. Neither the secret service command, nor the army command could independently make the decision to use force on the Union's territory without Gorbachev's sanction. And he flagrantly declared that he didn't know of the events in the Baltics, nor in Tbilisi, nor in any other hot zones...

Sapozhnikova: *Did you realize that morning that the 13 casualties would be pinned on you?*

Golovatov: No. This happened after I returned to Moscow. Initially there was the news that there weren't casualties, but injuries – someone got under the wheels or tracks of the military vehicles when they moved in through Vilnius. And they weren't talking about 13 people, but 5-6 killed by gunfire.

Sapozhnikova: *Right now it is no longer a secret that Lithuania needed a sacred sacrifice at that moment. Audrius Butkevičius, who was in charge of the Department of National Defense at the time, confirmed in an interview, that since 1987 he was acquainted with the color revolution theorist, Gene Sharp, and that American emissaries were coming into Lithuania. Why did no one know about the set-up provocation from the Lithuanian side? Why was it a surprise that there were gunmen firing from the roofs?*

Golovatov: I think that the Lithuanian KGB at the time didn't have the agent network which could clearly relay the information to the chairman on what exactly was planned. There were assumptions, but no hard information. If I were informed of the possible use of weapons from the Sąjūdis side – then wouldn't I have placed snipers and stopped the gunfire from the roof? Having sniper rifles with night sights, it wouldn't be hard to find the sniper...

***

MARSHAL YAZOV:
Former USSR Defense Minister

Why was Marshal Yazov Put on the International Wanted List?

It would have been too easy to just write that after getting a postal envelope from Lithuania and reading "Notification of suspicion" next to his name, Soviet Union marshal Dmitry Yazov was deeply surprised... It is hard to surprise a man after he lived past 90. Especially a man like this – the last USSR marshal,[5]

Marshall Yazov is accused by the Lithuanian government of "intentionally murdering 13 people" when in reality he was never in Vilnius.

who had been through the World War and spent two years in prison[6] under suspicion of treason. But the accusations that came to the home address of the former USSR Defense Minister said that in January 1991, Yazov had "conspired" with the KGB Chairman Kryuchkov and Foreign Minister Pugo, as well as 54 other distinguished people, to "organize a plot in an attempt overthrow the constitutional order in the Lithuanian Republic"[7] and "intentionally murdered 13 people" and "caused physical pain and inflicted heavy bodily harm" upon hundreds more... All of this done without ever being in Vilnius in his whole life.

Bringing Order to Lithuania

Sapozhnikova: *Allow me to take you back to the events 25 years ago, when the foundations of the Soviet Union started crumbling and the outskirts started shaking. What did you do in Lithuania?*

Yazov: Let me tell you a story on that: while in France in October 1990 (on the invitation of the French Defense Minister) I was meeting with the President. I left the meeting and there is a group of 10-15 people with Lithuanian flags. And they immediately ask me: "Mister Yazov?" I reply "I am no mister". "Well whatever? Comrade Minister!" – "Yes?" – "We have reports that your troopers are attacking a hospital in Kaunas."

Later I found out there were a few dozen soldiers who deserted from the Soviet army; all were Lithuanian. They were probably being prepared for an armed team. Our troopers brought them back to their divisions. So resisting the open fact of their desertion and insubordination was already seen as an "attack" in the West.

In December 1990, Landsbergis and Director of the Department of National Defense Audrius Butkevičius attended the fourth session of the USSR Supreme Council in Moscow. And out of the blue they invited me and the commander-in-chief of the Ground Forces, Valentin Varennikov, to the office of the Lithuanian SSR permanent delegation in Moscow. I asked for Gorbachev's permission. He said: "I don't give a damn, go there, listen to what they want". We went there and the talk seemed neutral. Then they asked a direct question: if our people rise up, how would the army respond? I told him that there are no specific instructions concerning that. If they order it, we will isolate everyone who is against the Soviet regime.

Sapozhnikova: *And then January 1991 came...*

Yazov: Things were looking grim in Lithuania. Around 9 January, Gorbachev invited me, Kryuchkov and Pugo to talk about the necessary measures to stop this cesspool of anti-Soviet activity. The President of USSR, as the guarantor of the Constitution, obviously had that right. On the next day he gave the order to bring Lithuania into line. We had the 107th Rifle Division under the command of General Uskhopchik there, and the head of artillery was Colonel Maskhadov [who later led the Chechen separatists].

I sent General Varennikov and Deputy Defense Minister Achalov there, who was supposed to take over my position as defense minister, as I was nearly 70. They reported on the mass riots and the advance of our column to the TV center in order to support Alpha Group. The TV tower was constantly broadcasting anti-Soviet propaganda, everything was criticized and ridiculed. A small team of 30 Alpha operatives was sent there, specifically to take the tower. And they needed the assistance of the troops. We moved out a few units from the 107th division. We didn't even make it there as the ambulances started moving out from there. At the same time, the army column started getting hit by rocks, bottles with flammable liquids and there was gunfire from a nearby roof, aiming at the crowd and the APCs. The soldiers hid in the armor.

By morning, it turned out that 13 local residents had been killed and Lieutenant Shatskikh from the Alpha Group was mortally wounded, and had been hit in the back... The prosecutor-general's men arrived. I ordered the military doctors to the site. We wanted to examine everyone: who was wounded, where and how had it happened? But neither the prosecutors, nor doctors were allowed to see the bodies. The Lithuanians desperately needed to prove that we were the cause of all this.

Varennikov and Achalov reported that they didn't fire a single shot. But they were shot at.

Sapozhnikova: *Vilnius had local police and KGB. With such a selection of law enforcement, why was it necessary to call in the army?*

Yazov: The thing is that on 11 March 1990, the Lithuanians had already declared themselves independent and the local law enforcement agencies had stopped working. Everyone, including the KGB, took orders from Landsbergis.

Sapozhnikova: *Was everything set up in a way to drag the army into the mix?*

Yazov: Everything was set up to cause mass discontent. They had to get the Soviet troops out of Lithuanian territory. How does one do that? Spill blood and provoke them. That is what they did. They outplayed us. Killed their own in order to win.

"At Least No One Killed Anyone"

Sapozhnikova: *The newspapers called the Vilnius events a rehearsal of the August Coup in Moscow against Gorbachev.*

Yazov: A lot happened before the coup. You could say that the Politburo ceased to exist at that point. When Gorbachev became president, he created the Politburo from the Republics' communist party secretaries. Lithuania's communist party split into two, so it had two representatives. Each one was trying to be independent. And the newly-developed Charter of the Union of Sovereign States[8] did not have unanimous support. Gorbachev thought that a few republics would sign the document and the rest wouldn't be able to do anything about it. And so on 19 August 1991, he called the first secretaries of the five Central Asian republics and Russia in order to sign the Union Treaty. The others didn't agree.

We knew about this, all of the ministers did, including the Prime Minister, Valentin Pavlov and Gorbachev's Deputy, Gennady Yanaev. It should also be mentioned that the Union Treaty was published on a Friday night, when everyone left to their dachas. No one read it during the weekend. And they had to sign it on Monday. To put it simply, Gorbachev et al. wanted to fool them.

As a considerable government majority, we gathered at a KGB site to discuss the situation. It was critical, with the events in Azerbaijan and Armenia, with the Armenians taking over Karabakh and the Azerbaijanis clearing out all of the Armenians from Baku. Not everything was okay in Fergana, Kyrgyzstan and Uzbekistan, Crimea, or Georgia, where the Meskhetian Turks wanted to claim their lands. Altogether the situation was stressful, mainly with national issues.

Instead of taking means to stabilize the situation, Gorbachev started developing the treaty of sovereign states. Shaimiev (Tatarstan) and representatives of the other republics started wondering: how are we any less, we also want independence. How else were the republics inside Russia to react? We also considered the issue unresolved, so signing the treaty would be a means to destroy the Soviet Union.

17 August, Shenin, Baklanov, Varennikov, Plekhanov and Boldin arrived at Foros to meet with Gorbachev. I was to remain in Moscow, so if we got hit by missiles, someone would be there. Gorbachev refused to meet with them for a while, but when he eventually did, he asked "Why did you come?" And everyone explained that he needed to take measures to preserve the countries, that the will of the people is the highest will for the government.[9] He cursed at them and told them they could do as they pleased. That was Saturday.

Sunday 18 January, I organized the protection of the TV center in Vilnius, but no one came to speak on television. Instead, the station ran Swan Lake.

And then suddenly the Airborne Troops commander, Pavel Grachev, calls me and says that Yeltsin requests guards. I sent a battalion. I couldn't imagine that that would be used that as proof of the army wanting to attack the White House. Then they showed the movie: Mstislav Rostropovich is sitting there with gun and a soldier is sleeping in his lap... No one was even planning to attack them!

We gathered in my deputy Vladislav Achalov's office and Marshal Akhromeev came to ask what was happening. I told him that nothing big was happening – just us wanting to stop them from destroying the Soviet Union. But while Gorbachev was against declaring a state of emergency, the comrades were wondering how to stop the signing of the treaty by the five republics. I went to the Kremlin to see Pavlov. The treaty signing was aborted, and once again, we flew to Gorbachev. I knew that I would be arrested upon my return to Moscow, I was informed of this via telephone right on the plane. Soldiers in police uniforms were already on the airfield. Barannikov [the head of the RSFSR[10] police] invited me to a room along with prosecutor Stepankov. "Are you armed?" he asked and I replied "No." He added "Then you are under arrest."

I could have told them to go to hell and gone for the car. Achalov called me on the phone: "We can take over the airport if you want." And I said "No." If we took over airfields then we could have started a war. I didn't go there. And at least I didn't kill anyone.

And Again, They Shot From the Roofs!

Yazov: In Lefortovo, it became clear that three men died in Moscow. And again, someone was shooting from an attic. But our soldiers couldn't shoot. So it means that they shot with the approval of either Yeltsin or the American embassy.

Sapozhnikova: *Just like in Lithuania... By the way, during the operation in Vilnius, did you keep track of all rounds fired?*

Yazov: Not a single one. No one fired a shot; we hadn't handed out live rounds. When they started investigating, there were only rifle rounds, PPSh submachinegun rounds and hunting rifles.

Sapozhnikova: *Gorbachev said that there needs to be an investigation in Vilnius, you took that literally. And what was the situation later on? On the night of 12 January and 13 January, when the operation was underway, did you report this to him or was he unaware?*

Yazov: Gorbachev knew everything. He said "undertake measures", and I will repeat, I sent Varennikov and Achalov there. Also I called Uskhopchik and told him that they were now responsible for everything. No one from the military went there until 13 January. And not only did no one shoot in the city, they did not even go into it, as to not provoke the situation.

Sapozhnikova: *Was the operation plan developed beforehand or was it a spontaneous decision?*

Yazov: Nothing was planned in advance. It wasn't all of Alpha that went there, just 30 operatives. And not all of the division, maybe one battalion, no more. It was reported that a lot of ambulances were going around town. But no one amongst us knew how many were dead or wounded.

Sapozhnikova: *Did you report to Gorbachev that night?*

Yazov: I reported at all times. When he called, I reported.

Sapozhnikova: *This was the third conflict on Soviet territory. Before this, blood was spilled in Baku and there was a shady story in Tbilisi. Was the technique the same or were the conflicts drastically different from the Lithuanian one?*

Yazov: I'll explain. In January 1990, Gorbachev called for me, the USSR KGB Chairman Kryuchkov, and Interior Minister Bakatin, ordering us to immediately fly to Baku, declare a state of emergency and bring order. We immediately set out to the Chkalov airfield and were in Baku in two hours. Someone took down the TV broadcasts. In 2-3 days, we restored the *First Channel*. But the Popular Front was already setting things up and ordered to close the door for the military. And I get a report that the APC are traveling with the hatches sealed, because there is gunfire from the windows and roofs... The 295th Motorized Rifle Division was on high alert. Soldiers were lined up at the square of the "Krasny Vostok" military settlement. Someone opened fire on them from the roof of a children's hospital. A few soldiers were wounded and killed.

Sapozhnikova: *Gunfire from the roofs once again? But we had a whole collection of the smartest specialists. Why didn't anyone see that the same tactic is repeating itself time after time?*

Yazov: Could anyone of ours even get into an attic near the Vilnius TV tower? We weren't allowed there. The same thing happened in Baku. The gunner was in the hospital that was outside of the military settlement's limits. By the time we arrived at the hospital, there would have been no one on the roof.

Perestroika: Lift Off with No Landing

Sapozhnikova: *Is the Tbilisi army shovel story from the same line?*

Yazov: That one was a bit different. The Central Committee bureau and the First Secretary Patiashvili got together and decided to ask the Commander of the Transcaucasia Military District, Igor Rodionov, to liberate the square from the protesters. The soldiers advanced in a line and stones started flying on them immediately. They protected their faces with their army shovels. The armored vehicles were driving the protesters back and it was the people who stomped on each other. Later, the very same Patiashvili spoke at the Supreme Council sessions and said that troopers chased down an old lady for 3 kilometers... Then they announced that people died from suffocating gas. The chemists ran tests and there were no gases found on the spot. All of the casualties were from the crowd stampeding, but the army still got the blame. Patiashvili, who made the decision, blamed it all on Rodionov.

Sapozhnikova: *Why didn't you deflect this information attack?*

Yazov: We did all we could. But they sent Shevardnadze to figure it out instead of me. And they "figured out" that allegedly the army was responsible for everything. Then there was also the Supreme Council commission headed by Sobchak, which established that people indeed died in the stampede. But they also blamed us for sending in APCs, saying that we should have used the radio and told the crowd to go away. Simply put, they found a way to blame the army.

Sapozhnikova: *So, in just two years there were multiple operations aimed at discrediting the army. Why didn't you make this public back then? Or did the public not want to listen?*

Yazov: We couldn't do anything without the Commander-in-Chief's knowing about it. Gorbachev had it tough: the country had too many problems at the time. And with Tbilisi, he personally gave me my mission, the same with Baku and with Vilnius. When Perestroika started, no one knew what it was. Writer Yuri Bondarev said in one of the sessions: Perestroika is somewhat like an airplane that has taken off, but doesn't know where to land, because no airport is designated. Same thing here, they announced Perestroika, but what does it mean and how will it end? As it was the destruction of the Union.

Sapozhnikova: *Are you preparing a defense? What is it like to suddenly become likened to a war criminal? Or maybe you're indifferent to what the Lithuanian prosecution thinks?*

Yazov: Of course, I am not indifferent. But protect myself, how, exactly? I was never in Vilnius and I need to go there to prove that I didn't kill anyone? They will just say that I gave the order. But I gave the order, "bring order" and you could interpret that in a lot of ways. Nevertheless, we didn't shoot anyone.

What do they want to try me for?

(Interview conducted along with Viktor Baranets)

***

GEORGY OSTROUMOV:
Gorbachev's aide

"The Model for Breaking Up the USSR was Borrowed from the Baltics"

"Mikhail Gorbachev had nothing to say about the events in Lithuania. He has said everything," his press secretary replied tiredly to another, probably the millionth and hopeless, request to get an answer from Gorbachev on whether he gave the order to "bring order" to Lithuania or not.

Alexander Gamov from *Komsomolskaya Pravda* has had multiple interviews with the first and last president of the USSR.

And on my request he asked him a few questions. Here is what Gorbachev said:

> All of the talks about me puppeteering or executing some kind of scheme, as well as me organizing the coup... What kind of a fool would Gorbachev be? We made a program on how to escape the crisis; it was even supported by the Baltic countries. We prepared a new treaty and published it in the newspaper. The party had a plenum in July, and another congress was scheduled for November in order to introduce the reforms. We were on this wide road... And I ask, with this sensitive, but positive process underway, why would Gorbachev want to shoot from around the corner on some, and then on the others? Could it be that they misunderstood Gorbachev? Could it be that they knew his weakness and called it indecisiveness. But as soon as people started getting killed in riots – well that's Gorbachev... Sometime after all of those events, there was an anniversary of the Alpha Group's foundation. A group of the Alpha operatives went up to me and said: "Mikhail, we published a book!" and everything was described there. And it turns out that aside from the Politburo decision, Yazov and Kryuchkov also decided to gather forces and be ready for a chance to strike.
> - In Vilnius?
> - In Vilnius. The plan was written by hand in a textbook.
> - Back then, did they report to you that the shootings around the TV tower were Sąjūdis provocations and not the work of the Soviet soldiers and Alpha?
> - They told me even back then that there were shots in the back.

That is how that interview went. Mikhail Gorbachev won't say anything about that story.

So instead, his aide Georgy Ostroumov will act as his voice, seeing as he agreed to face the music, unlike his boss.

August Coup Rehearsal

"Gorbachev was the least interested party in the Vilnius events turning out the way they did," said Mr Ostroumov confidently, immediately as he entered the office.

Sapozhnikova: *But could the troops have acted on their own?*

Ostroumov: They weren't acting on their own! According to the documents that were uncovered after Gorbachev's resignation, the troopers sent him excerpts from Mikhail Boltunov's book, where he talked about all of it being a purely a State Committee on the State of Emergency's military operation. Gorbachev had absolutely nothing to do with the operation. He didn't give any orders, nor could he give them. Because it was a rehearsal of the August Coup. That is what I think.

Sapozhnikova: *It seems we understand this rehearsal differently. I was told this story that a few years ago in the Białowieża Forest Alexander Lukashenko hosted a conference on the 20th anniversary of the Soviet Union's dissolution. And the former head of the German Democratic Republic, Hans Modrow, took to the stage in front of the whole place and said "During the August Coup I was in Foros next to Mikhail Gorbachev's dacha. I saw the August Coup on TV and thought that Gorbachev was arrested. I went out and ran down the road near Mikhail's dacha and saw... that he was taking a peaceful stroll with his wife Raisa, along with the guards, smiling and laughing!" How are we to make sense of that?*

Ostroumov: Gorbachev was showing that public that he was healthy! On the famous press conference, where Yanaev's hands were shaking, it was said that we would be presented with documents speaking of Gorbachev's sickness. When Raisa Gorbacheva heard of this, she had a stroke because she knew of the KGB's methods and how they could make a sick man from a healthy one. Scary things were being planned, but not one doctor agreed to give a false paper on Gorbachev's illness. Gorbachev's top brass and Yeltsin were playing the same game. One side needed to smear Gorbachev with various violent actions, and the other needed to get rid of him. The people had yet to hear of these events, but there were already protest movements calling for Gorbachev's retirement.

Yeltsin Was in a Hurry

Sapozhnikova: *Back to Lithuania, where the fateful events were underway. Commander-in-Chief Gorbachev finds out that the special forces were dispatched to take over the TV tower against his will and people were killed. Why doesn't he fire Yazov and Kryuchkov, why doesn't he punish the leader of Alpha?*

Ostroumov: When Gorbachev found out about the Vilnius events in the early morning, Kryuchkov was the first one he went to. Kryuchkov said that he never gave such a mission. Then Gorbachev went to Yazov, who in turn said that the operation was requested by garrison chief Uskhopchik, which is quite suspicious. Boris Pugo said there was no order from Moscow to send the tank column to the TV tower. Gorbachev tasks the prosecutor's office to investigate this.

Sapozhnikova: *Well if that is what happened, then you needed to gather the Politburo and just arrest Kryuchkov and Yazov right in the office. Why wasn't that done?*

Ostroumov: It is not as easy as it seems. Do you remember what was happening in the streets of Moscow at the time? You could hear the howls and calls for Gorbachev's retirement. In that situation, Gorbachev didn't see that as a possible course of action.

Sapozhnikova: *If I follow your version of the events, then the tragedy in Vilnius happened completely without Gorbachev's participation. Who also took no measures, didn't fire Kryuchkov and Yazov, didn't exclude them from the party and didn't arrest them. If all that is true, then Gorbachev made the biggest political mistake and pre-emptively dug a grave for himself, which later led to his resignation and the August Coup.*

Ostroumov: I would watch my words about a grave, but altogether, I agree. You also can't discount the Yeltsin factor. The model of the Soviet Union's dissolution – namely the idea that the Russian laws are above the Union ones – was directly taken by Yeltsin, from what he said in the Baltics. But going back to the August Coup. They published Kryuchkov's personal letter to Gorbachev, where he asks for an audience and repents for what he has done. There is also the Yazov interrogation. And suddenly the turning point in the whole case – they start changing their testimonies and blaming everything on Gorbachev. You are doing the same thing now – trying to pin it all on Gorbachev. And he is the one who got the least out of it. On the contrary, Gorbachev didn't want to lose Lithuania. He saw it like this: you need to act within legal bounds. And at that point, there was a law on how to exit the Soviet Union. We must agree on the rights of the Russians and the Russian-speaking population and not just cut ties and jump off, as if getting off a bus. Who stopped that? Yeltsin, who was in a big hurry…

Breakthrough or Defeat?

Sapozhnikova: *And the fact that Gorbachev closely conversed first with Reagan and then with Bush and trusted them completely? Did he understand that the Americans were playing him?*

Ostroumov: Two great superpowers with the fate of the world depending on them started talking to each other with trust – that is Gorbachev's colossal breakthrough. But who outplayed who is a big question.

Sapozhnikova: *There were two groups around Gorbachev: one of them was liberal – Yakovlev, Shevardnadze – and the other was later closer to the August Coup. But Yakovlev was always close to Gorbachev. And he said numerous times, that his goal was to "break the back of the thousand-year Russian statehood and destroy the communist system from within."*

Ostroumov: I have never heard Yakovlev say that, but if he did, then that is just absurd. You can't trust words, trust the documents. I clearly remember how Yakovlev spoke of Leninist-Stalinist fascism. We shrugged. But the idea that Yakovlev was an architect of the Perestroika is a huge exaggeration. Right now everyone is acting like during the August Coup and blaming everything on Gorbachev. It is stupid, counterproductive and provocative.

"He Paid for It"

Sapozhnikova: *If Gorbachev got word that there were gunmen on Vilnius rooftops, why didn't he move to protect Alpha?*

Ostroumov: That is one of the reasons why he didn't retire Yazov and didn't persecute anyone. Because there was outrage against Gorbachev and against the Soviet Army.

Sapozhnikova: *Why didn't Gorbachev accuse the Lithuanian government of the provocation?*

Ostroumov: He was receiving contradictory information from different sources. And he was weighing in on implementing presidential rule there. By not implementing it, though, Gorbachev avoided civil war in Lithuania.

Sapozhnikova: *Then why did he send troopers there?*

Ostroumov: Go ahead and say that Gorbachev is responsible for everything, that he is a traitor, like the newspapers write. I am not going to refute that.

Sapozhnikova: *But his fault as a political leader is obvious....*

Ostroumov: Gorbachev's actual responsibility in the events that happened is undoubted, but he paid for it.

| Chapter Two |

THE LITHUANIAN SYNDROME 25 YEARS LATER

The scenarios of all emergencies of the former USSR were similar: Mikhail Gorbachev constantly slept and seemingly had nothing to do with anything, the military resolved issues on its own, and the civilian population just sang songs, with colored ribbons attached their chests... But here is the interesting part: in December 1991, Gorbachev left the stage, while the drama throughout the territory of the former USSR continued. Especially, nonviolent coups. The suspicion that for the first time we had encountered the color revolution tools in the late 80s in the form of Estonia's Singing Revolution in the Baltics appeared long time ago. But for some reason, on the Tallinn streets, I didn't bump into the American, Gene Sharp, the author of all these tools. As it turned out, he had to be sought in Vilnius, rather than Tallinn.

AUDRIUS BUTKEVIČIUS
Minister of National Defense, Lithuania

"We ruined the picture for the Russians"

This became evident from the interview with political strategist Audrius Butkevičius, who was the Director of the Department of National Defense in the early 1990s. By the way, he is being named as the main orchestrator of the January 1991 drama.

Gene Sharp's favorite student Audrius Butkevičius successfully used his teachings in the field.

He has a striking and extraordinary personality -- one of his majors was psychotherapy. In 2000, he gave a rather explicit interview in the Lithuanian paper *Obzor*, in which he admitted that on 13 January 1991, he deliberately aimed for civilian casualties. He held no regrets, since the deaths "delivered a powerful blow to two main pillars of the Soviet authority, the army and the KGB," which never recovered. "Yes, I planned to place the Soviet army in a very uncomfortable psychological position, so any officer would feel shame for being there." We have to admit, he did a great job... Later Butkevičius said that the *Obzor* journalist made everything up and even went a little crazy, but didn't demand the paper to do a retraction.

We met several times, each time going back to one subject, so the conversation below is compiled of several interviews. We argued and debated, clearly understanding that we will forever remain on different sides of the barricades, yet, nevertheless, it didn't stop us from talking, because a smart and experienced adversary deserves respect.

It Wasn't a Revolution!

Sapozhnikova: *I would die to see a man who saw Gene Sharp in person!*

Butkevičius: I not only saw him but was a guest at his house! In mid-90s, I worked for a whole year for him in Boston, at the Albert Einstein Institution.

I began to exchange letters with Gene Sharp and his colleagues back in 1987. Back then, I was working in a psychology and sociology studies lab at the Kaunas Institute of Cardiology. I took an interest in psychological warfare. Sharp had developed a technique that was able to use large groups of people in acts of civil disobedience. I was getting into politics at the time, so I got interested.

Sapozhnikova: *How did you manage to freely communicate with foreigners at the time of total control, as they call it?*

Butkevičius: We had letters. People were travelling abroad. The Lithuanian emigration was quite massive. First time I saw him, Sharp was already in Vilnius. He arrived in February 1991.

Sapozhnikova: *At the pivotal time of Estonia's Singing Revolution?*

Butkevičius: It wasn't a revolution. It was another wave of the national liberation movement. After the Polish-Lithuanian Commonwealth was partitioned, we had rebellions every 30 years. In 1795, in 1830, and so on.

Sapozhnikova: *What we observed from 1988 to 1991 on the territory of the Baltics, was it a color revolution crafted by the classic recipe of Gene Sharp? The one that was repeated in Serbia, Ukraine, Kyrgyzstan and Georgia?*

Butkevičius: Absolutely not! We employed many of the techniques Sharp described. But these techniques were being used by people in different countries, the Buddhist monks, the students during the resistance in Czechoslovakia and Poland, and even in various states of Africa. Sharp simply combined all that experience and created a solid theory, designing a real psychological warfare strategy, where civil disobedience is used as a primary weapon. He was crafting a tool for people to fight the regime for their ideals. It is not a scientific approach, but rather a religious one.

I was happy to be seriously involved in the process. Having medical education with a psychology major, I understood how to use the idea. And that power is very dependent on people. Once a man stops obeying, the strength of authority completely fades away. To teach a man not to be afraid, to act as a team, that was my goal. Sharp never organized such things himself. We had a good partnership: on one side, people were willing to adopt his theory, on the other side, we had Sharp's books and insights. And on our side we had a good organizational force.

"We Outplayed Moscow"

Sapozhnikova: *Did you work in all three republics simultaneously?*

Butkevičius: When we began, he had no contacts in Latvia and Estonia. We practically assumed the role of disseminators of his ideas. In the 90s, I became the Director of the Department of National Defense, later the Minister of Defense of Lithuania. In establishing this department, I was resolving an issue of how to act. Should I emulate the strategy of a big state or should I create a petty army with 19th century muskets, thinking it can do something against the Soviet troops? I decided for sure that we can't afford the mistakes our fathers and grandfathers made.

For us, it was crucial to utilize the tools of psychological warfare. Before the August Coup in Moscow, using the techniques of civil disobedience was our main strategy. We had small armed units; their purpose was not to let people say that Lithuania wasn't resisting occupation. Sharp was one of the most useful people, who came at our aid. A lot of speculations are going on around his name without understanding that he only formulated key principles.

Sapozhnikova: *But Sharp's techniques exclude bloodshed. Blood got spilled on 13 January in Vilnius...*

Butkevičius: You misunderstand. The option to use armed forces or to cause physical harm is excluded. But if you are talking about moral, psychological, economic, financial force, the opposite is true – such option serves as the lead engine. We knew quite clearly what actions the opponent would take, and hoped for a conflict in Lithuania between Lithuanians and Russians, and for the army to arrive to restore order for the sake of protecting the Russian national minority.

The Soviet security services prepared for the events to fall under this scenario, and invited foreign journalists to Lithuania to witness the lawfulness of the use of military force. But we outplayed them in a different way: we convinced the local Russians not to participate in the game on the side of communists. Gorbachev and his team had everything ready except one thing – the Russians, who were to go to fight the Lithuanians, didn't show up. And, since the order was already issued, the tanks rolled in and charged right through the crowd of people surrounding the TV tower. The foreign journalists and camera crews shot the whole scene. We didn't need to stage anything.

Sapozhnikova: *Then why do they call you the orchestrator of those events?*

Butkevičius: In reality, we just switched only one frame in the opponent's plans, we didn't allow the local Russians to participate in Moscow's script, and ruined his picture.

Precisely that was my direction. I mean, it wasn't me, who gave an order to fire guns in the peaceful city! I accept the responsibility solemnly for us using the nonviolent struggle techniques in a situation where people could die. I have many Russian friends, who were beside me that day. I was organizing a so-called international battalion with many Russians, 500 men from Moscow and St. Petersburg. They joked that I would rally them first against tanks and APCs. Because afterwards I could have dragged all of Russia into a war on communists. And they were right, I would have done it.

"The Shooters Weren't Ours"

Sapozhnikova: *At Algirdas Paleckis' trial, the witnesses testified that people did not die at the hands of Soviet troops. Bullets were flying from the rooftops, into people's backs.*

Butkevičius: Quit this nonsense. I can present you with a thousand witnesses claiming it was the other way around. Paleckis just has some kind of a support group made up of people, who lost everything during the collapse of the Soviet Union. Now they talk rubbish.

All the bullets, extracted from the dead or wounded, are in a case file. As a person knowing what was about to go down, it wasn't in my interest to take actions that would help the opponent to justify a moral, psychological or legal right to attack us. I can only speak for my party: we didn't shoot and had no intentions to do so. If someone proves that there were certain shooters, we have to investigate, who dispatched them. I knew exactly what was going to happen. Aware of the Soviet armored vehicles preparing to enter the city, I briefed the National Security Council. We adopted a decision to use civilians. I always accept responsibility for using the nonviolent struggle techniques in a situation when people could die. But such a decision was made. And saying that our side used something additional, like fire, is totally stupid. I pose a counter question: who gave an order for armored vehicles to move into the city? Who gave an order to fire tank guns?[1] I didn't do it!

Sapozhnikova: *Not you... You, understanding, that there might be carnage, nevertheless, sent your people to the TV tower with your nonviolent methods, understanding, that they might die.*

Butkevičius: Yes. I am not running away from this responsibility. I will tell you more: if we would have executed a different technique in defense of our state, a lot more people would have died. For instance, if we had decided to defend ourselves, using old guerila warfare methods and firing outdated guns. Or if we had thought of playing toy soldiers, then more people would have died. In our case, this many died. And the responsibility rests on the people who rammed pieces of military hardware into a peaceful city.

The Army Lost Face

Sapozhnikova: *Does your conscience bother you?*

Butkevičius: Answer me, was I in charge of the tanks? Did I give an order to deploy military hardware? Did I command tanks and guns to fire? When seeing this, I thought that the people in Moscow had gone mad. They could act like that only if they wished to help us gain independence at the fastest pace. What happened after the Soviet troops in Vilnius attacked a peaceful city and unarmed people? The army was humiliated.

Sapozhnikova: *But in your interviews, you clarify that that was one of your objectives, to undermine the two last pillars of the Soviet power, the KGB and the army. Which means, you bear a share of the responsibility...*

Butkevičius: The Soviets themselves made the same mistakes, whenever they could. Who sent them against the people in Prague? Or in Budapest? I want you to understand, that when we stopped Gorbachev and his team, that was more because of your and your Russians' deeds, than ours. You had to be complete fools to react to the events in such a fashion. The Soviets just didn't comprehend that it wasn't year 1956 in Hungary or 1968 in Czechoslovakia. They didn't get it that they were standing in front of CNN and BBC cameras and TV journalists from the whole world.

Sapozhnikova: *By the way, how did you manage to pull so many of the press into Vilnius?*

Butkevičius: The KGB was stationed at the borders. It was the Soviet authority, who pulled all the folks here to showcase a totally different picture than the one actually happening. They wanted to demonstrate the battle between Lithuanian nationalists and the Russian-speakers. But we extinguished that possible conflict, and the army charged into a totally peaceful crowd.

"I Was Against All the Showing-off"

Sapozhnikova: *Are you satisfied with what happened with the country you built?*

Butkevičius: Obviously, not. I am not happy with the fact that Lithuania had lost the most important thing we fought for – independence. Back when Lithuania was joining the European Union, I was among the few who believed that we shouldn't do it. When Lithuania went out of its way to adjust to European standards, getting into debt, we were vehemently opposing it. We criticized the government all the time for the debts, which piled up in Lithuania. The government didn't build and didn't create anything new that could jumpstart our country to the next level. Everything was squandered and embezzled. The fact that Lithuania today obediently listens to the masters from the European Union is also one of the biggest sins of the current Lithuanian authorities. I can say the same about NATO. The government constantly covered itself with the words that NATO will help us. The issue of security was put aside. The authorities were showing people four drunken pilots from Romania who did air policing missions over Lithuania as if it was a great security achievement coming from NATO. Yes, I was against all that showing-off, to put it bluntly. I guess, that is why I don't play in today's politics.

Sapozhnikova: *But, if you are so unhappy with the current state* *of affairs, why don't you, as a political strategist, once again remember Sharp's techniques and use the colored ribbons? Forgive my humor, if it offends you.*

Butkevičius: It is not humor, and it doesn't offend. It is a totally different game. People are fooled too much. Without a very large amount of resources not a single political strategist is capable of changing the situation. We lost thousands of the most active people. Everyone who could go to the rallies and stand up for themselves, left. It is a lot for a nation of 3.5 million to cut off 500-600 thousand of its best workers, the most adventurous people, who could take matters into their own hands and aren't afraid to live in a new place. We lost the opportunity to use them in the domestic battles in Lithuania. This is the saddest part.

***

GENE SHARP
American Political Analyst and Apostle of Non-Violence

The "father" of the theory of a nonviolent change of power – Gene Sharp – and the Author. It is hard to believe that the USSR could be destroyed by this frail old man.

"The Baltics Are My Doing"

...You could say it took me several years to walk up to this house in the suburbs of Boston. I have been walking since the time when I first saw the Baltic Chain, when on the far end of the Soviet Union, Estonians, Latvians and Lithuanians joined hands to show the world that they wanted to leave USSR. The striped national ribbons were flickering like little colorful snakes in the cold wind. It was sincere and beautiful. I would even write that tears were pouring down my eyes, but only to say that the sight can cause such a reaction once in a lifetime. As for the second human chain, which I later witnessed in the Georgian city of Batumi in 2008, two weeks after the August five-day war, and the third, which spread across the Garden Ring, Moscow, in the winter of 2011, for some reason my eyes reacted differently. It is known that for the first time, history appears in front of us in the form of a tragedy, the second time as a farce, and the third time, as a caricature of a technology tested once before.

The sense of déjà vu struck me more than once – in the revolutions dubbed Orange in Ukraine, Rose in Georgia and Tulip in Kyrgyzstan. Nowadays even the schoolchildren know about the techniques of nonviolent toppling of regimes, described in the books by American professor Gene Sharp. His 198 methods of nonviolent action (ribbon-wearing, prayers and worship, symbolic "reclaiming" of land, hunger strikes, human chains, etc.) pop up on the TV screen almost every day, sending gestures from Chişinău, Cairo, Kiev. A question: what came first – a chicken or an egg? Did Professor Sharp simply record the details of this phenomenon or did he impose his "colored" techniques on the world? The question demanded an answer. I wrote a letter to his organization, the Albert Einstein Institution. The reply from Boston was brief: come over.

...A Spanish-speaking neighborhood, where the wind was carrying scraps of paper across the streets, didn't look like a place suitable for a research facility. The house, where Professor Gene Sharp lives, with the first floor occupied by the institute, had neither a plaque, nor a sign. Two tiny rooms were practically stacked to the ceiling with books and documents. Marx, Lenin, Mahatma Gandhi, the books and posters in all languages – you could practically see that the owner of the cabinet was wise and old. So old, he needed a magnifying glass to look at the computer screen.

"I mumble when I speak," chokingly apologized Gene Sharp, a very old man, who looked like a monument, 84 at the time. "But if necessary, for you I will repeat five or ten times."

This would be handy indeed. We could talk forever, how, with his techniques, the USSR was dismantled more than twenty years ago.

Cracks in the Monolith

Sapozhnikova: *Do you know, Mr. Sharp, how many people in Russia died after the collapse of the state? How many emigrated? How many perished in ethnic wars?*

Sharp: "Is that so?" he was sincerely surprised. He had a habit of covering his mouth with his hand when he spoke, so it seemed as if he was panting all the time.

Sapozhnikova: *You founded your institution in 1983. Did you know back then that the Soviet Union would collapse?*

Sharp: No, it was impossible to predict. At least, I couldn't.

Sapozhnikova: *Who, in your mind, destroyed the USSR – Gorbachev, Sharp or the Russians?*

Sharp: Neither. There is an essay on this subject by a scholar Karl Deutsch, called *Cracks on the Monolith*. He is an American of German origin, a Harvard professor. This book, published in the US in 1957, contains a chapter about totalitarianism I quote in my book *From Dictatorship to Democracy*. And, at the time when the

Stalinist regime still existed and controlled virtually everything, Deutsch wrote that the system had problems, and noted 7 or 8 of its weak spots. I don't think that the essay somehow affected the Soviet Union... I mean, I suspect that the USSR wasn't dismantled by Gorbachev or me. Really, who am I? A small man.

Sapozhnikova: *When did you start visiting our country?*

Sharp: I am not good with dates. Surely I was there in 1991, and believe that I returned once more a year or two after. I initially only flew to Moscow, attended two conferences at the Soviet Academy of Sciences. One was concerning the ethics of nonviolent action, the other was about its history. We brought along promotional copies of the book *Civilian-based Defense*, which was underway for publishing at Princeton University. We gave them away to the representatives of the Baltic states; they took the books to their respective capitals.

Sapozhnikova: *Can you recall, who exactly did you give them to?*

Sharp: I always mix the names up. The Estonian State Minister Ravio Vare. Some people form the government of Latvia. Audrius Butkevičius, the then-Director of the Department of National Defense.

Sapozhnikova: *I was living in Tallinn at that moment and could observe your techniques with my very own eyes, as well as its results, not suspecting who was behind it. Recently I read in one of your interviews: "The Baltics are my doing!"*

Sharp: The three states began nonviolent struggle by themselves, I had nothing to do with it. They had a history of guerilla warfare against the Soviet occupation, the Nazi occupation and again the Soviet occupation. They decided to gain independence via the nonviolent path, without my influence whatsoever.

Sapozhnikova: *But how did you bump into each other?*

Sharp: Very simple: they invited us. But, apparently, you are trying to tie these events with my persona? It is a mistake. It is connected with my ideas, but not with me personally. The idea of a type of struggle can reach many different people, yet nothing can happen in their countries. If the Balts were strong enough to achieve their goals they would probably use violence. But they were weak. Their strength rested in the masses of people that were thinking alike. Actually, the ideas laid out in my books come from the deepest past. You see a portrait of Mahatma Gandhi of the wall – I learned a lot from him, although, of course, I never met him.

Provocation as a Goal-achieving Method

Sapozhnikova: *Let's get back to the Baltics. Do you remember the tragedy in Vilnius, January 1991, when 13 civilians and a Soviet officer died around the TV tower, and the Soviet army was blamed for everything? Is it true that you came to Lithuania a couple of days before the beginning of the assault and gave advice to Lithuanian freedom fighters?*

Sharp: I gave no advice! I don't know who is spreading these rumors. I arrived only after everything happened. And before that only met them in Moscow.

Sapozhnikova: *And how do you like the theory, that Lithuanians wanted to gain independence so much, they decided to speed up the process by organizing a provocation, and your favorite apprentice, Audrius Butkevičius, was behind the plot?*

Sharp: Oh, no! I know him perfectly – he would have never done anything like that. He was a fully-devoted proponent of the use of nonviolent methods of struggle. Excuse me, but it sounds like Soviet propaganda. The Soviet Union continues to invent fairytales to justify the things it should be ashamed of.

Sapozhnikova: *But I read in one of your books a phrase, which* said – *"if you wish independence, you must be ready that someone of your associates will die..."*

Sharp: I meant a different point – authoritarian governments and dictatorships are very dependent on violence, police or military, otherwise you won't hold out long as a dictatorship.

When popular movements begin to threaten them, even using only nonviolent action, you shouldn't be surprised that the regime will be killing people off to cease the movement. Nonviolent struggle actually doesn't mean that you are safe. It means that less people might be killed, than when resorting to violence. And less than if you wouldn't do anything at all. The Chechens acted unwisely, when they chose violence to achieve independence, because Russia is more powerful. It makes no sense to choose armed struggle, when your opponent is that strong. But if you use only nonviolent methods, the authorities won't know what to do with you. Because if they unleash force, it will cause an immediate international reaction. In other words, if the Chechens hadn't used force, there would have been less casualties and more chances of victory.

Sapozhnikova: *Some think, that the events of 13 January 1991, in Lithuania, were a rehearsal for the August Coup in Moscow. Testing the waters, so to speak... Do you agree?*

Sharp: I was talking to many people from the Baltics back then, and can tell that their goals were quite limited – the resumption of independence. They never thought of broader ideas, like the destruction of the USSR. Never. Whoever imposed this idea on you that the people were shot by Lithuanian snipers doesn't know anything about Vilnius and the TV tower. The snipers couldn't fire at the demonstrators! That hill had no tall buildings around.

There were houses a bit further, five-story or similar, but no buildings standing in the direct vicinity of the tower. People were gunned down not by snipers, but by Russian soldiers. Your government occasionally does things that shouldn't be done, then again so does the US government. You don't necessarily have to become a traitor to accept it.

Sapozhnikova: *But there is no evidence that Soviet troops were firing near the tower! Besides, there were casings found from rounds, fired from WWII-era guns...*

Sharp: Every government has its excuses. And every time something despicable is done, excuses appear: oh, we didn't do it, somebody else did it, and so forth. You, obviously, can believe what you want. But I object to facts being distorted.

Who Taught Who?

Sapozhnikova: *Let's talk about your theory. Do you know that it is being used for not-so-righteous goals? The techniques are universal: you can oust the government, but opposition, too.*

Sharp: But of course I know! People can go on a hunger strike to achieve something bad. But I believe that it is better to go on a hunger strike to achieve something bad, than killing for the very same goal. In the former case, the only victims are the people on hunger strike themselves.

Sapozhnikova: *Did you manage to create a system of countermeasures so your methods wouldn't be used to damage the society?*

Sharp: Only in general terms. Naturally, you have to resist. Nonviolently. There are limitations to my abilities.

Sapozhnikova: *What do you feel, by the way, when revolutions, woven with your techniques, fail? In Ukraine, the Orange Revolution seemingly won, thanks to your recommendations, and then what? The new democrats, who assumed power instead of the old authority, began doing the same things as the previous rulers.*

Sharp: I didn't monitor the situation in Ukraine. But in the last part of my book *From Dictatorship to Democracy* it is said that the toppling of a regime doesn't provide the full solution of the problem. Those who conduct revolutions must be aware so the new regime won't become a dictatorship and won't be similar to the previous regime. The problem is not in toppling the regime. You have to clearly understand how to prevent the takeover of power by a certain political group. How to withstand a coup, provoked by the CIA, how it, for example, happened in Chile. Or in Iran, when the Ayatollah came to power. Or in Russia, in 1917, when power was seized by the Bolsheviks. We are the only organization that had laid out a methodology for how to counter a coup. By the way, the few things I know about the methods of wielding nonviolent struggle I learned from Leo Tolstoy among others. He had a theory of political power – tyrants enjoy only the power given to them by the people. If the people disagree, a dictator loses power. So you have to think through, who taught who, I taught you, or you, the Russians, taught me.

Sapozhnikova: *Can you guess that your name in Russia suffers from certain degree of demonization?*

Sharp: Oh, look, what a demon I am! Three heads, 14 hands... I am that strong! With a large office and many employees. This is hilarious, really.

Sapozhnikova: *Maybe, people mean that you are responsible for the collapse of the USSR?*

Sharp: This is a good joke! You assume I, alone, could have toppled an empire, the biggest country in the world, with millions of people, with a giant bureaucracy, the KGB and the army? This is ludicrous. Ludicrous! And people attribute this to me, to an old man? I can't even walk without somebody's assistance! The Soviet society's problem was that an old man was menacing it? In that case, the society had very big problems... This is your domestic affairs, which have nothing to do with me. If I wasn't born, if I didn't exist at all, these problems would still exist.

"We Give Advice to No One"

Sapozhnikova: *The US authorities utilized your techniques multiple times – why didn't they acknowledge their value?*

Sharp: I don't deserve any pay, because they don't use my methodology. They imposed an economic boycott of Cuba, for example. But it is something used for hundreds of years. I didn't invent it. To change the regime in Iraq, the Americans called the military for assistance, not me. I received no money from the US government. Only once I got an indirect grant through one Harvard professor, who, in turn, got a grant from the Pentagon to study untraditional means of resolving conflicts. Our institution, as you see, has neither a building, nor staff.

I don't teach, I am not a teacher. I do research, analyze and publish results. If people are interested, they can learn. Various visitors come here, receive books, and nothing happens in their states. We never tell people from other states what to do and in what order. Many get here and ask: please, tell me, what to do, let's say, in Venezuela. I respond, "No. I don't know the situation in your country like you do. But I know the principles of nonviolent struggle. We are giving you a guide called *Self-Liberation*. It is precisely designed for you to learn what you don't know. And, while combining it with what you know, and with the ability to think strategically, you will make your own plans." The book *From Dictatorship to Democracy* was actually written for Burma. Now it is sold in 34 languages.

Sapozhnikova: *What are your wishes for the future revolutionaries?*

Sharp: Stop, think, study and think again before you begin doing anything.

***

"The paternity test showed that Gene Sharp isn't the father of the color revolutions," I wrote down a beautiful phrase in a notepad. I stopped to think. Professor Sharp in person didn't match the image, nor by the income level, nor by physical appearance. He wasn't proportional to what he did. The much-lauded Albert Einstein Institution was comprised of himself and two employees, helping him in monitoring mail and editing books. They piled up like mountains on top of everything, including the fridge. "Actually, Gene Sharp's dictionary costs 100 dollars, but we will sell it for 20," offered his assistants with the voices of door-to-door salesmen. Sharp didn't let me and the photographer inside the three residential floors, so we, unfortunately, couldn't film for history how he waters his famous orchids. "I have a mess there. Here I keep it tidy more or so…" he explained shyly, glancing through the paper mountains on his cabinet table, to which, at his 84 years, while barely walking, he descended every day to work. He had the sharpest mind with a practically complete physical helplessness.

I wrote down another paragraph: "So this is what Mr. Sharp is like, living in Boston suburbs, on the street, where the wind moves the trash around, working in a cabinet, stacked with papers. A man who created a system that can make the world go round, and in the end of his life, regretted it and attempted to stop the young revolutionaries from ill-conceived actions."

In the evening, I reviewed the material and couldn't understand anything, as if the effect of hypnosis had worn off. How could I have fallen for the charm of his mind and not notice the slogan on the Albert Einstein Institution booklet – **"Consulting government ministers, MPs and volunteer organizations on the development of nonviolent struggle, like in Lithuania, Latvia, Estonia and Thailand"**? Turned out, Professor Sharp had his hands in the Velvet Revolution in Czechoslovakia[2] as well as those in the Baltic states, the first color revolutions in the former USSR?

And yes, I forgot to remind him: there are, indeed, tall residential buildings near the Vilnius TV tower, from whose rooftops snipers could fire…

***

VLADIMIR OVCHINSKY:
Interior Ministry Major-General, Doctor of Legal Sciences

"The USSR Leadership were Consciously Destroying the Country"

It is paradoxical, how a famous criminologist, Interior Ministry Major-General, Doctor of Legal Sciences Vladimir Ovchinsky knew the whole truth about the event in Lithuania back in February 1991. Together with political expert Sergey Kurginyan he had published a famous investigation called *The Lithuanian Syndrome* in February 1991, upon returning from Vilnius, where he was stationed right after the events. He wrote, "It is evident that the bloodshed possibility was modeled beforehand by the Landsbergis advisers because, at the moment of the takeover of the television, the tapes, created prior to the assault, went on air from autonomous radio stations, broadcasting in multiple languages that 'blood was shed in Vilnius and a military coup happened at the TV Tower.'"

The information, which journalists years later had to collect bit-by-bit, had beens obtained by Ovchinsky and Kurginyan, analyzed and published 25 years ago, but amidst the then-existing democratic euphoria no one wanted to listen to them.

Another Lie by Gorbachev

Sapozhnikova: *How did you get to Vilnius, what status did you have and to whom did you later report?*

Ovchinskky: The story began much earlier, when the ethnic conflicts started emerging, the first being the Karabakh conflict. The Minister of Interior Vadim Bakatin established the Emergencies Department in the All-Union Research Institute of the Interior Ministry. The department was directly subjected to the USSR Interior Ministry Central Operational Command and, through the command, the data was forwarded straight to the minister himself. The Central Operational Command was headed by Vladislav Nasinosvky, a very experienced agent, the man who was one of the leaders of the Cobalt Group in Afghanistan. He supervised us in terms of administration and operations. We first worked in Karabakh, later in Tskhinval, then in Moldova. When, in 1990, Lithuanians declared independence, certain forces within the CPSU and the government of the USSR were interested in having independent channels of objective information. So we reported directly to the Politburo, the Chairman of the Councils of Ministers Nikolai Ryzhkov, the Chairman of the KGB Vlamidir Kryuchkov, and to Leonid Shebarshin, head of foreign intelligence. Back then it was called the First Main Directorate of the KGB. That is how I, a police officer, completely suddenly was dragged into the analysis of the political events in the country.

We entered Lithuania as journalists and worked for several weeks in 1990, collecting data among nationalist and extremist forces. We had some knowledge of how American political strategists and experts from European states acted. Most certainly, there were members of the secret services from NATO. And since we worked very intensively, we attracted the notice of the local KGB. They even attempted to apprehend us once, mistaking us for foreign nationals. Afterwards, we worked together with the officers of the Lithuanian KGB with complete mutual trust. So when the events around the TV tower occurred, people died, and a storm of noise and distress broke out on all-Union television and radio outlets, which immediately sided with the Lithuanian separatists. As a result, public opinion was artificially transformed into an uproar to rally the society against the armed forces and the secret services. Here is the picture: Soviet airborne troops attacked unarmed people, murdered 13 of them, seized the TV tower and did everything without an order from the HQ... There was a kind of mayhem. Yuri Prokofyev, the First Secretary of the CPSU Moscow City Committee, and Oleg Shenin, a Secretary of the CPSU Central Committee, worked closely with our group. They asked us to urgently head out for Lithuania and to conduct a snap collection of the data of what actually happened in Vilnius. I went there together with an independent political analyst, Sergey Kurginyan, whom I met in Karabakh, after which we started to cooperate in analytics exchange.

The first thing we understood was that the Pskov airborne troops acted not by themselves, but under a direct order of Gorbachev and the Defense Minister Yazov.

Sapozhnikova: *Which means, the statements that he was sleeping and didn't know anything are…*

Ovchinskky: Brazen lies. It is another one of Mikhail Gorbachev's lies. He personally had issued an order to seize the TV tower. After the seizure, the first report was delivered to him. We were told about this by the KGB operatives of Lithuania, who witnessed how the airborne troops reported to Kryuchkov, Gorbachev and Yazov how the mission was accomplished. They didn't kill any locals. Only Lieutenant Shatskikh died, who was, apparently, gunned down by the Sąjūdists. We knew this from day one. That is the first point.

The second point is that we absolutely clearly established that covert US intelligence groups were operating in Lithuania. They were made up of ethnic Lithuanians, who held US citizenship, fought in various countries as members of special forces, served in the military intelligence, CIA and other US secret services. But they were all retirees by the time they appeared in Lithuania, arriving to their historic homeland to help establish the democratic foundations. We couldn't formally call them CIA agents. But everybody understands that if a person is part of the secret services, it doesn't matter, whether he retires or not.

It is a frequently used trick, especially in US secret services. The so-called Qatari task force, which stormed Tripoli, was up to 90% formed of retired agents of European and US secret services. Basically, they were mercenaries. The foreign covert groups in Lithuania had their own battle groups. They taught people how to make Molotov cocktails, so if a real invasion happened, a real civil war would start. The territory of all the Baltic states had weapons caches that remained from the times of the last Forest Brethren.[3] Yet, the most undercover units were located not in Lithuania, but in Latvia, and we also reported that directly to the leadership of the country and the party. We also knew then that the victims near the Vilnius TV tower were mostly killed by snipers, probably, firing from hunting rifles.

Treason Came From the Top

Sapozhnikova: *Then how did everything get twisted so much that the blame landed on the Soviet task force?*

Ovchinskky: Everything was known from the very beginning. We arrived early in the morning and were walking down the Vilnius streets – there were barricades, smoke, people with armbands wandering around, checking documents. The situation on the ground reminded of a revolutionary war, of some kind of a revolutionary city... Then I called the local KGB officers and met with the few Russians who remained there. By that time, almost half of the KGB of the Lithuanian SSR had defected to the Sajūdists. Only the Chairman of the KGB of the Lithuanian SSR was sitting in his office, a modest man in glasses, whose last name was Tsaplin. Tsaplin was the one who ordered his subordinates to provide us with documents so Moscow would know the truth. They brought in case files; we retrieved photos of the American covert agents that led the local resistance. The photos later got published in the *Moskovskaya Pravda* newspaper.

For us, the most important thing that we established was that the airborne troops acted on behalf of the order issued by Gorbachev about direct presidential rule,[4] which was supposed to be enacted but wasn't. And there was supposed to be a command coming for the National Salvation Committee from the Politburo of the SPCU Central Committee, but it never came about. No civilians were killed during the Russian tank and troop assaults on the TV tower and TV Center, all people were murdered by the Sajūdist snipers and the agents of Western secret services. The US and NATO covert groups actively operated on the territory of Lithuania, and the whole situation unfolded just like in Sharp's books.

Sapozhnikova: *This, too, you knew back then?*

Ovchinskky: - Of course. I have known his name since the late 80s when I was just starting to be involved in that type of activities.

Sapozhnikova: *Then, if you knew all that, why couldn't you counter his techniques?*

Ovchinskky: We reported everything. The only person, who decided to take legal action on the data, was Yuri Prokofyev. He said, "I have a rebellion in the city, the party committee is going down, people believe the Lithuanians and what the TV shows". He assembled a lot of party workers in a large hall in the party city committee building and asked me, Kurginyan and several others to speak. They didn't let us go for, I guess, two hours. We told them in great detail about our impressions from Lithuania and the Baltics. Someone from the Bureau stood up and suggested that everything should be published in *Moskovskaya Pravda*. We had written a piece called *The Lithuanian Syndrome*. Everything was described in two articles that came out with a wide circulation and these were cabled to Gorbachev, all Central Committee members and the government. We later reiterated everything during the session of the Presidium of the Council of Ministers of the USSR. The classified parts we reported personally to Kryuchkov as the KGB Chairman. Everything that could have been done, we did.

But what could there be done if the treason came right from the very top, and Gorbachev and Yakovlev's goal was to let the Baltics go?.. Right know I believe that the whole operation of seizing the TV tower was a show to give the Baltics an opportunity to leave. When someone wants to strengthen the union, he acts as was done in Hungary and Czechoslovakia. I am not going to pass judgment on how right or wrong that would have been, but it is a part of our history. And when someone desires to get an opposite effect, he acts like Gorbachev and Yakovlev acted. What happened in Lithuania is a micro-August Coup, a type of provocation that helped to separate Lithuania and later the whole Baltics from the USSR. So if, let's say, some CIA leader had showed up and said that he would work for us, it still would been impossible to do anything, because the leadership of the USSR was deliberately destroying the communist party and the country, the USSR, that it represented.

The USSR-Dismantling Mechanism

Sapozhnikova: *Is that what you meant, when you wrote in your article that you could sense the presence of CIA and our secret services in Lithuania?*

Ovchinskky: Yes. What are the Popular Fronts of Latvia and Estonia, and the Lithuanian Sąjūdis? The late Boris Pugo, who officially committed suicide, while serving as the Minister of Interior, personally told me this (we had very informal trusting relations). I asked him, "Comrade Minister, how did it happen that you, serving as the Chairman of the KGB of Latvia, allowed the Popular Front and nationalist, pro-fascist structures to emerge in your republic?" He told me that when he was the First Secretary, nothing of the sort took place in the republic. But Gorbachev recalled him to Moscow and asked, "Why aren't the democratic processes happening in your domain? Lithuania has Sąjūdis, Estonia has the Popular Front, even Moscow has its own Popular Front, while you have no democratic movement. Assist these processes."

And Pugo started to assist. He assembled all the agents, working in artisan and sciences circles, and began telling them to establish a front, similar to the ones the Estonians and Lithuanians had. Everybody was dodging. No one wanted to do it. One literally fell on his knees, almost kissing Pugo's shoes, saying, "Why do you want to bring me down? We will establish everything, get people out on the streets, and you will arrest us, maybe, even execute by firing squad".

So, all the Popular Fronts were initially created through the Fifth Directorates of the KGB of the USSR and the KGB of the republics. Every single one! Later the process was hijacked by the US and NATO covert agents and local nationalists. The process was triggered, and the people who initialed it got ousted and compromised. The agent dossier of Kazimira Prunskienė[5] had been already released in Lithuania. She later denied the allegations, saying that she wasn't involved in active complicity with the KGB, but her political career went down in flames... It was an act of treason from within the KGB of Lithuania. This is why I am emphasizing that it was a double-sided project of ours and foreign secret services. No democratic revolution in the USSR would have happened, if Gorbachev and Yakovlev hadn't started a mechanism to dismantle the CPSU.

Stupidity or Treachery?

Sapozhnikova: *How did the plan of the 12 January operation land on Landsbergis' desk?*

Ovchinskky: Yakovlev personally handed it over to him.

Sapozhnikova: *Do you have proof?*

Ovchinskky: When I was transferring a totally classified report, written after the Karabakh events, to Yakovlev through the Interior Ministry leadership, the report fell into the hands of Armenian and Azerbaijani nationalists. When I was reporting about fascist organizations in Latvia to the country's leadership, the Interior Ministry leader issued a command to fire me from service. I miraculously stayed on the job.

Sapozhnikova: *The price hike, which took place in Lithuania right prior to the TV tower events, was too a part of the scenario?*

Ovchinskky: I assume, it was a common economic mayhem.

The key element was to deploy troops, carry out a violent action, murder people and blame it on the airborne servicemen. And to turn the ones in doubt into the opponents of the USSR. The goal was reached via provocation, organized by Gorbachev and Yakovlev, and their accomplices in the ranks of our secret services.

Sapozhnikova: *Where else do you, as a professional analyst, see the provocative nature of the situation?*

Ovchinskky: We didn't conduct an official investigation. We didn't have powers to do so. We met with people from the Lithuanian Communist Party and the KGB, who did political analyses – they all were in a suppressed state of mind. But the general notion was that the order to storm the TV tower was issued by Gorbachev, who later disavowed it and set everyone up, virtually making them criminals. The airborne troops didn't kill anyone, and those Lithuanians, who got murdered, were killed either by snipers, or by the foreign secret service officers. Just like in 1993, when, apparently, no one shot the police from inside of the White House,[6] but... someone did shoot! My university associate was shot through the lung from a sniper rifle, he became disabled for life. He was shot in the back from the side of Kutuzovsky Avenue, while standing in defensive formation near the White House. The same methods were used in Vilnius. People got shot to place all blame on the Alpha Squad and the airborne troops. Exactly the same thing happened during the Tbilisi events: people got killed in a stampede, while the rumors spread that they were killed with army shovels. Not a single death from an army shovel was recorded. It was all made up by Georgian nationalists. People didn't need to be dispersed, no one did anything. Gorbachev gave the order.

Sapozhnikova: *Out of stupidity or treachery?*

Ovchinskky: He did everything consciously and deliberately exacerbated the situation. It was not stupidity; he is a very smart man.

Sapozhnikova: *Then, please, try to explain what happened to our society – it just swallowed everything without choking?*

Ovchinskky: Our society was behaving as normal. During the August Coup, I was in Anapa with my family and saw how the people reacted. When the coup was declared, people cheered and said "finally"... Later Boris Pugo recalled me to Moscow, and I saw the reaction of the people at the airport – everyone was saying that some order is being finally installed after Gorbachev's universal mess. No one knew that it was another provocation, organized by Gorbachev himself. The majority of the people, in March 1991, voted for the unity of the Soviet Union. Afterwards, three criminals signed a worthless piece of paper that dismantled the state. The traitors, sitting on the Supreme Council of the RSFSR, virtually unanimously welcomed it. So you shouldn't allude every time to the people. The people understood everything perfectly. Everything was done by a clique of traitors, who appeared on the radio, on TV, in print media.

This Was Not Like in the Movies

Sapozhnikova: *Why didn't you continue the investigation?*

Ovchinskky: Where and with whom should I have continued it? The USSR was already gone. I fled Vilnius with photos, given to me by the Lithuanian KGB. Four years later, the Deputy Chairman of the KGB of Lithuania, Tsaplin, was killed. The colleague, who handed me the documents, was made an outlaw and went hiding for a long time. He was placed on a wanted list later. I don't know his fate, he vanished. He was abandoned by our FSK, later by the FSB[7]... There were many similar people around the republics. When he brought me the documents, the excerpts from the operational case files I later gave away to Kryuchkov, at the train station restaurant, we saw that we were practically encircled by the Sajūdists. We then reordered our food – it is a psychological trick intended for the psychology of the village people: if we made an order, it meant that we aren't going to leave. I went to the bathroom and jumped out of the window on the second floor. I left with the documents and ran through the square.

Sapozhnikova: *What should we do right now with the truth that is now floating on the surface?*

Ovchinsky: Such truth exists not only with regard to Lithuania, but in any other state in the post-Soviet space. Look up the alternative report that we were preparing with Kurginyan about the Tbilisi events, or the alternative report on Karabakh. For me, the Lithuanian events weren't the main thing. It was simply one of the episodes of the tragedy, happening with the destruction of the USSR. Did people die? Yes, but after that people massively died in ethnic conflicts in the post-Soviet space. No one is saying that in Tajikistan, when the so-called Islamic democratic revolution happen, which was endorsed by Yeltsin and his circle, 150,000 people died. I am stating the exact number. My close friend, Timur Rakhimbayev, was first the Deputy Minister of Internal Affairs of Tajikistan, and then became the head of the Khujand Directorate of Internal Affairs. He later was blown up on a plane in the Emirates along with the Khujand clan. This concerns not just the 13 Lithuanians shot by the Lithuanians themselves. It is about the thousands of people slaughtered in Kyrgyzia. It is about the thousands killed in Chechnya… Should you remember Lithuania, when such tragedies occurred on the territory of Russia? I will never forget the villages, burnt to the ground, which I saw right after the fighting between Ossetians and the Ingush, when I was an aide of the First Deputy Minister of the Interior, and we flew over the territory on a helicopter. It was hard to believe that it wasn't the movies… It was all one chain of treason and betrayal committed by the leaders of our country.

***

EDUARDAS EISMUNTAS
Chairman of the KGB of Lithuania

The above interview needed to be fully comprehended. The question raised by Vladimir Ovchinsky could be answered only by one man – Eduardas Eismuntas, the Chairman of the KGB of Lithuanian 1987-1990. And I managed to find him in order to ask him the question:

Sapozhnikova: *Could it be that the secret services weren't aware of the US political strategists operating in the late 80s? And the color revolution, which then was called the Singing Revolution, was prepared completely openly?*

Here is what he replied:

Eismuntas: Everyone saw and knew, but what could we do, if the emissaries arrived through Moscow? All the money came from Moscow, too. The local KGB was completely helpless.

It wasn't Lithuania who began the movement for democratization. Everything was unraveling, but was under control. Then came the great reformer Gorbachev, and it all began... All the doors and windows became open: emigrants and intelligence officers poured in, so did the money. Then there was a visit of the lame US intelligence agent, Alexander Yakovlev, who gave a clear sign: do what you want. Everyone got that: instead of limiting yourself to the talk about democratization, you could talk about leaving the USSR. No matter how often I wrote or reported to Kryuchkov, I saw that the process was uncontrollable, and nothing could be done anymore.

We decided with our colleagues from the KGB of Latvia, Estonia and Moldova to go to Moscow to report the facts on the ground together. They told us, "Don't panic, everything is under control..." I returned, filed the report and resigned. I couldn't act against the law and didn't want to. The Baltics aren't guilty of the collapse of the Soviet Union. It is the fault of Gorbachev and his team. So, in January 1991, I sat at home watching TV. No one informed me – I would have talked them out of the assault, if I had been aware. Dragging in the army was an utter stupidity. What fool gave an order to assault the TV tower? You could just cut the cable. The most powerful intercept station in Europe was located near Kaunas, from where we were able to broadcast not only to Lithuania, but to Latvia and Estonia.

| Chapter Three |

AND THEN THEY CALLED FOR DED MOROZ…

Every New Year celebration in Lithuania starts with children drawing tanks all throughout the week before the anniversary of the January tragedy. You could say that the Vilnius TV tower has gained a cult following, an illustration to the most heroic page of the contemporary Lithuanian epic. Everyone is okay with the official version because all of the state ideology is based upon it. Heaven forbid you accidentally forget that mournful date, the people will rally against you. A few years ago, Valery Gergiev had a concert in Kaunas scheduled on the exact day. The maestro was somewhat shocked to see people protesting the music outside the concert hall, but didn't cancel the venue, and, as polite man, even gave his condolences from the stage. After that incident, Lithuania started wondering: do the Russians even have the right to celebrate the Old New Year while all of Lithuania mourns? I have personally seen visitors of a Vilnius restaurant drop by on that day, 13 January, for a good time and then simultaneously move the forks and salads aside on the host's command to give a moment of silence. And then cheerfully call for Ded Moroz, the Russian Santa Claus…

No one is really against mourning: 14 people had died and 13 were young men who bought Landsbergis' calls to protect liberty and believed Butkevičius words that all shots fired will be blanks. However, this is not about the victims of the Lithuanian "heavenly hundred", but the ones who are responsible for their death. The "Soviet aggression" legend is hard-wired into Lithuania's modern history with the TV tower becoming sacred: there are memorial lessons about it, there are sports competitions in its honor, pyres in the city squares and children's drawing competitions. Out of the few hundred colored pictures on the street stands near the Lithuania genocide victims' museum – with a lot of tanks, TV towers and scary Soviet men in gray coats – two really tug at the heartstrings. One has a Soviet solder taking a Lithuanian boy's wooden horsey away. And in another someone there at the Vilnius tower is being run over by a tank, but instead of Soviet flag, the tank has a Russian one... No one corrects these mistakes, the path Lithuania chose for its future aligns perfectly with it.

It would be wrong to rob the people of this pretense for unity in national spirit. It was easier to discredit the source of the questioning, which was opposition politician, Algirdas Paleckis.

He wasn't really inventing anything new, he just repeated the opinions voiced by other sources. But it raised quite the commotion. Paleckis was tried for "denying Soviet aggression". He won the first trial in January 2012. But the offended TV tower defenders wrote a letter to the judge demanding that he punish the renegade. You can understand where they are coming from: they all received medals, pensions and lands for their feat. For twenty years, they have been telling their children and grandchildren how they beat the fearsome Soviet dragon. And now it turns out that the dragon wasn't as scary as the legends and instead of fire, it breathed old embers. And the next court used a few wrong words ("As it turns out, our people were shooting our own") and fined Algirdas Paleckis three thousand euro. The European Court of Human Rights in Strasbourg, where Paleckis appealed, replied to him that "the issue was of little importance", demonstrating their lack of care for freedom of speech and Lithuania itself.

So figuring out this 25-year-old situation falls upon those who really care – the Lithuanians and Russians. And maybe those who also care about the "color revolutions" yet to come.

ALGIRDAS PALECKIS
Opposition Lithuanian Diplomat and Politician

Algirdas Paleckis and the 21st Century Inquisition

Lithuanian political scientist Algirdas Paleckis was on trial for a few words said on the radio.

Before Algirdas Paleckis said his famous words on the radio, a similar thing had already been directly mentioned in the books of at least three people: Juozas Kuolelis, Vytautas Petkevičius and Valery Ivanov.

Why did he garner such a heated reaction?

The reason is in his name. The writer Petkevičius passed away, pensioner Kuolelis is celebrating his 85th birthday, and the twice-imprisoned Ivanov is named "Ivanov" and that just says everything. No one would follow them, so they aren't dangerous. But enter the young and colorful heir to the famous Paleckis family, whose grandfather helped add Lithuania to the USSR, whose father was an MEP (Member of the European Parliament), while being a diplomat and journalist in Soviet times – and you could say that Algirdas' future was set before he was even born. To say nothing of his stellar education, fluency in four languages, bright career in the Lithuanian MFA, foreign assignments and everything else a member of the political elite should have.

Everything except his opinions. They don't fit into the current Lithuanian political landscape. Sounds like a premise of a bad movie, but it is true. Having been on diplomatic assignments, being elected into the Seimas, the Lithuanian parliamentary body, having worked as a vice-mayor and receiving two state awards (the French Order of Legion of Honor and the Order for Merits to Lithuania – which was later revoked), around his mid-thirties, the man comes to a realization that the world is unjust and you "have to live life in a way where it is not torturously painful". His political views take a left turn from the social democrats; he speaks the long forgotten words of social justice and even organizes his own party.

Well, the ghost of the left idea has gained extra popularity in Europe during the global financial crisis. But no one thought that it could materialize in this country, which spent the last twenty years fighting everything communist with a passion. But it materialized in the form of the young Paleckis.

In January 1991, as a university student at the time, he didn't have any doubt who was responsible for the events at the TV tower. The Soviet Army, of course... What had to happen for his opinion to change completely from the public one in more than twenty years?

A Gulf with No Swimming

Sapozhnikova: *Where did your opinions come from, when faced a completely "right wing" informational backdrop?*

Paleckis: First I followed in my father's footsteps, diplomacy seemed like a calm and comfy gulf. And I wanted to swim and be in the center of it all. That is why I decided to leave the Lithuanian MFA. One of my main motives was the wide-spread social injustice and inequality in Lithuania after so many years of independence. The people don't deserve to live like this.

Sapozhnikova: *Personally, what do you remember from the events of January 1991?*

Paleckis: I was 20, a student of Vilnius University and child of the Glasnost era. Of course, I was also under the effect of Landsbergis' propaganda; he was the leader of the nationalists and skillfully manipulated the image of Russia, the Soviet Union, as Lithuania's eternal enemy. We believed in naiveté that Perestroika would be the bridge to a new super society from the stagnation society. And when the national awakening began in Lithuania, we were absolute romantics. But because my father was one of the leaders of the Lithuanian Communist Party I knew a bit more, about the power struggle happening up top. Sąjūdis quickly turned from patriotic to nationalistic.[1] The witch hunts started and our family was also terrorized. By around 1991, I had developed an immunity to all of it. Maybe that is why, unlike many other Lithuanians, I wasn't affected by the mass psychosis, I didn't go to the tower, I looked at what was happening near the parliament and then went to study for my exams. And the suddenly there were gunshots, shock and anger at the events and those partaking in them. That stereotype of Soviet soldiers killing Lithuanians, *Lithuanian* citizens, stayed for a long time.

Sapozhnikova: *With you specifically or with society?*

Paleckis: I grew up in the family of a Soviet Lithuanian diplomat, I spent my childhood in a Soviet school in GDR. As a teenager, I lived a few years in Moscow. So, while being a Lithuanian, I was an internationalist. But the atmosphere in Lithuania was heavy, the Lithuanians had developed a negative outlook on everything Russian and Soviet. But when the new government concluded the privatization and the population was impoverished, heavy doubts started arising.

Sapozhnikova: *The illusions concerning democracy fell apart with the overall disappointment in capitalism?*

Paleckis: Sąjūdis was initially called a movement in support of the Perestroika and socialistic update. But when Landsbergis took charge, the movement made a sharp turn to the right and into nationalism. I have experienced this with my family, the attacks on my grandfather, who had already passed away. Sąjūdis used real psychological terror, which was covered with the fight for independence and democracy, but really was just a struggle for power. Its leaders included a lot of turncoats, which was disappointing for a movement which started so good – for Perestroika, against privilege – but by 1989 it turned into pure nationalism, Russophobia and caveman anticommunism.

A Law with Retroactive Effect

Sapozhnikova: *Next morning, after the January events, almost no one doubted that everything was exactly as Vytautas Landsbergis said it was. How many years did it take for alternative information to start appearing?*

Paleckis: Everyone was shocked and they accepted that version as truth. Television showed the murdered people, and despite the fact that there wasn't a single shot that showed tanks running anyone over or Soviet soldiers specifically killing anyone – they were just pushing a path for themselves with their gunstocks – but still it affected the psyche.

The first one to doubt was Vytautas Petkevičius, a famous and vibrant figure in Sąjūdis and the Perestroika. He wrote a memoir, *Ship of Fools,* where he debunked many myths about Landsbergis, Sąjūdis and 13 January, being the first to declare that it was hunting bullets and that everything was planned and executed by Landsbergis and Audrius Butkevičius, the Director of the Department of National Defense. There was a whole series of his interviews in the press, but we chose not to give any thought to it, setting it aside as something Petkevičius got wrong due to his old age. Then, in 2010, there was a book by Juozas Kuolelis, who had been a political prisoner for a few years along with the other leaders of the Lithuanian Communist Party, which remained aligned with the CPSU. They were political prisoners, charged with working for another state.

Sapozhnikova: *In 1990-1991, was Lithuania only recognized by Iceland and living on the USSR's money?*

Paleckis: Exactly. When Juozas Kuolelis was on trial, he had access to the documents of the Lithuania forensics, which plainly states that out of 13 civilian casualties, 5 or 6 were killed by hunting rounds fired down at a 50-60 degree angle. And you can't write this off as enemy data, this is the Lithuanian forensics team! The question is: who used hunting rifles and Mosin-Nagant rifles to shoot down from above? If it were the Soviet soldiers, then that would be AK rounds, and they would have been shot from the front. But the forensic experts determined that the bullets went down the neck. In the same book, titled *The Case on the Verge of Two Centuries*, Kuolelis wrote that he read witness reports in the trial documents, who saw people in sports gear who were shooting from the roofs of 5-story and 9-story buildings. They tried to silence this book in Lithuania as well. It came out in 2010, at the same time as the law banning the denial of Soviet occupation and aggression in 1940 and 1991.

A Common Enemy

Sapozhnikova: *What problems could they possibly have with you? You merely repeated what others said?*

Paleckis: Being the vice-mayor of Vilnius, I have encountered the surviving witnesses of those events – people who lived near the TV tower, who have told me of the provocateurs shooting from the roofs and how some burly men told them to approach the tanks fearlessly, because they will only have blanks. Even though many went there of their own volition - you can't deny that the rise of national and patriotic emotions was used against Lithuania itself. November 2010, I received an invitation to take part in a radio show on Lithuania's problems, on where the roots of poverty and inequality were. And when one of the guests started talking about the Sąjūdis saving all of us, I decided to remind him that it wasn't all that clean-cut. And I used the events of 13 January 1991 as an example, saying the words that sent the Lithuanian elite into a panic.

After that broadcast, the Seimas members and the ruling party wrote to the prosecutor about me. And there was a criminal case started about me denying and belittling the USSR aggression against Lithuania and insulting the victims. However the question of who "our own" were was debatable: that was during the Soviet times, the Lithuanians didn't have national [Lithuanian] passports. Even Romualdas Ozolas, Landsbergis' right hand man, later wrote in his memoirs that Landsbergis' cynicism was limitless – why was he so quick to bury those victims? Why didn't he finish the investigation on who killed, how the killing happened and under what circumstances? Why was it never established who those instigators were, who rallied the people to the TV tower even when they knew that there would be gunfire? It turns out that the people died in deception – they were invited to a singing revolution and told that the gunshots would be blanks.

But no one was interested in that. The collective responsibility was put onto the Soviet army, the accusation verdict saying that the Soviet soldiers willingly killed people. The saddest part is that none of the Sąjūdis leaders were at the TV tower. They were all barricaded in the Supreme Council. Landsbergis had a plane and pilot ready to take him out of Lithuania. The pilot was Rolandas Paksas, the future president of Lithuania, who would later face an impeachment organized by Landsbergis. Quite ironic.

Sapozhnikova: *What did you lose after that big controversy? Friends, work?*

Paleckis: Lost or gained, it is a matter of how you look at it, you never know how it will work out. I didn't think that the government would be stupid enough to start persecuting me. Of course I lost some of my supporters, who couldn't handle this challenge. My family stood strong, though my father and brother try to keep separate from me. But I can understand that, because what I said is too difficult for Lithuania. The politicians have made a religion out of the 1991 Incident. It became a dogma: the Russians are killing Lithuanians. Russia is the eternal enemy and Lithuania belongs with the West, which is always democratic – and whoever doubts this must be imprisoned. That is why millions, if not billions of money were sunk into this version. When I said that the earth is turning, as in "our people were shooting our own", the 21st century inquisition started.

Sapozhnikova: *Would you rather you never said that phrase?*

Paleckis: There is no answer to that... It produced results. Lithuania started cleansing itself of some of the ideological stereotypes. I hope those words, that cost me so much, will give an impulse to a new understanding of patriotism: the bitter truth is always better than a sweet lie. Genuine patriotism is being free of prejudice. The official version is very convenient for the current government to justify the economic failures. There is an enemy – Tsarist Russia, the Soviet Union, and now Putin's Russia – an enemy that is always harming Lithuania and always at fault for everything. And as soon as economic problems arise in Lithuania, the Russophobia and anti-communism button is pressed. And the people unite once again, because they have a common enemy.

Under that logic, the Lithuanians should be uniting right now, because they have a new common enemy – Algirdas Paleckis. But everything did not go as planned. Because Algirdas Paleckis also brought 12 witness to court, who confirmed HIS version of the events and not the official one.

"Blame It All On the Russians and It Will Work"

...I can't wrap my mind around this: how will the 13 January 1991 "Soviet aggression" trial, which started in early 2016, go about gathering witness testimonies, of which there are thousands?!

Initially when I started recording these interviews on the events of that January night, I thought I would be writing a classic journalistic investigation on how the events near the Vilnius TV tower and TV center really happened. I started interviewing the witnesses and I broke – in their versions the Soviet tanks multiplied geometrically and ran over dozens, no, thousands of people! The soldiers and officers seemed "high," a word which would appear during the cynical 90s and definitely not the last years of the innocuous Soviet Union. Someone's memory had a lieutenant in Soviet uniform shooting Lithuanians in the gut, others seemed to recall Landsbergis and Butkevičius in the crowd, while they never were there, and some recall smoke grenades going off and killing people... What can you say: human emotions multiplied by time and amount of consumed TV shows can truly make for a most impressive result.

So I abandoned that work – let the historians and prosecutors piece together this tragedy's details bit by bit. This book is about Lithuania, the one that grew on the ruins of the construct that fell 25 years ago and the machinery of political repressions that was activated surprisingly quickly thereafter. In fact, it happened almost at the same time as the national Lithuanian flag was raised over Gediminas' tower.

But here's the question: what do you do with the witness testimonies gathered and brought to court by Algirdas Paleckis? All of those who remembered the picture that doesn't fit with the new censored script? They have no chance of making their memories known in the press, because due to the law banning the denial of Soviet aggression, you just can't deny that very aggression, even if you have seen what actually happened with your own eyes:

- **Kristina Bradauskienė, mathematician and programmer:**
Hearing Landsbergis' call to protect the TV tower and hearing that people from all of Lithuania were brought in, me and my friend made two casseroles of hot food and set out to feed the protectors. The mood there was almost disco-like – right until the moment the Department of National Defense told us that tanks are coming our way and didn't ask us to hold hands. Then we heard the hum of the heavy vehicles and saw the tanks and APCs start driving up from the side of the residential area. The tank drivers were very skilled – I was horrified when they drove to the crowd at high speed yet managed to stop at nearly half a meter away and only the inertia [they jerked as they stopped] gave away their speed. I saw gunshots from the house across the way, they were visible in the night because they were tracer shots. If it were the Soviet soldiers then they would have run us over with the tanks and we would have a lot more victims.

- **Pavel Lagodny, ex-military:**
On that day, Landsbergis was on TV and the radio all day. I myself was in a basement, but called for everyone to go to the TV tower. And then when I went along with them I saw the gunshots start from the five-story building no. 37 on the street that is now called the 13 January Street. There were flashes and people fell, they were either trying to hide or were wounded/killed. On the second or third day I went to the hospital and saw a crowd of children. And I saw they have a bag of gun casings. I myself, have held a casing from a 16-caliber round, fired from a PPSh with a circular magazine, they had them back during the war and were still in the army up until the early 50s, the modern army didn't use them. I also saw casings from Mosin-Nagant rifles. I'm sorry I didn't take them back then. Although… even if I did show these casings today – who would believe me?

- **Boleslavas Bilotas, ex-Sąjūdis**
I remember it perfectly, how and when the slogan of liberating from the Russian yoke started. We needed to free ourselves from

the military garrisons which were here and make the people rise. So they would come to and say: we don't want the Russians! And how to do that if this was never a problem: we didn't even know who was Russian and who was Lithuanian?

I didn't know of the events at the TV tower until the next morning. I came to the Sąjūdis HQ and Vytautas Petkevičius was loudly saying that our people shot our own. I saw, "Then this will be an international scandal! Moscow will find out, send a commission and the army, and in a few days we will all be in Siberia!" And he says, "Who will figure this mess out at this time? Blame it all on the Russians and it will work…"

The funeral was most pompous, all of Lithuania gathered and the mood wasn't anti-Soviet, but anti-Russian. At work, they were very pleased that Lithuanian blood was spilled by the Russians. We could now demand: "Russians, get out of Lithuania!" And that was exactly what happened, they gathered up and left without a single shot and we remained.

We even made a deal back then, that it would be best to remain silent and not talk too much. If they would have not asked me this in court, I wouldn't have told you anything even today. I thought this was the honor of my homeland, so I didn't disclose it. And it weighs on my conscience, because I see how Paleckis is taken to court for nothing and those who ran our factories into the ground are never tried for anything. I am even ashamed of it…

- **Jaunutis Lekas:**

On that day, all of my family was near the parliament, my wife and four kids, the youngest being 10. I returned home, wanted to lie down, but the children screamed, "The tanks are coming!" We left our daughter at the neighbors and ran to the TV tower. The tanks were shooting blanks, lowering the barrels and sounded off a bang, but only from the cannons, no one was shooting from inside. They started pushing us out – there was a line of soldiers in front of me and they all shot the ground. They were live rounds, it would have gotten grim! Then I noticed the five-story buildings – that, as if three people were shooting a film. And four bangs from the middle of the house.

I recently met a neighbor on the street and he said that he apparently still has various round casings at his house. I asked him to give me his address and he replied, "I'm scared!" Lithuanians now are scared of their own shadow. The euphoria has passed. They fooled us, just like they did with the Perestroika. They promised us that we would be gods, and it turned out to be the opposite. We gained independence in order to disappear. We barely have enough population and we sold 53% of the land to foreigners. A people without land, without a state – just props. We were fooled flawlessly, telling of freedom, but it turned out the opposite... Before we sold out to the Germans, then the Soviets and now to the Americans. It turns out we weren't protecting a TV tower, but a concrete pole...

All According to the Designer's Vision

...Once again 13 January, I and Danguolė, a witness of the January 1991 events, went to the Vilnius tower, but it wasn't the 20th century, but the 21st.

The twenty-something years have changed many things: there are wooden crosses at the tower's base, and small obelisks where the people died, their passport photos displayed in the vestibule museum.

"Look here," says the guide, pointing at the small stone poles, "People died not only in front of the tower, but also behind it, on the opposite side of residential house. The shots of the 'unknown roof snipers' couldn't have hit them there. Which means they were all killed by the troops!"

Now that is convincing argument. It is as if it still reeks of death near the TV tower...

The story's drama dictates that I should note that Danguolė is worried. But that is not so: she has worried enough, in court, about three times. The first time when she testified at the Algirdas Paleckis case. The second and third times, when she was the one on trial, for telling about what she saw with her own eyes, and not read in the papers:

DANGUOLĖ RAUGALIENĖ:
Witness to January 13 events

Raugalienė: I lived close to a TV tower, and I went there, because I felt like I had to. During the day and the evening, Vytautas Landsbergis showed up in the Seimas windows and the people chanted: "Landsbergis, Landsbergis!" And I chanted as well. And when the tanks started moving in at night, I started dressing on my way and told my brother that we had to be there. Things were hectic inside, as if everyone had wings. When we made it to the TV tower, the tanks were only turning towards it. The tank crews were peeking out from their vehicles, like on a parade. Someone started shooting above and only then they hid inside.

Sapozhnikova: *Above from where?*

Raugalienė: From the five-story building and the nine-story one. The bullets flashed and you could see their tracers in the night. Then the worst part began: there were young men standing near the chain link fence, illuminated by the tank projectors. You couldn't see their faces. I only saw the silhouettes drop down and heard screams of someone being killed... There were people walking through the crowd and proposing that we don't leave and instead go there, where the bullets were whistling by, saying that "They are shooting blanks, they definitely won't kill you!"

Sapozhnikova: *But at that moment as you saw people fall, you had no doubts that the Soviet soldiers killed them?*

Raugalienė: The soldiers on the tanks definitely weren't shooting. Because if they were, then there would be nothing left of that district of Vilnius. We shouted at them, calling them murderers and were even excited when someone started shooting the tanks from above, because we thought we weren't alone and help arrived.

Sapozhnikova: *When did everything come together into something different from your first impression?*

Raugalienė: When I came home and told about this to my father. He told me to forget about what I saw and never tell anyone about it. The next day I bought flowers and once again went to the tower. And then the image of the falling silhouettes flashed before my eyes... For a whole year I have avoid this place...

Raugalienė pointed at where the fence used to be. And then she starts thinking and adds:

Raugalienė: You know, the obelisks on the place of the deceased are set up wrong! Loreta Asanavičiūtė (some men in the crowd pushed her towards the armored vehicle and she pressed to a chainlink fence- G.S.) was run over completely elsewhere. And there aren't even any obelisks near the chain-link fence where I saw the people fall!
Nobody demanded it be historically accurate – it seems the memorial signs were set up by a designer's intent. So it would look good...
The Vilnius TV tower now serves a different goal, an ideological one. So it must be milked for all its worth.

Two of the witnesses in this list – Danguolė Raugalienė and Jaunutis Lekas – were charged with false testimony after they published their accounts of the events. But Lithuania's Supreme Court acquitted them completely.

Not in Chekov's style

"Do you realize that you have insulted everyone? The people ran to the TV tower with no call to action! You have spat into their soul!"
Algirdas Paleckis has heard a lot of that from classmates, friends and parents.
It is understandable; to many Lithuanians the January 1991 events have become the crowning emotional event of their entire lives.

And how is a man to live with this newfound knowledge that events unfolded differently than the papers say? How to align it with the big picture, without ruining the harmony?

Another question is whether you can call the time-cemented legend of "Soviet aggression" with no place for any alternative viewpoints "harmonious"?

For the next interview, I went to the theater, in hopes of hearing the formula for that harmony, for the sake of which people died 25 years ago and now have Vilnius streets named after them. Who should I turn to if not the writers, painters and actors? To line up for the truth, which they usually feel visits them first?

And after the things I have heard, I realized that there was no rush: there was no harmony in Lithuania and none on the horizon as well. The interview with set designer Valentinas Tudorakė of the State Small Theatre of Vilnius is presented in order to illustrate the Lithuanian society in 1991. And where it has gone in the last 25 years.

***

VALENTINAS TUDORAKĖ
Set Designer, State Small Theatre of Vilnius

"We Smoked Like They Do Before a Battle in the Movies"

Tudorakė: Two days before 13 January 1991, we did the premiere of the Cherry Orchard play by Chekov. And the second one was to commence in two days, but due to the events, we decided to delay it a few days. It was a time of high spirits, mass unity: the play would distract from the main events that required the strength of the whole nation. It must sound pretentious, but that is exactly how it happened. Right now, after more than twenty year have passed, many things appear differently, especially with the expectations of those who were in the events not coming to pass. I was 36 at the time.

Sapozhnikova: *How did you end up near the TV tower?*

Tudoraké: There was a call to gather by the Seimas. It is not like it was a call to protect it with our bodies, but it was suggested that the more people show up, the less likely the Soviet forces would be to take any brutal action. The Russian-speaking population, in particular the Yedinstvo party led by Valery Ivanov, tried to start fights in order to prove that it was not safe to be there and that a military lockdown was necessary. I, as well the rest of the theater troupe, constantly went to guard the Seimas. Everything was going fairly calmly: if it were the Summer, then it could pass off as a hobby gathering or a club. My mother came to Vilnius from another city in order to also partake in the protest meetings and events. She brought me a warm winter coat even though it was not that cold by then.

Everyone had their radios and TVs on, and new information was coming in constantly. I decided to take a bath, a minor detail, but it will be important later. My mother called me and said, "Sonny, they are calling everyone to the TV Tower, we must go!" I said that my hair wasn't dry yet and she said, "Dry it up fast and come, we need the people's help." I dressed and went there on foot. For a few hours, it was calm around the tower, the people were singing folk songs and dancing so as to not get cold. Around 11 pm, I heard that something was happening. There was a group of men at the TV tower's steps, one of them had the Lithuanian national flag in his hands. At the same time, there was a sound of engines from the side and few IFVs[2] showed up. They turned sideways to the fence, running it over, and surrounded the TV tower in a tight ring. The gap between the vehicles was so small that if someone wanted to go away, they would have to slip between them. They were turning the turrets, lifting the cannons and made various threatening gestures. And then a few trucks rode in, with armed soldiers rushing out of them, and advancing in a line. The first thing they did was start breaking cameras and beating the journalists and only later did they get to us. I remember me and my neighbor were smoking hastily, like before a battle in the movies. There was a feeling of catharsis. A feeling that this was my purpose and destiny. We all clung together, no one stepping away, and if someone got hit in the head and lost consciousness, he would still be held up by the others...

The soldiers ran up and started shooting the glass above us, it shattered, but we still didn't move out of the way. Then they launched a smoke charge and the people stepped aside. Something blew up and a piece of the glass window fell off and hit my head. I lost consciousness. They were trying to take the flag away, it was constantly given from one man to another, but still stood above the group of people near the entrance. One old man, gray in the hair, shouted in Russian, "What are you doing? What are you doing?" When I came to, some young man and a woman took me up by my hands and pulled me from the encirclement and led me away. There were ambulances there and they were stocked full, some were being treated on the spot and some driven away.

"It Was the Peak of All of My Life"

Sapozhnikova: *You said that a lot were wounded. With what?*

Tudorakė: First, they shot from the cannons. I think those were blanks, but still something was shooting out of that, and a piece of plastic hit me in the leg. Second, people were getting beat up. Even before the glass fell on me, a gunner hit me in the back with his gunstock so hard that I keeled over.

Sapozhnikova: *Did you see the troopers or the Alpha operatives kill people?*

Tudorakė: I can't say I saw them point a gun at a specific person, shoot him in the stomach and he died from, but they were firing live rounds, that much is certain. They were either using the guns as intended or used them to clobber people on the head.

Sapozhnikova: *The case files say otherwise...*

Tudoraké: What file? Paleckis is being shady when he says that our people were shooting our own. A great political figure! Why is he telling his fairy tales about some kind of Mosin-Nagant rifles?

Sapozhnikova: *But the forensics reports made by the Lithuanian side state that five people were killed with Mosin-Nagant rounds and hunting rifle conversions and not Kalashnikovs!*

Tudoraké: I categorically declare that that couldn't have happened.

Sapozhnikova: *But the forensic report was made by Lithuanians!*

Tudoraké: I know how people can be! If everyone is so good and honest, then where do these Paleckises keep coming from? His grandfather made sure that a third of nation rotted in Siberia with the help of collaborationists like that.

Sapozhnikova: *But he brought 12 witnesses to court, who all testified that they saw people shoot from the roofs!*

Tudoraké: It is obvious that those are the ones who had a good life under the Soviets. Those who received trips to the resorts of Mineralnye Vody or Yalta. One can't simply go to the Black Sea nowadays. And they could do it back then.

Sapozhnikova: *Right now in Lithuania, not everyone can afford that...*

Tudoraké: I agree. But these are different things. It is economics. The world is imperfect and there is no justice within it. Right now we are being choked by everyone, and also Russia with its oil and gas. Thank God we managed to get away from you with the oil. We will find an alternative to the gas and the Russia will be completely inconsequential to us!

Sapozhnikova: *You are wrong to think that Russians start their days thinking about Lithuania. Remember this well and pass it to the others: not a single person in Russia wants to be feeding you again. But tell me, did you personally gain or lose anything from the USSR's collapse?*

Tudoraké: I have gained freedom. That is the most important feeling for any man. What could be better than knowing that you have possibilities? Not everything is progressing as we would want it to, those who were at the tower have gained a lot more than they lost. I remember that moment in history as the peak of all of my life. As a spiritual rise. So any theories and retellings I see as a personal insult. They rattle my soul and it hurts.

"A Lot of People Just Went Away Somewhere"

Sapozhnikova: *So do you think anyone was actually shot from converted hunting rifles and Mosin-Nagant rifles?*

Tudoraké: My personal opinion is that it is all made up. There could have been provocateurs. As if the KGB wasn't here? The whole history of the Soviet Union is built upon blood and lies!

Sapozhnikova: *So you don't have a single good memory about the USSR?*

Tudoraké: Why shouldn't I? I studied in St. Petersburg. And I have friends in Russia. I have nothing against the nation or the people. Only against the feeding organization that destroyed people with a passion.

Sapozhnikova: *And what about your Forest Brethren destroying 25 thousand of your compatriots? The Lithuanians have also managed to leave a mark on the 20th century in terms of cruelty.*

Tudoraké: Which people were sent to camps the most? There were whole railway cars of people being shipped out of Lithuania. A third of the nation was destroyed, if not more. Take the Soviet statistics.

Sapozhnikova: *Here are the statistics: out of the 3 million population of Lithuania, 130 thousand[3] were exiled to Siberia. The majority of them returned. And saying you lost a third of the nation is completely untrue.*

Tudorakė: I can't recall perfectly, it was a long time ago, but I watched on the situation before the war and after. And a lot of people just went away somewhere.

Sapozhnikova: *Well, for example, 196 thousand Jews were killed by Lithuanians.[4]*

Tudorakė: Outright killed? Lithuanians? (At this moment, my interviewee was confused, not believing me. But he quickly regained composure – G.S.) And how many fled West? They are also lost to Lithuania.

Sapozhnikova: *And the ones fleeing today? Is that also the Soviet Union's fault?*

Valentinas Tudorakė was silent. I had one more question.

Sapozhnikova: *Is the phrase "our people were shooting our own" enough for Algirdas Paleckis to become an outcast in Lithuania society?*

Tudorakė: He is a complete outcast! [He rejoiced.] As soon as news about him appears on TV or in the theater, we all think the same thing: "Hang him!"

* * *

That answer could be a find for any theatrical director and it saved me a lot of time and a whole chapter. In any case, it became clear just what kind of mechanism was activated in Lithuania right after the August coup, with them announcing a hunt for all of the "formers" – communists and journalists, swat, patrols and the military – everyone who could have gotten in the way of their new "bright future" which they never did reach.

This was a hate mechanism familiar to us from World War II. There was no need to invent anything new.

| Chapter Four |

THE GREAT LITHUANIAN WITCH HUNT

It was curtains for Lithuania on 21 August 1991, when they started arresting communists and their sympathizers. The corpse of the GKChP[1] was still warm when they came knocking at the apartments of those who didn't consider the USSR a "criminal state" and tried to preserve it. The speed at which yesterday's friends and colleagues turned on those with whom they had sat at the same table is truly astounding. The overblown feeling of revenge is also quite surprising: the Lithuanian state wasn't yet functioning, wasn't acknowledged by anyone and de-facto didn't even exist yet, and the revolutionary neophytes were ready to see an enemy in anyone who wasn't with them. The great Lithuanian witch hunt had begun.

The "enemy of the nation" lists had hundreds on it: district party committee secretaries, journalists, policemen, SWAT members – everyone who was naïve enough to try and defend the honor of the USSR to the end. Dozens of Lithuanians in August 1991 had to leave their homes forever, in order to avoid penance for something they never did. The personal stories of their separations from their small and heretofore warm homeland are the truest picture of the Great Lithuanian Eclipse Days, when black turned to white and vice versa.

The worst awaited those who stayed behind. They came for them as well. And 8 (!) years after January 1991, a trial was started in Vilnius, which was known as the "red professors" case. Of whom there were six, but one of them – Ivan Kucherov – did not live to see the trial. Another one, the editor-in-chief of the Soviet Lithuania radio station, Stanislav Mickevic, didn't show up in court for his verdict; being a citizen of Russia, he managed to hide there. Communist Party of Lithuania CPSU platform secretaries Mykolas Burokevičius, Juozas Jermalavičius and Juozas Kuolelis took the brunt of it (and they will have the next chapter dedicated to them). Two other accused – former policeman Jaroslav Prokopovich and former Director of the CLP Central Committee publishing Leonas Bartoševičius – legitimately served their 15-month sentences. The court did not take the age of the defendants into account; Jermalavičius was the youngest at 54 and the eldest Bartoševičius was 73, who was in court in a wheelchair.

"I am asking you to let me die at home. I am a very sick man. After the operation, I have constant headaches. I can't sleep during the day, nor during the night... I have never stood against Lithuania... I am not a political figure. I am not guilty of anything. I ask the court to acquit me and take my health into account," begged Bartoševičius. But it was in vain. They counted the time he spent in the pre-trial detention facility, but when the verdict was issued, they made him remain in prison for 6 more days before letting him go.

All of their good deeds done for Lithuania were forgotten. Two doctors of sciences, three cultural workers and one distinguished police worker were put on trial, and "civilized Europe" didn't bat an eye at the whole thing. PACE[2] representative Andreas Gross visited Mykolas Burokevičius in prison, but politely chose to say nothing. And the acting director of the UNESCO Office of International Standards and Legal Affairs, John Donaldson, wrote to the Russian Union of Journalists (which tried to defend the journalist Stanislav Mickevic) saying that the Communist Party of Lithuania on the CPSU platform was a "rebellious group" and that "Lithuanians were deprived of freedom of speech and freedom of press for half a century, from 1940 to 1990."

The details of the trial of the red professors were documented for history by another political prisoner, historian and philosopher Valery Ivanov. First he was imprisoned for three years for leading the Lithuanian-Russian-Polish organization Venibe – Edinstvo – Ednost, which opposed Sąjūdis. And when he was set free, he wrote the book, *Lithuanian Prison*, detailing how he did time in the triumphant "Lithuanian democracy", locked in a torturous 2 meter by 78 centimeter box in maximum security solitary confinement. That landed him in prison again. The official version states that he insulted the memory of the 13 January victims. But really, he was punished for doubting the official version that states that people died due to the Soviet military. And for disclosing the great Lithuanian secret: that the "red professor" trials, militiamen trials and his own trial, which are all used by Lithuania for years in an attempt to create a second Nuremberg trial on communism, are all held together by newspaper articles and have no proper foundation to them.

One time, the two political trials coincided and Ivanov's court had the former leaders of the CPSU platform CPL brought in for questioning. It was 11 April 1994.

From Ivanov's diary:

> Today is a special day for us. The former First Secretary of the CPL Central Committee (CPSU) M. Burokevičius, former head of the ideology department of the CPL Central Committee (CPSU) J. Jermalavičius and CPL Central Committee (CPSU) advisor I, Kucherov have arrived from the Lukiškės prison to testify. It was three months from when the Lithuanian secret services kidnapped the CPL leaders from Belarus. The prison had yet to leave its mark on their bright faces. Only Ivan Kucherov, who had spent 9 months in confinement, looked pale and disorientated.
>
> When they were escorted one by one into

the courtroom by the police guard, we stood up from our seats in honour of those who fought for the unity of our great country and at the most important moment, took the responsibility for a socialistic future, those who were brazenly betrayed by their direct nomenclature leader, the CPSU Central Committee General Secretary and President of the USSR, Mikhail Gorbachev.

Right now they are part of the same drama, worthy of Shakespeare. Brought before court, they testified that they loyally served the country that they were citizens of until December 1991.

...The performance came to a close but the stage play continued on its own. And if Shakespeare found out that 25 years after the premiere [January 1991 events – G.S.], Lithuania still had the actors brought on stage for the final scene called the "Poster trial", then he would have turned into a Stanislavski and shouted "I don't believe you!"

VALERY IVANOV:
Historian and philosopher

"I promised to pick up my son from kindergarten and disappeared for three years"

I pretty much had just one question for this man, but it was the most important one: on the third day of the August coup, 21 August 1991, when democracy blossomed in the Baltics like red poppies and the first arrests began, the smart ones started fleeing Lithuania. Why did he, Valery Ivanov, stay?

Ivanov: I had no other option. First of all, I didn't kill anyone. My struggle was purely political along with the organization I led, which was officially registered. I, honestly speaking, couldn't even

Valery Ivanov, never got his son Adrian to kindergarten. He was arrested on the way there.

assume that I could be persecuted. And furthermore, everyone knew I was a single father, my wife died of cancer a few years ago and I had a small son on my hands and I was my mother's only son. I thought that they would call me in, maybe scold me and interrogate me, but why would they imprison me? Alas, I had to go through all of the circles of hell.

Sapozhnikova: *Were you still in that illusion up until the day of your arrest on 27 November 1991?*

Ivanov: Yes. I was taking my child to kindergarten, and two people approached me. I understood that they were there for me. I had previously made arrangements with my friends: if something were to happen and I would be taken somewhere, then they would try to let my friends know, so they would take my son, Adrian, to Russia, otherwise they would blackmail me with him... And it happened just like that. I was arrested. Took me to the prosecutor straight from the kindergarten. I asked them to let me go home to at least take some of my things. They didn't let me. I kissed my child and told him I would pick him up at six o'clock and was gone for three years.

Indicted under Soviet Law

Sapozhnikova: *What were you charged with?*

Ivanov: First they didn't know what to charge me with, so they tried using the 105 Article, as if I killed some person called Mr. Kanapinskas on the night of 13 January 1991. Then it turned out that he had been taken to the hospital even before I had arrived at the TV and Radio Committee building with my filming crew. I am an experienced man, I worked as an ambulance team member because I wanted to be a doctor at one point, so I know how to do all of that paperwork. The documents are very strict. And I told the investigators that Kanapinskas was driven away at 2:10 am, where they found him, and the militiamen and camera crew, which I was with, arrived at the TV and Radio Committee only at 2:30 am, which was documented. Therefore, I had an alibi.

Sapozhnikova: *So what was the official reason for keeping you in prison for three years?*

Ivanov: For "creating an anti-government organization and anti-government activity". Article 70, a political crime from the Soviet times.

Sapozhnikova: *So it turns out they passed a verdict using Soviet laws? Did they have a postponement for a single father or a suspended sentence?*

Ivanov: No. I immediately told them: you know I have my son in kindergarten and I need to pick him up in the evening? They knew all of it, of course... When the investigator left the office, I quickly called my friends from his phone. They probably specifically set it up, so I could make that call. And that was it. I was taken to prison with four assault rifles pointed at me, to ensure that I didn't escape.

What is Soviet Power?

Sapozhnikova: *I know an interesting fact from your biography, that during those three years in a prison cell, you were not just wasting away with no benefit for yourself or society. When you were given access to your criminal case files, you diligently copied all of it to your notebook, day by day, page after page. That is a real feat, because Lithuania doesn't allow anyone near the files of the 13 January 1991 incident.*

Ivanov: It is because I am an educated man and was well-schooled in history in Warsaw University. They taught us to work with documents, make proper conclusions and look for information. However, there is an important detail: I refused to testify. I was the leader of the organization and any word of mine could have hit other people, who would also be dragged into interrogation. And that is why they took me to Šiauliai, and pressured and beat me so hard, that I spend a month in the Šiauliai prison hospital... Before I left prison, there was a provocation aimed at me, where I was probably meant to disappear. So, probably if I hadn't held out, I would have been killed by my cellmates. At one point, one of them asked me, "Are you for Soviet power?" I replied "yes". And they gang up on me, I try to defend myself, but see one of them has a shiv. I sit there and think: fine, beat me up, let me be beat up and then you will have no alibi. But when they saw I wasn't reacting, they stopped. And in two hours they took me away.

Sapozhnikova: *So how did you figure out that you needed to copy the documents?*

Ivanov: I started copying them when the investigation was over and we were given access to the case files. And when I was in prison, I kept diaries, which I later published as a book. It was printed in small numbers, it sold out immediately and became a rare item. But after, I made a presentation in the Russian State Duma, repeating that there is no evidence of the Soviet soldiers killing anyone. There was a member of the Lithuanian embassy there. And when I returned to Vilnius, they immediately started another case against me; this time it was for the book. And I got a year for that.

Sapozhnikova: *For revealing a state secret?*

Ivanov: What state secret? I just wrote that the facts in the documents just don't add up. They don't add up at all. And I'm a philosopher who builds his philosophy on math, so I am very precise.

Writing the "Wrong" Book

Sapozhnikova: *Why did you even return to Lithuania? Did you not foresee how it would end?*

Ivanov: I foresaw it well, but what could I do? I know I am innocent. Jesus Christ also did good and look at where he ended up. I had ideals I looked up to: do good and have no fear, if you get evil, it is still not a reason to be afraid – you will pass through it and triumph in the end. And triumph I did.

Sapozhnikova: *Your book* Lithuanian Prison *was probably reprinted multiple times, since you were sent to prison for it?*

Ivanov: No, because it was wrong book. It didn't fit in with the ideological moment in Russia, or in Lithuania. It was 1996. The Baltics were considered "paragons of democracy" back then. Getting out of prison, I talked to Andreas Gross, a PACE representative, who visited me in prison, gave him my book, outlined how many dissidents were in prison at the time, I had a file on that. But I could have just let my file flow across the Neris river through Vilnius. No answer, no response at all.

Sapozhnikova: *So they knew of your predicament in Europe? Why did they not act?*

Ivanov: It is a mystery to me as well. I was visited by many people and nothing... I did my time in full.

Sapozhnikova: *Why wasn't it considered possible to criticize the Baltics in Russia or Europe? Lithuania joined the European Union with the infamous Red Professors case and official political prisoners!*[3]

Ivanov: That is the main question. Honestly, I don't know how to answer it. The biggest surprise is that these events happened on the territory of the Lithuanian SSR and under Lithuanian SSR jurisdiction. On the night of 11 March 1990, Sąjūdis proclaimed Lithuania's independence and adopted the 1938 Constitution, according to which Vilnius and Vilnius region were not part of the Lithuanian Republic at the time and Kaunas is the new capital. But no! People who were in the Lithuania SSR, citizens of the Lithuanian SSR and living under Lithuanian SSR rules were tried for doing acts that contradict the laws of a different state – the Lithuanian Republic... Just imagine if say, Amazonia has tribes that eat their people for breakfast. We grab a tribesman, fly him to Vilnius and try him by our laws, asking him on why he ate his unlucky fellow tribesman? A circus. During the trial I asked them one question, tell me the name of at least one person, a Soviet soldier, who killed your relative? Or at least a number of the tank. Tell me and I will repent and self-chastise. But no, they tell me they don't know. And yet I was convicted for offending the memory of the deceased.

I feel sorry for them: they can't prove anything, because they have no evidence. But how to create any? Loreta Asanavičiūtė [she died under the tracks of a Soviet tank, according to the official version – G.S.] was made into an exemplary victim – she was taken to the hospital still conscious, said her home address before the operation, she also had a cardiogram taken at 7 am 13 January, and at 1 pm, she was already up for autopsy... And I have seen the autopsy report – she didn't have a single broken bone. How can you run over someone in a tank and not break a single bone? Talks of snipers on the roofs were around since the very first day after the January tragedy. And the writer, Petkevičius, with whom I have spoken personally many times, openly spoke of 18 border guard Lithuanians, who apparently shot from the roofs. I'm not sure that the trial of USSR, which is happening right now in Vilnius will include these facts.

"I Demand They Find the Killers"

Sapozhnikova: *Is it dangerous for you to give this interview?*

Ivanov: Why should I be afraid? My son has grown up, his mother is in a better place. If you don't live by the truth, then why live at all? I am not denying the death of those people on the night of 13 January 1991. I feel for their loss and offer my condolences. But I demand that the killers of these men be found. And they haven't been named. The same way that no one proved that those border guards in Medininkai were killed by that unlucky SWAT officer from Riga, who is now serving a life sentence in a Lithuanian prison. He was locked away, just because. Some director wrote in a script and during the finale, someone has to take the fall...

Sapozhnikova: *Would it be correct to say the following: during the late '80s a large number of Lithuanians were your potential allies and didn't want Lithuania to leave the Soviet Union, however their minds were turned around with one historic falsification?*

Ivanov: I wouldn't say that their minds were turned around. If they were turned around in favor of Lithuania, then right now, we wouldn't be seeing this mass exodus of its population. Lithuania's population was 2.5 million before the war. During the collapse of the USSR it was 3.8 million. Now we have dropped lower than pre-war numbers. But the internet still keeps saying that we shouldn't fear the country dying out and instead turn our fears towards Russia. Lithuanians aren't Russophobes, I was born there, I know the people, I love the people. Until Sąjūdis and the inflation of that nationalistic bubble, everything was normal. My wife was Lithuanian. Can you believe it, I was married to Miss Lithuania and her face was even one of the symbols of Sąjūdis. For the past 25 years in Lithuania, there hasn't been another international organization similar to the Venibe - Edinstvo – Ednost, which I led and was tried for.

From Valery Ivanov's prison diaries:

…So, I am in a pre-trail cell on Kościuszko street in Vilnius. Saying my farewell to Adrian in the group, I didn't know that they wouldn't allow me to pick him up, as I usually did at 6 pm. I didn't know that I would be in the pre-trial cell №1, with naked wooden bunks, in 6 square meters with a rectangular window pointing at nothing. The glass block covering the cell's window only let a dim light inside. The instinct to meet my son at kindergarten, reflective of the responsible care for him which I had exercised over the years, was weighing on me. All of my thoughts were of Adrian. I counted that my son was 5 years, 10 months and 4 days old today. Yesterday, when they took me from the Lithuanian Republic Prosecutor-General's office, I managed to tell my friends to look after him. Today I was calmer, as I was sure that my son was not left in trouble, but cared for and fed. The hope that everything will be alright with my son calms me. There is some noise behind the door, there are new arrivals at the cell next door. They brought them out to take their fingerprints. They are also Russian. You can't near any Lithuanian speech at all.

Punishment is already underway, even though they have yet to prove that I am a criminal. Is that not the sign of the local totalitarian government? Instead of letting active participants of non-extremist political organizations at least speak their mind in the mass media outlets, combat the political opposition arguments and prove that they are right – the government just locks them up. This is state political terrorism!

...And releasing them – they won't do it. I asked them to do it for my young son, who is suffering without a father. Adrian is so little and he has had to go through so much: his mother's death, hardships, insults and hounding of his father. Oh God! The great Fyodor Dostoyevsky wrote about a "child's tear"... Are we really still so uncultured and uncivilized?

... I will note an observation I made that night. Which I consider important. The ambulance cars imitated a mass evacuation of the wounded from the events near the TV and radio center (KRTV). This could be seen in the fact that the medical vehicles, which came to Konarskio street every five minutes, stopped in front of it, and after standing there for a while, quickly rode away, flashing the lights and sounding the siren. And they didn't pick up anyone from the streets, because the doors remained closed throughout the time it stood there. I think it was a devious plan of the organizers, which would show the foreign correspondents, who were fluttering about with their video and photo cameras the widespread victims of the "Soviet army mopping up the peaceful civilians." As odd as it may be, but a lot of journalists came to Vilnius in advance and, unlike us, took very precise positions for their reports from the impending events. The blue signal lights of the ambulances and the screech of sirens, the roar of the army armored vehicles, the rare bangs of the blanks fired from the tanks, all of it created the suitable setting. It excited the emotional crowd of Lithuania nationalists, heating up their urge to protest about the presence of Soviet Army personnel...

...A day of mourning. We, along with one guy from the Moscow TV crews, picked out the needed registration cards from the video storage list, 19 of them, with recording of symphonic music, which fit the scene. They have pieces by Bach, Chopin, Mozart's Requiem, etc. Then we went into the vault, however none of the videocassettes were in video storage. We had to work hard, but we managed to get the appropriate music and clips. I think what we did is an important discovery that reveals that someone in the TV and Radio Committee prepared for the events of 13 January beforehand, which included human casualties, took the tapes from storage and drove them out of the TV building. I must admit, they were quite meticulous in expecting human blood to be spilled and the act of sacrificing human lives will be at hand...

...During all of the court trial, in front of the Lithuanian Supreme Court, across from the cage where we were sat, there were 41 of the so-called public prosecutors. This crowd had 16 demanding the firing squad and the others were saying "try them by the law" or "compensate the damages".

Only one, a conservatory student and eye witness of the events of that January night near the KRTV building said, "Even if they are guilty, then God will judge them. I forgive them…"

…The unforgettable moment of meeting Adrian on 15 June 1998. He is standing on the other side of a long broad table in the meeting room, divided into sections by transparent Plexiglas walls, and he is looking at me with surprise and a certain shyness. And I look at him. At one point I read his look, his thoughts, "Here is my dad, he is different, not the same as I saw him last in kindergarten, back then, long ago. And he is dressed different, gray in the hair, but the eyes are his…"

Or maybe it was me looking at him and thinking that way?

… I interrupted him and said "Come to me" and after some encouragement from his grandma, he, awkwardly came over the table and into my hands. I pressed him to me, felt his strong, but small heart beating, it had to endure a lot. I stood up slightly, and cradled him in my hands, calming him down for a while. And he calmed me. We were happy at that moment. Tears ran down my cheeks. We were together again."

***

IVAN KUCHEROV:
Professor and Doctor of Law, deceased

Conspiring to Take Over Power With the Help of the Militiamen

"My meek homeland, clear-eyed land! What woes hath

descended upon you? Our false prophets hath gotten you drunk, and a foreign fiend brought his poison."

... You have to be a very romantic in order to write like that while in prison. Or really love Lithuania.

Both of those can be said about professor and doctor of law, Ivan Kucherov. If he had lived to see his trial, then he would have been tried for treason. Although it is not certain who betrayed whom – he betrayed his homeland or his homeland betrayed him?

Like many others, he left Lithuania for Belarus right after

Doctor of law Ivan Kucherov proved that the data in the forensics report was falsified. This discovery cost the professor two years in prison.

the August coup, when the first arrests and searches started, and avoided the madness of the first wave of repressions. The trials started and fell apart – the first ever political prisoner in Lithuania's recent history, the First Secretary of the CPL Mažeikiai District Committee was acquitted after serving 7 months in prison. CPL Central Committee workers Nikolay Gribanov and Sergey Reznik, who were released in the court room, both got a monetary fine. The stature of those thrown in cells (militiamen, ordinary communists, Russian-speaking activists) was low: the group was lacking a diamond, a banner, whose determination would justify all of the New Lithuanian regime's mistakes.

And this role was given to Professor Kucherov – unexpectedly and crudely, because he was not in hiding and regularly arrived in Vilnius for interrogation, replying to all court summons. And one day, in July 1993, the cage slammed shut.

Seven Bullets and One Body

A day after his arrest, he wrote an open letter to the then president, former First Secretary of the Communist Party of Lithuania, Algirdas Brazauskas, posing a few uncomfortable questions:

- How many foreign secret service specialists arrived in Lithuania, along with Mister Andrew Eiwa?
- Who were they working around and what were they doing?
- Whose idea was it that during Summer 1990, the Lithuanian media started a propaganda campaign, stating that only spilt Lithuanian blood will unite the Lithuanians?
- Who orchestrated that campaign?
- Who sent armed men unto the roofs near the TV center and why were they shooting at the crowd?
- Why was the extent of casualties falsified along with the autopsy reports?

Of course, Brazauskas didn't answer him and probably didn't even read the letter, but that is not important here.

The reason for Kucherov's arrest was the last question. It was that question that got Ivan locked up in prison for 20 months.

The issue at hand is that body of one of the victims, Ignas Šimulionis, contained seven bullet wounds. It was strange: how could a man get so many gun wounds at the same time from different sides?

Kucherov, a respected voice in forensic examinations, was asked to comment on photos and official forensic files. The reply of the experienced forensic expert was clear-cut: "The wounds were inflicted in an artificial environment. The shots were fired at the dead body at point-blank or almost point-blank range." Isn't it silly to assume, wondered Kucherov, that during the night time shooting, the shooters being on different sides of the victim and at a distance away from it, shot at the exact same moment at the exact same victim.

But that is not all. The official report from 6 February 199, signed by the chief of the Republican Bureau of Forensic Examination, Antanas Garmus, had another revelation: "...in addition to that, the victim (Šimulionis) has cerebrocranial trauma. Multiple fractions of the skull cap and back of the skull mean that the head was pressed between two surfaces in a sideways manner. This kind of trauma is commonly seen when run over by the wheels of a vehicle."

What could that mean? Only that Šimulionis' body was shot seven times after it was ran over by a car.

Garmus and non-Garmus

It wasn't hard to find Antanas Garmus in Vilnius; even after so many years, he was still working as a forensics expert, however, now in a private bureau under his own name. Garmus was most friendly over the phone: "Send any questions!" Which is what I did, sent him a copy of his own report from 25 years ago over email. The reaction was surprising: "I have received it and this is my first time seeing it, I don't recall ever signing something like this. I ask that you do not disturb me anymore," he added dryly.

But I did not relent, "I think you are very frightened by something. There is a big difference between your good will in our previous conversation and your cold reply. The signature is yours, there is also a photo of this document, but now that all of Lithuania is doubting your report, you are being intimidated. Am I right? Maybe you will reconsider and give future generations some clarity on who is actually lying in this situation?"

It seems that he is a honorable man, because he replied again. As sincerely as he could:

"Stop talking nonsense, I am seeing this paper for the first time and the first I have heard of it, as well. And I didn't talk to anyone. That is all."

The original of this report, which is 5 pages, is in the Lithuanian Republic Prosecutor-General's Office criminal file 10-09-057-96, tome 8, pages 126-30. Signed and stamped...

A Coup in the Minds

But this is not about him, but about Kucherov. That phrase about Šimulionis being already dead when he was shot seven times from different guns is the key to why the professor was persecuted, covered in vague criminal case words on how he was the "main ideologue" who was "planning to overthrow the government". There was nothing to overthrow – independent Lithuania existed only in the hearts of Lithuanians, and not all of them. The coup was only in the minds of those who decided to fill out the "anti-government organization" list with not only the Lithuanian Communist Party, but all other opposition organizations and mass movements. "Even the Slavic University, which I helped create as the dean of the law faculty! If I had read it in the papers, I wouldn't have believed it and considered it a hoax!" said Kucherov in his articles, which he wrote literally on his knee, in a prison cell, trying to get the people to see the obvious:

> The Lithuanian Supreme Court bill from 11 March 1990 and the USSR Presidential decree

[on their illegal status] led to the following socially harmful consequences:

Lithuania's population ended in two crisscrossing and active at the same time political and legal systems [the Soviet Union one and the separatist bourgeois one], split between supporters and opponents of these systems and confronting powers. These legal acts are at the foundation of the rapidly worsening socio-political crisis, which led to the January 1991 events. After 11 March Lithuania was de jure and de facto part of the USSR up until September 1991. The declared independence was not recognized by the USSR, nor the world community [excluding Iceland, I believe]. Moreover, many legal acts in Moscow were adopted by the Lithuanian government. So saying that someone took part in the activities of a different state is just causing confusion: at the time, USSR and Lithuania were a single state.

Nothing like... "the winners" stomping "the defeated" with a devilish passion, continuing to say that Lithuania is in a state of war with the USSR...

Only for Madmen

But at least someone at some point should have noticed the obvious absurdity of accusing the "red professors" of conspiring to take power with the aid of the militiamen? Kucherov was patient and with the lenience of a teacher in a school for the insane repeated in accessible language:

It is known, that military men execute the directives of their commander-in-chief and their direct military superiors, and not some civilians. The Vilnius TV tower, which they took over and for which the militiamen came to provide protection, was not the residence of the Lithuanian leadership. You have to even come up with that: a triumvirate [Burokevičius, Jermalavičius, Kucherov] sends out armed men to take over the storehouses of a paper and a TV tower instead of the residence of the Supreme Council or the government! Wouldn't it be more logical to assume that rattling sabers is the dastardly ruse of the commander-in-chief and his entourage in order to set-up the – much hated by the democrats – SSR's armed forces for public criticism?"

It was all for nothing: unlike Kucherov, the investigators did not have a sense of humor... In addition, the professor couldn't publish his arguments in the new, independent Lithuania. Even Russia and Belarus at the time were not quite sober, being permanently drunk on "democracy." But Kucherov wasn't just writing for no one, even though the pro-communist press were the only ones brave enough to publish his prison notes. In order to understand what was really happening in Lithuania in the early 90s, his conclusions at the time, read today, are priceless.

Sacrifice, According to Kucherov

"Summer 1990, the Lithuanian media, as if on order, started milking the question of how to attain "complete independence." The grim ideologue of the Sąjūdis, Romualdas Ozolas, a Russophobe and reactionary, bluntly stated in his writings: only spilt blood will unite the Lithuanians and raise them up against the USSR. In multiple publications only one thing was the dominant point: the army is the enemy of independence and thus casualties can't be avoided. And Landsbergis never missed a chance to rouse the people to fight the USSR and its army.

Simply put, Lithuania's population was psychologically "zombified", prepared to make sacrifices unto the altar of freedom.

And the same time, armed groups were being hastily formed. But if there is a negative idea of sacrifice, then there are plans on how it will happen.

On how the 13 January 1991 sacrifice plan came to be is supported by these facts:

- People in Independence Square were being prepared for death day and night: shoddy barricades were built, the people were roused up, the radio and TV were inspiring them with patriotic songs and reports, a priest absolved those present of their sins.

- There was still no shooting on the streets, but the Lithuanian radio started reporting in the main European languages, repeating several times that blood is being spilled on the streets of Vilnius, there aren't enough medical supplies, transfusion blood and doctors... Turns out this message was in preparation for the sacrifice scenario.

- As soon as the motorized troops moved out, Department of National Defense head Butkevičius knew where it was headed, calling the unarmed people to protect the TV tower, assuring them that the soldiers don't have live rounds. Another question: why not ask the people to wait, the soldiers would leave!

- The investigators knew well that there was fire from the roofs near the TV tower, from the forest: what if the soldiers really have blank rounds! Someone really wanted the TV tower takeover without casualties.

- Because the mass sacrifice would not have happened, someone had the idea to announce those who died of a heart attack, died in a car crash, which is also known by the investigators.

The sacrifice on the altar of Lithuania's independence was planned ahead by the political backstage entourage of Landsbergis, which was later supported by Gorbachev's entourage. It was he who set up the military in order to raise the prestige of the Lithuanian "democrats."

This was written 3 September 1993.

But alas, this was all for naught. It was never published, they didn't want to hear any alternative opinion in Lithuania. What was left was poetry – Kucherov published his poems under the pseudonym Yan Grach, which wasn't a secret to anyone, so the poems had the same fate as the articles.

A Ballad of the Unnamed War

«...Шестая часть земли в огне горячих точек.
И ставят короли на карте мира прочерк.
В неназванной войне нет фронта, нет и тыла.
В неназванной войне jдна на всех могила..».

"…A sixth of the land aflame with hot spots.
And the kings cross out the world map.
The unnamed war has no front, no behind lines.
The unnamed war has one grave for all…"

These and other poems, as well as articles written by Professor Kucherov in Lukiškės prison were given to me in January 2015 by his son, Igor Kucherov. with the words: "You need these materials more. You can use them as much as you need for as long as you need." We talked a lot about his father then, on how he survived in Vilnius prison and how he lived out the rest of his life in Minsk, when he was paroled early, because he was deathly ill and had mere months to live. And there was no one to return the weighty folder of cut-outs and poems, because in Spring 2015, Kucherov Jr. passed away as well. This is his last interview.

KUCHEROV JR., deceased
Son of Ivan Kucherov

Sapozhnikova: *How did you family end up in Lithuania?*

Kucherov Jr.: We lived in Minsk, then my father was offered the position of deputy director of a forensic expert research institute. There was also an offer to go to Volgograd, to the High Militia School, but Lithuania was closer, three hours by train and the family council decided that he would go there, settle in and then get us there as well. But when I was in 10th grade, my mother died. The question was whether to take me to Lithuania or let me finish school. But because dad didn't get an apartment in Vilnius and lived at his office, it was decided that I would finish school in Minsk and would try for the institute. That is how it turned out, we lived in different cities. Every weekend, he would come to visit me or I would visit him. He showed me Vilnius from end to end.

Sapozhnikova: *As a child, did you register any national tension in Lithuania? Could you imagine that things could unfold as they did?*

Kucherov Jr.: I have relatives on my mother's side in the Donbass. And when you come there, you feel yourself at home. And here, it is as if you are kept at a distance. Even when going to visit someone as a guest, you feel that you are different and you are tolerated at best. All Lithuanians, with whom I have talked to, treated Russians exactly like that, even though everyone held a post and were near the party feeder.

Sapozhnikova: *When exactly did it start going downhill? Did you make any attempts to get your father out of Lithuania? Why didn't the emergency button work?*

Kucherov Jr.: He felt it all! But he was such a patriot of the Soviet Union, so he started fighting all the signs of nationalism with all of his enthusiasm – making speeches, calling the citizens to unite in order to preserve the Union. So, he was immediately in opposition to the new government, but he thought he was protecting the lawful government. He considered it his duty to do everything he could to save the Union and Lithuania would remain part of it.

Gorbachev Was an Agent of Influence

Sapozhnikova: *Did he feel that closer to January 1991, the Lithuanian pressure cooker was about to reach a breaking point?*

Kucherov Jr.: He always came to visit me and share impressions. Of course, no one could even assume that it would come to shootings and bloodshed. But he did say that things were going bad and blamed Gorbachev. We argued with him, because when Gorbachev came to power, we applauded that the old men had finally gone and there was an energetic ruler. And my dad told me, "He is an agent of influence, he will do all he can in order to break up the Soviet Union." He said that openly, rather than whisper it. I thought to myself, how is he not afraid?

Sapozhnikova: *What did your father tell you about the events of 13 January, except that dead bodies were shown at the morgue tables?*

Kucherov Jr.: That is exactly what he told me. He talked about it even before the newspaper articles began, that they were shot in the back, that there were snipers on the roofs and shot at their own. And those who weren't down, were finished off at the morgue. He even drew the bullet paths for me.

Sapozhnikova: *Was he persecuted specifically for that report?*

Kucherov Jr.: As a whole for his activities, the crowning achievement of which was that very "coup", because when he was officially accused, he was said to be one of the main organizers and the troops were secondary... So three communists organized a coup and called the army in for support. And he was considered the main ideologue. He was a professor back then, a doctor of law and taught at the High Party School.

"I Don't Know Any Other Country Than This…"

Sapozhnikova: *Did he understand that the USSR's end was predetermined?*

Kucherov Jr.: He said that when they took the TV tower, the military gave a plane and they went to see Gorbachev, so he would call for a state of emergency in Lithuania. They flew in at evening, sat there all night and were then told that there would be no meeting. And they flew back. Gorbachev had already made his famous declaration that the local separatists were raging and he had no idea about it. So, he took the Lithuanian side! My father then exclaimed, "Would you look at that…?" And then always said that Gorbachev had to leave, because he would lead to not just all of the Baltics leaving, but the whole Union falling apart. When the August Coup happened, he welcomed it. And then in late August 1991, when I was at work, I received a sudden call, "Hello I am in Minsk at the train station." I picked him up and took him to my place. And that is when he moved in with me, because he realized that it was done…

Sapozhnikova: *Was he depressed?*

Kucherov Jr.: No. He was never depressed. On the contrary, his energy buoyed him up! He was constantly talking about how you have to fight. Never handed in his Soviet Union passport. He said, "I don't know anything, I am a USSR citizen!" Then this came back to bite him in prison, because a lawyer came in and offered Belarussian citizenship, it was a way for him to liberate himself, and he replied, "I know of no such country. There is the Soviet Union!" It turned out that neither Belarus, nor Russia could take him. And he did additional time with his Soviet passport.

They Executed not Him, But a Poem

Sapozhnikova: *And how did he get into Lithuanian prison, if he managed to leave and lived in Minsk?*

Kucherov Jr.: From time to time he secretly sneaked out to Vilnius through some of his personal channels. I asked him, aren't you afraid? In summer I went to Ukraine to my relatives and asked him: "I beg you – don't go to Vilnius without me." He said "okay." And I come back from vacation and find that he is not home. And then they told me: your dad is arrested... First, we thought that they would figure it out and release him, because the charges were absurd. In addition, the investigator was his direct student! And then that investigator was replaced with the ardent anti-Soviet, Kęstutis Betingis, and he threw the book at him.

Sapozhnikova: *What conditions was he in, while imprisoned and how long was it?*

Kucherov Jr.: Two years, from 1993 to 1995. The first six months they didn't let me see him. And then a few times it was like this: I come to Betingis and he refuses a meeting. I finally managed to see my father in January 1994. I went to see him when I could. Two times they took me off the train and did not allow me to enter Lithuania. Then they started letting me through, and the investigator would begrudgingly allow the meeting. My dad said that he once wrote a poem, but he had criminals added to his cell. They didn't beat him, but the poem that was only in hand-writing was torn page after page. That was his most significant shock from prison... Why did he write under the pseudonym Grach? Because he was born in the Smolensk Oblast and everyone in their family was black-haired, so the village would talk about them like they were a flock of Rooks. It was unwise to use his own name. He did teach at a Party school, but not lyrical poetry. That is why he took the pseudonym. He lived by his poems. The first thing in his life was politics and protection of the Union and the second was poetry.

To the Last Second...

Sapozhnikova: *Did they let him go because he was ill?*

Kucherov Jr.: Yes. But not immediately. First they diagnosed him: stage zero, cancer without metastasis. I then went to Betingis and asked him to release my father for treatment. I told him, "We have a specialized clinic in Belarus". And he told me, "Bail is 50 000 dollars," of course we didn't have that kind of money… And they kept waiting until autumn when the zero stage went into the first stage. They wanted to treat him in Vilnius, but my father openly said "Igor, they would gut me on that table. Not let me wake up. So I will only go for treatment in Minsk."

Sapozhnikova: *How did you get him out of Lithuania?*

Kucherov Jr.: Being in prison, he finally got Belarussian citizenship. In order to not tempt fate any further, we had Belarussian embassy workers come to get him, who took him straight to Minsk. The bail was paid by Belarus on Alexander Lukashenko's personal decree. There was a condition: after treatment, he would need to return to court. And then he died. Belarus raised the question of returning the bail, but I don't know how that was resolved. When my father was arrested I went to all of the offices, I went to the Foreign Affairs Ministry and to Stanislav Shushkevich, and wrote to prime minister Vyacheslav Kebich. I went over to everyone and no one turned me away.

Sapozhnikova: *How was your father during his last days?*

Kucherov Jr.: Enjoying his freedom. He sprang back to life, spread his wings, started writing poems again. Literally before the New Year he had his first operation – cut out two thirds of his lung. He got over it. Signed out. Had grand plans. He found work, was invited as a consultant at the School at the Presidential Affairs Department. He read lectures and was proud of it. Sadly, in March they found metastasis in his second lung. It was surgically removed as well. That is when his health was really bad. But his spirit wasn't broken – even after that he was preparing to go read a lecture. I tried talking him out of it. He looked at me in surprise, his work was stimulating him to live. It was his last lecture, everyone was listening with bated breath... Then he was sent back to the hospital and didn't make it out this time. I went there every day. During the last time I was there, he said he wrote a poem. He could barely speak any more. I leaned down and he read it to me for 30 minutes. It was just soul-rending. His roommate later said that on his deathbed, he was reciting poems. He read and read until his voice ceased. To the last second...

Иван Кучеров (Ян Грач)

Лицом к лицу

Когда тебя скрутила жизнь
И к роковому тянет часу,
В комок энергии сожмись,
Сожмись в критическую массу.
Что тратиться по мелочам
На покаяния, на грезы?
Предстань судьбе и палачам
Лицом к лицу, но цельным, грозным!
Перед судом глаза не прячь,
Не горби перед стражей спину –
Ведь взгляд твой плазменно горяч
И мудр, и ты подобен джину.
Кто смог держать таких в плену?
Ты – сгусток лазерного света –
Пройдешь тюремную стену,
Расплавив на руках браслеты.
...Когда тебя скрутила жизнь,
а прессинг перешел пределы,
держись! Что мочи есть держись!
Ты – Все! И свято твое дело.

Ivan Kucherov (Yan Grach)

Face to Face

When life twists you
And the hour of doom approaches
Curl up in a ball of energy
Curl up into critical mass
Why waste time on minor details
On repenting, on dreaming?
Face your fate and your executioners
Face to face, but whole and awesome!
Don't hide your face at the trial
Don't bend your back for the guards
Because your gaze is as hot as plasma
And wise as if a genie
Who could ever hold you prisoner?
You are a cluster of laser light –
Passing through the prison walls
Melting shackles on the hands
…When life shatters you
and pressure is beyond all limits
Hold on! Hold on with all your might!
You are everything! Your work is just.

| Chapter Five |

ROMANTICS VS. TRAITORS

This is the ugliest story of the book, because it is a story of treason. I am talking about the Red Professors Case. The so-called Red Professors were four 100% Lithuanians, scientists, who were convicted for their beliefs and fell victim to prosecution for not wishing to succumb to the establishment-imposed nationalism. You will read later about one of them, a second Ivan Kucherov (no relation to the previous one), this one a forensic medical examiner who didn't survive to see the trial.

Another of them, Juozas Kuolelis, was first banned from Lithuania by travel restrictions, and later was given a five-year prison sentence.

Two other men, Mykolas Burokevičius and Juozas Jermalavičius, were kidnapped and extracted from Belarus by the Lithuanian secret services in violation of all existing laws.

Their trial completely rocked the history of the three countries and one Union. First, of Lithuania, who sentenced its best sons, renowned intellectuals, to 12, 8 and 6 years in prison. Second, of Belarus, which violated the laws of brotherhood. Third, of Russia that, in an attempt to cleanse itself from the "red stain", swallowed the events without choking. Fourth, of the European Union that "didn't notice" the Lithuanian punitive "democracy", and accepted Lithuania as its member, disregarding the fact of there being political prisoners in the country. The case also touched the United States of America, which ended up involved either way.

Only the elderly convicts themselves deserve admiration, because they jointly refused to sign a petition requesting pardon, for which they would have had to plead guilty. They were only guilty of not changing their views, which, at the time, was a rarity.

MYKOLAS BUROKEVIČIUS:
First Secretary of the Lithuanian Communist Party

"I didn't come to bow down to Lithuanian bourgeois nationalists"

Professor Burokevičius was imprisoned for 12 years for his beliefs.

...Honestly, I didn't assume that eventually I would decide to publish this interview. When I met Mykolas Burokevičius several years ago, he wasn't in his best shape. He was forgetful, repetitive and spoke with phrases that seemed as if they had just come from scientific textbooks. It was touching to see his convictions, but he was too frail and old. I didn't want him to go down like that in history, because there were things he deserved respect for. For instance, for the 12 years he had spent in prison after Belarus surrendered him in 1994 to the Lithuanian secret services. A professor, Doctor of Sciences, an idealist and a geek from the "communist national park", he was once an excellent talker. But, unfortunately, not so during our meeting, so I shelved the tapes, not thinking I would come back to use them. And then he passed away on 20 January, 2016, and the clamor was unleashed. "One of the 1991 coup masterminds died," wrote the Lithuanian press...

Excuse me, what coup? In 1991, Lithuania was part of the USSR, and its official independence came into effect on 6 September when the USSR recognized it. Or, if you wish, on 2 September, in case the US recognition weighs more. Which means, the January coup, in a classic sense, with thousand-people rallies, TV hysteria and the Supreme Council compound, occupied by armed volunteers, was organized not by Burokevičius, but by someone else. Judging from comments online, the coup headline confused not only me. Many thought that the other mastermind, the "Brussels musician", as many in Lithuania call Vytautas Landsbergis, had died. And only after reading the news did they understand that it was actually his polar opposite...

If you don't give a man the chance to speak, even if it is posthumously, his name will be drenched in lies, as has happened on other occasions, with no witnesses left.

A Communist Party romanticist, Mykolas Burokevičius, after leaving prison, decided not to run anymore and to quietly let the years pass in his apartment, in the company of his sick daughter and wife. What he said in the interview was secondary. To record a persona for history, this is important. I rang the doorbell. I succeeded, although Burokevičius already wasn't that bright – he forgot things, wandered in childhood memories and dug too deeply into terminology. But from time to time it looked like he was rising back to the surface from the depths of memories. And then, along with a trail from the portions of lectures on scientific communism, all-too-familiar from the student days, came the important stuff.

There Was No Order

Sapozhnikova: *What, in your opinion, happened in Lithuania in late 80s and early 90s?*

Burokevičius: Basically, the former Communist Party of Lithuania broke into two parts – the international part of communists, about 40 thousand people, stayed loyal to the positions of Marxism-Leninism and elected me as their First Secretary, and the smaller part, fronted by Algirdas Brazauskas, took the path of national restrictions and moved towards social democracy.

Sapozhnikova: *After the August Coup, during the searches, your letter to Gorbachev dated 7 January 1991 was found, where you allegedly requested Moscow to intervene in the Lithuanian situation…*

Burokevičius: No, it wasn't like that! I raised the issue in front of Gorbachev several times, but it was framed differently – in making decisions, he must consider the special aspects of Lithuania. He must consider the national and historic specifics of the development of the Lithuanian nation and the Lithuanian state.

Sapozhnikova: *Am I correct that they tried to make you the chief mastermind of a military solution in Lithuania in January 1991? And you are saying that the letter dealt with a totally different subject?*

Burokevičius: Anything, but military solution! There was not a word about military options. The thing is, Lithuania was a part of the Baltic Military District, which was commanded by the General of the Army, a Hero of the Soviet Union, Valentin Varennikov. Later he became the First Deputy Defense Minister of the USSR, while his original position was assumed by General-Colonel Fyodor Kuzmin. They were very smart people. The events in Vilnius were provoked by the Lithuanian bourgeois nationalists, who were inspired by the West. There is no reason to blame the Soviet Union and the army. You must consider that Lithuanian extremists more than once attempted to break into the military facilities. The relations between the army and nationalists got really heated. It later led to conflict.

Sapozhnikova: *Then how did the people die on the night of 13 January, 1991? There were 14 fatalities, and you can't move away from it!*

Burokevičius: You have to consider that the nationalists shot the people that died. You can't pin everything on the army. It would have been a crime and a distortion of historic reality. Varennikov and Kuzmin preserved people from both sides. How everything came about, nobody can tell now. There is an opinion that Lithuanians were firing at Lithuanians. There is an opinion that the patrolling troops were firing, when the protesters attacked the crowd control barriers. But there was no order of the garrison commander to use firearms. I can confirm it. I had a military base phone number, which I used to connect with Moscow and the army. The army called me, too, and asked: what should it do? People were breaking everything around, jumping, shooting… It was evidently a provocation by the Lithuanian bourgeois nationalists.

A very bitter class warfare was going down in Lithuania. An intelligent man always knows that it can lead to armed struggle. Which is why the Lithuanian nationalists hated the Soviet authority, made up dirty things about the people who were working and creating Soviet Lithuania, and even espoused strong hatred towards the top-ranking officials of the socialist establishment, like Antanas Sniečkus, Justas Paleckis, Mečislovas Gedvilas. They intrigued and plotted against these people, so the class warfare in Lithuania took place not only in 1945, but after the war as well.

Gorbachev Didn't Respond

Sapozhnikova: *Where did so many foreign media crews come from in Vilnius in that tragic night? Who invited and let them through?*

Burokevičius: This question, probably, is not for me. I can only say that it didn't take one day for Landsbergis to devise the January events. Because the class essence of the struggle boiled up so much that the fight between the people standing for progress, and people standing for regress and wanting the return of the bourgeois formation, was unavoidable. Capitalist states, Germany, the US, France, espoused bitter hatred toward the Soviet authority and Lithuania, and provided various assistance to the Lithuanian bourgeois nationalists.

Sapozhnikova: *So, you think, that night foreign reporters were summoned by Landsbergis to record the planned provocation?*

Burokevičius: There is a large share of Landsbergis' actions that affected the whole thing. Why did I say a "large share"? Because foreign imperialist states, having sensed the critical state of Lithuania, also participated. It was a question of the political system. And nationalists, headed by Landsbergis, relied on Western bourgeois regimes.

Sapozhnikova: *On the night of 13 January, 1991, were you in contact with Gorbachev?*

Burokevičius: When the events started to unfold, I began calling, but Gorbachev wasn't responding. I transferred my protest via telephone. Gorbachev hid, as I would say. He avoided the meeting. I was the only one in Lithuania having a direct line with Gorbachev. So I didn't need to ask anyone, I would just pick up the phone and he would answer.

I Grew Up Underground

Sapozhnikova: *After the August Coup you had to leave Vilnius. Were you threatened?*

Burokevičius: I received threats before, written, spoken. There were provocations. It was clear that if I was the First Secretary of the Communist Party of Lithuania, nationalists would arrange various provocations, and that we wouldn't be forgiven for defending the Soviet political system. It happened due to the fact that, after the war, fascist clandestine agents stayed in Lithuania. So it is not the Soviet political system that is at fault for what occurred in January 1991, but the bourgeois activists, who were left behind from the Smetona regime, and the people, who fought the war on the side of Hitler's Germany. The class warfare in Lithuania went down very violently. More than 40 thousand civilians died, an absolute majority being peasants, who received land from the Soviet authority.

You have to know the nature of Lithuanian bourgeois nationalism. Its nature has ties with fascism, against which not only communists fought, but most progressive people. Later they ruled in the Lithuanian Soviet government. With heroes like Paleckis, Sniečkus, Gedvilas, Lithuania came to be a developed socialist state in the Soviet Union. Lithuania didn't lose its statehood! Only the content changed: a bourgeois system became socialist. Why did everyone stay silent when the German fascists occupied Lithuania and established their own institutes? The Soviet authority is hated by Lithuanian nationalists. I am Lithuanian. My father was Lithuanian. And all brothers are Lithuanian. You shouldn't attribute negative activities to all Lithuanian people.

Sapozhnikova: *You have lived a long life, and I can't say that it was a hundred-percent happy life, because you had you endure* *many challenges. If you could change or rewrite something in your biography, what would you redo?*

Burokevičius: It is impossible to rewrite anything because a man lives only once, and must answer for his own actions. My position was influenced by such historic events as my brother's and father's fight against the bourgeois Lithuanian fascist regime. I grew up in a family of underground resistance fighters, the members of the Communist Party. My brother Jonas became a Komsomol member under a fascist regime that persecuted him for it. He was arrested in 1914 for communist views, and sent to a labor camp. But he didn't break down, he stood by his positions and, in 1941, participated in establishing the Soviet authority. When the war began, Hitler's forces and Lithuanian bourgeois nationalists executed him by firing squad. They shot him with dad and mom. She was still alive after a bullet, so they bayoneted her. My other brother, during occupation, was confined in a Kaunas prison.

Who Will Have the Last Laugh?

Sapozhnikova: *You got an actual 12-year sentence for your "crime", right?*

Burokevičius: Yes.

Sapozhnikova: *Were you offered the opportunity to ask for pardon?*

Burokevičius: More than once.

Sapozhnikova: *And you?*

Burokevičius: What about me? I am not a traitor to my nation. I am a member of the working class. Communists of Lithuania shouldn't petition a bourgeois government. My brother was a Communist Party activist, and when he was arrested, I sent no petitions. My father was a communist, too, and he didn't go to bow down to the bourgeoisie. So why should I do it? I vehemently rejected them. They offered me the opportunity to petition two or three times, even in writing. I didn't bow down, because neither my father, nor my brother did so. Prison is prison. If you will be all in tears, you will die quick. You have to find a way to survive. You have to find strength in yourself and fight.

*

He did fight. He fought illnesses, poverty and mockery. Or, to put it better, he paid no attention to them.

The mockery, however, ended much faster than the life of Mykolas Burokevičius, subsiding with every utility bill, every liter of milk spilled on the ground by farmers due to the absence of demand for milk, and every one-way flight ticket to Europe, booked by children and grandchildren of his fellow citizens. They will still have to find out how the times will be laughed at by the one who will get the last laugh.

***

JUOZAS KUOLELIS:
Secretary for Ideology, Lithuanian Communist Party

"Not Lithuania destroyed the USSR, but Moscow"

An investigator gave Kuolelis a rude welcome "You were the Goebbels of the party, but act like you had nothing to do with anything?"

It was the summer of 1994, three years after the Communist Party of Lithuania on CPSU platform was dismantled. In the party, Kuolelis was the Secretary for Ideology.

It would be wrong to say that he awaited this, although he did live under travel restrictions. It wasn't a big deal: he had nowhere to go anyway, had no reason to travel and didn't have the means – he had been stripped of his honestly-earned pension

The absurd accusations against Juozas Kuolelis were apparently enough for 6 years in prison.

right after the August Coup, and his old car was seized by the authorities.

In August 1999, Juozas Kuolelis was convicted. He was put on trial for his position, not for his actions. Even if he had wanted to, he couldn't "organize a group of servicemen of the Pskov Air Assault Division of the USSR Defense Ministry" to "seize the students and the teaching staff of the Vilnius Pedagogical Institute", and, rallying the 42nd Division of the Interior Ministry's internal troops, seize the Press House building...

But this indictment, nevertheless, got him 6 year in prison. He spent 5 behind bars and was released in 2004, when Lithuania had already joined the European Union. He was freed because it would have been too embarrassing to be an EU member, while having political prisoners... On the single positive note – while in prison, Juozas Kuoliles wrote a book, *Pro kalėjimo grotas* (*A Case on the*

Verge of Two Centuries). So the condensed stupidity, which he noted in Lithuanian court documents, won't fade from history. And the truth of how he tried to convey the whole absurdity to the European Court of Human Rights, and the only proper response out of all existing letters and signs would be an ellipsis, as a symbol of a post-Soviet man's disappointment in the "civilized Europe".

"Kuolelis v. Lithuania"

Sapozhnikova: *What were you sentenced for at the end?*

Kuolelis: For "creating anti-state organizations and inciting the January 1991 events". The Communist Party was branded as an "anti-state organization". My speeches on radio and television *after* the events were regarded as incitement. That was how it went.

During December of 1990 up to New Year's Eve, I was in Laos vacationing with my wife. I returned when the atmosphere in the republic was already tense. Then I spent a week in Moscow – the Academy of Social Sciences had training courses for the party ideology managers from all republics, and I studied there. On 12 January, I arrived in Vilnius, and there was a strike. The trains weren't operating. I caught a cab in Naujoji Vilnia and headed home. Despite that the National Salvation Committee was set up in December, when I was away not only from Lithuania, but from the Soviet Union, I was assigned as having organized named, deemed, charged with it. All my arguments in court weren't considered, and I got sentenced to 6 year in prison.

Sapozhnikova: *On the next morning after the events, did you hear other theories of what happened? Or was everyone around unanimously saying that the 13 Lithuanians were gunned down by the Soviet troops?*

Kuolelis: At first, everyone though that people died as result of the assault. But later, as time went on, it turned out that everything had happened differently. People came to us, at the Central Committee, and were telling that the soldiers of Landsbergis were the ones shooting, while the army had guns loaded with blanks.

Sapozhnikova: *So, it wasn't a secret right from the start?*

Kuolelis: But of course! Besides, when I was charged, I studied the court files and found the official forensic report, which clearly stated that people were shot from high ground. But that subject was banned later.

Sapozhnikova: *Did you have faith that Strasbourg court would rule on the case rightly?*

Kuolelis: I was convinced that the European Court of Human Rights would acquit us. The Strasbourg court studied *Kuolelis v. Lithuania* case for 8 years, quickly admitted the application, assigned a number to it, and, in general, took the issue seriously. The court was inclined to find a violation of the European Convention on Human Rights (ECHR) and to offer to help the parties to reach a settlement and agree to the payment of compensation. But later the Parliamentary Assembly of the Council of Europe condemned the communist regimes, the president of the panel of judges was changed, and the final judgment stated that there was no violation of the ECHR. I guess administrative pressure was applied.

Sapozhnikova: *Under an order from the top?*

Kuolelis: I believe there was such an order. I went to the Strasbourg court when Lithuania hadn't yet been accepted in the European Union. Later our delegation headed by Landsbergis pulled some strings... As it turned out, the European Convention on Human Rights doesn't protect communists.

"Even the Government Has Nothing to Govern"

Sapozhnikova: *When the Communist Party of Lithuania split, you supported the fraction that stayed true to internationalist positions. What is the source of your convictions?*

Kuolelis: You don't become a communist in one day. Nationalism was always foreign to me, and its rampant form, which appeared in Lithuania in the late 80s, for me was unacceptable. My parents were peasants, living in poverty.

If it wasn't for the Soviet authority, I would have never made it far outside of this hut that we are having this conversation in. I would have worked some hard manual job and lived all my life here, next to the picture of my parents and this icon – it was hanging when I was born, and I don't take it down. My cousin had lived all his life in this village, and he feels himself even happier than me, while I have travelled almost around the whole world.

I had an opportunity to be educated; I saw how Lithuania was reaching a decent level of economy and culture. All this, drop by drop, added arguments to my case. Lithuania, as poetess Salomėja Nėris wrote, was a "chiming string" in the Soviet Union. We were good at everything – culture, economy. Then the nationalist sentiments burst in, and it all went down... This malaise not only hit Lithuania. I see how Russia now chants "Russia for Russians!", just like we once chanted that Lithuania was for Lithuanians. This is not good.

Sapozhnikova: *I didn't encounter a single person in Lithuania who would look at the future with optimism. How do you see Lithuania in 15-20 years?*

Kuolelis: I don't know, will Lithuania ever snap out of it all, or not. People are leaving. No heavy industry is being created, and the one that existed is ruined. Mechanical engineering, instrumentation and appliances, electronics, light industry, everything was created during the Soviet regime. Now nothing is left, everything is bankrupted and looted. And if some manufacturing remains, it is in the hands of foreign companies. Here even the government has nothing to govern. No job creation, unemployment, the prospects aren't cheerful.

Witch Hunt for Communists

Sapozhnikova: *Is current Lithuanian intolerance towards dissent connected with the traditions of the First Lithuanian Republic, which was known for repressions against communists? It would seem like once you have gained independence, just focus on prospering and being happy! Why did the new Lithuanian state begin its reign with arrests?*

Kuolelis: They made up the idea that a coup was underway. On these grounds, all communists were imprisoned. The Communist Party is banned, communists are outlawed.

Sapozhnikova: *When the August Coup happened, did you already get the notion that the witch hunt would start?*

Kuolelis: Moscow was doing the same thing. If it wasn't for Moscow, I assume, there would have been no arrests in Lithuania. Bear in mind, back in the day it was trendy to hunt down communists. I believe that I was arrested for my post, not for my activities – they did it to elevate the status of arrestees. In the Communist Party of Lithuania, for a long time I worked in the ideological field, for almost 15 years I headed the propaganda department. I had no relation to the 13 January events, it was proven. But, apparently, there was a command from Brazauskas and Landsbergis to lock me up together with the others.

Sapozhnikova: *Why didn't the series of arrests lead to a wave of protests in Lithuania? People were afraid and poisoned so much by the propaganda that they thought it to be lawful?*

Kuolelis: I believe it was going on not only in Lithuania. Some kind of a mist fell on the whole Soviet Union. In Moscow, when the coup participants were arrested, I didn't see anyone protesting. There was a big confusion in the Communist Party in general, not limited to Lithuania. In such atmosphere, if anyone thought that it was wrong to carry out an arrest, he didn't dare to state his views.

Sapozhnikova: *Do you think, it was possible to stop the collapse of the Soviet Union? Or was it historically predetermined and didn't depend on us?*

Kuolelis: What do you mean, didn't depend on us?! We were betrayed by the entire Politburo, with the General Secretary in charge! The main reason is the treason at the top. Such a General Secretary shouldn't have been allowed to rule. I view Gorbachev as a number-one traitor. Lithuania didn't destroy our country, Moscow did. To be more precise, it was the Kremlin. James Baker (US State Secretary in the Ronald Reagan times) wrote in his memoirs, "We have spent billions of dollars on the destruction of the Soviet Union, but, most importantly, we found the traitors."

Sapozhnikova: *When we met several years ago, you hoped that common sense in society would prevail. Do you have less hope now?*

Kuolelis: Talking about the prospects, I believe that it will get worse from here. The world is walking on a slippery slope. Now I can't even go fishing, because everything is privatized. I arrived at a lake, and the person owning the lake called the police. And I got kicked out.

* * *

…For a man, whose life was spent in the USSR, the latter punishment seemed more severe than 8 years of travel restrictions and a few years of prison…

JUOZAS JERMALAVIČIUS
History Professor

A Shepherd from the Village of Slaves Becoming a Professor – This is What the Uniqueness of the Soviet Regime is All About

"I am a citizen of the Russian Federation," he said proudly right after meeting me at the door. And only then he stated his name.

He could hardly surprise anyone: about 146 million hold the same citizenship. Yet, his case was special. "I decided to acquire Russian citizenship in prison," Juozas Jermalavičius explained. "I

Professor Juozas Jermalavičius was kidnapped from Belarus by the Lithuanian special services and smuggled across the border without a passport.

was a citizen of the Soviet Union, and when Russia was declared its legal successor, I got a legal right to acquire Russian citizenship. The court verdict wasn't yet released, investigation was pending, and the Russian authorities already had a document from their judicial institutions verifying that my actions didn't constitute a crime! So Russian citizenship was granted to me before the delivering of the judgment by the Lithuanian fascist court." This is a story about how and why one divorces one homeland and marries another.

From Shepherd to Professor

Sapozhnikova: *Mr. Jermalavičius, I would like to confirm that you are a genuine Lithuanian and not some Joseph Yermolayev, planted behind enemy lines.*

Jermalavičius: I was born in Lithuania in 1940, in the village Vergakiemis. Its name can be translated into Russian as "village of slaves". I am proud to be born in Lithuania, although no man can choose a place of birth or his parents.

Sapozhnikova: *How did a "village of slaves" native become a Doctor of Historical Sciences?*

Jermalavičius: This is what the uniqueness of the Soviet regime is all about: a barefooted shepherd can become a professor. My parents were peasants. I could do all the farmers' manual jobs. I worked and studied after the war. I graduated from Vilnius University's Faculty of History. My second major was politics. I completed my master's, then my doctoral thesis. I became a professor.

Sapozhnikova: *Seems you had it all, until the things changed.*

Jermalavičius: I am fine now, too. The undeclared war, waged by the imperialist reaction against the Soviet nations, naturally, played a part in my fate. But I am a communist with a scientific mindset, who knows what is happening and understands the logic of world history. So for me there is nothing unexpected and inexplicable.

The Illusion of Freedom

Sapozhnikova: *In 1985-1987, when Lithuania got swept up by the winds of change, did you also understand what was going on?*

Jermalavičius: Naturally. I began to understand what processes started to unfold in the world and our country back in the late 70s. At the time, I was working in the Institute of the History of the Party at the Central Committee of the Communist Party of Lithuania. If you are doing scientific research, looking through the various data and constantly following the statistics review, you start noticing something. Specifically, the peak of industrial production in advanced countries occurred in the second half of the 60s. Starting from the 70s, industrial production began contracting. First, they started talking about an energy crisis and the limitations of the energy resources on the planet. In 1971, the direct convertibility of the US dollar to gold was officially suspended. The US dollar turned into a mere piece of paper. It became clear that the next escalation of the general crisis of capitalism was coming. Circa 1974, flicking though American journals, I saw a facsimile of the secret protocol of the non-aggression pact between the USSR and Nazi Germany, signed on 23 August 1939. It contained Molotov's signature done with Latin letters. Unbelievable! Under the German text, and under the Russian text! Since then, the US Senate, in mid-June, annually has been adopting various documents concerning the so-called "Soviet occupation" of the Baltic republics – Lithuania, Latvia, and Estonia.

By the late 70s, the whole world became engulfed in the propaganda of the necessity to redistribute the spheres of influence. The socialist states of Central and Eastern Europe were included into the zone of the US vital interests. The first fact of the undeclared war of American imperialism and its satellites against the world socialist system took place in autumn of 1980 in Poland. It was followed by an attempt to bring the Polish crisis to the Soviet Union though Lithuania. But it failed.

Sapozhnikova: *By the time of Gorbachev's accession to power, Lithuania was the richest republic of the USSR, very prospering. True?*

Jermalavičius: Undoubtedly. Socialist Europe had three pinnacles of living standards: Czechoslovakia, East Germany and Lithuania.

Sapozhnikova: *But people tend to remember late-80s Lithuania not because of the living standards, but because of massive rallies with tricolors.*

Jermalavičius: I believe, it is a manifestation of the crisis of consciousness. An eclipse of mind. Although, the rallies in defense of the Soviet regime were also massive.

When the Act of the Reestablishment of the State of Lithuania was adopted, my father laughed at the illusion of freedom. He said, "Well, now we will have complete freedom from oil and gas." He, of course, was a wise man.

Landsbergis Thirsted for Blood

Sapozhnikova: *Let's go closer to the events that led you to the prison cell and now - 25 years later – have suddenly become relevant. Is it true that already in December 1990 emergency doctors in Vilnius were given a notice to prepare hospitals for a large influx of the injured? Were there signs that said that the tragedy on 13 January 1991 was coming?*

Jermalavičius: Naturally, because before Vilnius we had similar events in Tbilisi and Baku. With what purpose were such bloody provocations instigated? The first goal was to discredit the Soviet army. A clash was being provoked. I can't imagine any fool who would deploy the Pskov Division for the offensive against a flustered protest crowd. It turned out that it was done under the order of the USSR President Gorbachev.

Sapozhnikova: *He vehemently rejects it.*

Jermalavičius: He has an irrational thought process. He never had an adequate perception of life. It is shameful for a president to claim that he doesn't know what is happening in his country. He knew everything he has been doing. The second reason for provocations was the defamation of the Communist Party. To shield the Communist Party of Lithuania, a rumor was disseminated about the establishment of the National Salvation Committee of Lithuania, which claimed to have assumed all power. Opponents' disinformation is a necessary attribute of war. In reality, there was actually no Committee. But, in the end, all imperialist agencies rose up against the proverbial National Salvation Committee, while the Communist Party of Lithuania stayed in the shade. The Soviet Union was destroyed in Moscow. Landsbergis, Gamsakhurdia and others were mere accomplices, local actors who played the same roles as did the top Soviet officials in the destruction of the USSR.

According to the transcripts, there was a discussion in the Lithuanian Supreme Council, should blood be spilled or not? I read them, they were published. So they knew about the prepared provocation.

In the evening before 13 January, a Military Council of Lithuania headed by Landsbergis was convened. It was given all authority over the republic.[1] Landsbergis, Butkevičius, Laurinkus (the Director of the State Security Department) voted for bloodshed. Professor Antanavičius, Associate Professor Stapelevičius and Jurgelis, who, too, was one time a Director of the State Security Department, voted against it. There was a discussion. Antanavičius argued that we could neither confront, nor assist the process of the destruction of the Soviet Union. The destruction was put into effect by the greater powers. "Do we have a right to demand victims?" he asked. Why should we sacrifice the youth? But Landsbergis thirsted for blood.

"We Were Fooled!"

Sapozhnikova: *What did you feel, when, 21 years after, Algirdas Paleckis appeared with his phrase "our people were shooting our people," and the truth poured out from all sides, just like a genie set free from the lamp?*

Jermalavičius: It doesn't depend on Paleckis. The truth can't be concealed.

Sapozhnikova: *So, it was clear to you right from the start that the Soviet troops didn't use firearms?*

Jermalavičius: Yes, they didn't.

Sapozhnikova: *Is this truth evident to many in Lithuania?*

Jermalavičius: You have to understand the people, too. Small proprietors and the common folk are easily prone to be fooled. But people didn't jump under the tanks, they were pushed. Loreta Asanavičiūtė didn't die under the tank tracks. She was brought alive to the hospital. She was pushed under a tank. Testimonies exist. I personally heard in the court how her friend talked about it. There are witnesses' accounts stating that the shots were fired from the rooftops into the crowd before the arrival of the troops. I read about it in the January events court files. The medical forensic examination determined the bullet paths – the majority died from the projectiles, entering from the 30-60 degree angles. The rounds were different, even from the old Mosin-Nagant rifle. Somebody fired from that rifle and killed a man. It was confirmed. For me, the important thing is this: early morning, of 14 January, a young Catholic priest approached me, and he had also been present near the TV tower. Disappointed and shocked, he kept on repeating, "We were fooled!" Shots were fired from the roofs, he had seen it himself. I believe him. Since he addressed the person of the opposite mindset (I was never a religious man, I was born free of religion and was a famous atheist in the republic), it means that his intention to tell what he saw was serious.

Sapozhnikova: *Audrius Butkevičius hinted to me in an interview that the shooters could have been the fighters of the Yedinstvo leader Valery Ivanov. The Russian community felt quite nervous in those days...*

Jermalavičius: They couldn't! Ivanov didn't have such people. I have known Ivanov for a very, very long time. He is a man of rallies, not a shooter. On the other side, Butkevičius could have organized it. He is very wicked. When he got released from custody, he testified against us. He couldn't even tell Burokevičius from Jermalavičius. To him we were the same. And when he was jailed for some kind of fraud, he gave a completely different account from the prison cell. What Butkevičius says, shouldn't be taken seriously – he was the one who invited people to the TV tower and publicly repeated, "Soldiers aren't equipped with live ammo, go on, don't be afraid."

A "Gift" For the American President

Sapozhnikova: *After the August events, you, like many others, had to flee and remain at large?*

Jermalavičius: For two and a half years I hid in the communist underground in Russia, Ukraine and Belarus. If I had been captured, I wouldn't be talking to you right now. I wouldn't be alive by now.

Sapozhnikova: *So how did you end up getting arrested in Minsk with Mykolas Burokevičius?*

Jermalavičius: I stayed there for no more than two and a half weeks. A summit of the Baltic communists was about to take place. In the morning of 15 January 1994, I arrived at the train station, met a person from Moscow, one of the leaders of the communist movement on the territory of the Soviet Union. We went to the apartment where Burokevičius lived. My landlady called and said that the police came to the apartment where I was living. The police asked for me. What to do? A bag packed with my things was standing on the balcony – I was always ready to leave immediately. I went to a trolley stop to meet some people. A police car rolled up, and a policeman with a man in plain clothes stepped out. The latter I had seen somewhere before. The policeman said, "You are under arrest." Burokevičius got lured out the same way. I was taken to the police station. The people from the Prosecutor's Office were already present there, while the arrest was conducted by a man with CIA ties.

Sapozhnikova: *Why did you think that?*

Jermalavičius: I was told that Lithuanian State Security Department had two units. One fought for national interests, the other did it for American interests. Even the salary was different. National service wouldn't have arrested us.

Sapozhnikova: *In what car were you driven? Not in the trunk at least? In a civilized way?*

Jermalavičius: No, no. Two of us, and two masked men on the sides. The man from the Lithuanian Prosecutor's Office sat in the front.

Sapozhnikova: *So, Belarus did everything to help Lithuania?*

Jermalavičius: I was told later that someone was allegedly paid 10 thousand US dollars – an equivalent of a two-room flat in downtown Minsk by the prices at the time – so no one would notice at the border that I was transported without a passport from one sovereign state, Belarus, to another sovereign state, Lithuania. US President Bill Clinton flew to Minsk that day, so everything was done in the shadows. But our kidnapping had led to a crisis of authority in Belarus, which resulted in two ministers losing their posts, Stanislav Shushkevich losing presidential election and Alexander Lukashenko becoming president. So I am glad that it turned out that way.

Sapozhnikova: *You have a remarkable sense of humor after jail…*

Jermalavičius: Everything is funny in this world. In 1991, the internal and external destroyers of the Soviet Union crossed the plane of what is acceptable in the world historical process. All their acts will unfold in exactly the opposite consequences. They will bury themselves. As a professor, I can give them an A.

Sapozhnikova: *It all had been wonderful, if not the eight years that you have spent in confinement…*

Jermalavičius: Oh, it is such a teaching academy, liberating a man from illusions! Through the bars, the world looks completely different. We sat in a cell, sang songs. Revolutionary… It is so useful for perceiving the world! Whoever hasn't been locked up in prison, won't become a serious revolutionary.

Sapozhnikova: *Is it true that the European Union lambasted Lithuania for the fact of having political prisoners, and you were offered the opportunity to write an appeal for pardon to commute the sentence, but you declined?*

Jermalavičius: It is true. Although I had only two weeks of prison left. Burokevičius and Kuolelis declined deliberately – we don't admit our fault. I was offered to at least partially plead guilty. They said, "You are known as a moderate communist. You will get two and a half or three years in prison, and then will become a member of the Seimas or a minister." But human decency to remain yourself costs a lot more. Once you sell out, you become a wimp. I always didn't care about politics. But being a wimp in life? No, no.

"An Agonizing Nation Doesn't Understand Its Own Actions"

Sapozhnikova: *Did you feel a threat to your own security, once you left prison?*

Jermalavičius: I survived an attempt on my life back in March 1991. They missed, shot up an apartment where I lived. When Burokevičius went for a walk near his house after a surgery, some young man jumped at him and punched him in the chest. Fortunately, he didn't strike the wound. There was also an incident with our associate, Juozas Tonkaitis. He was journalist and a very talented person. He was more than 80 years old, and had cancer. Somebody punched him in the back. He fell on the ground and died in a hospital. You shouldn't fall victim to the crime of some mentally-challenged people. An agonizing nation doesn't understand its own actions.

Although the majority, if you believe the polls, is inclined to leave Lithuania, still there are fanatics, living in a totally different world. If it will go on like that, the nation will be gone. It will perish. With the current situation in the world, far from everyone will survive the global crisis. Where is the Lithuanian nation heading? To the graveyard of history. There won't be another path. If it won't come to its senses.

It is impossible to survive the crisis as a single state, like in 1917. The way out is in the integration of the world, in its communion. But there won't be swift victories. The reactionary forces will have their say. It is the agony of the whole capitalist system. The whole old civilization, founded on private property. It has outlived itself. It was devised by the world scientific revolution in the second half of the 20th century, which facilitated the globalization of material production. And this globalization implacably collided with private property in the means of production.

Sapozhnikova: *To put more simply, what will happen to Lithuania and Russia?*

Jermalavičius: They will become socialist. Socialist revolutions will initially triumph in the majority, and then in all other countries of the world. Humanity can only go in the direction of its historical progress. Attempts to zigzag and roll back are degradation. Degradation isn't infinite, it is destined to fail.

*

At least we know it is clear why Professor Jermalavičius was isolated from Lithuanian society.
Because the society could believe him.

***

VLADIMIR YEGOROV:
Interior Minister, Belarus

"I Didn't Think There Would Be Such an Outcry"

The story of what happened to the speakers in this chapter touched two countries, Lithuania and Belarus. Both handled it differently.

Lithuania made political capital with it. The Prosecutor's Office staffers, who kidnapped the Communist Party leaders in violation of all imaginable and unimaginable laws, make speeches on TV, think of themselves as heroes and to this day boast of their "feats". The then-prosecutor, Artūras Paulauskas, and his accomplices built decent careers on the hunt. The Red Professors topic hasn't been brought up in Lithuania ever since, neither in literature, nor in the media pieces, to say nothing of the lack of attempts to at least apologize on the state's behalf and to dress in sackcloth and ashes for the fervency common in young Lithuanian democracy.

All of the ash landed in neighboring Belarus, where the

information about the two Lithuanian communists, one without a passport being transported in the back seat of a car over the border, sparked a high-profile controversy.

Those at fault, Interior Minister Vladimir Yegorov and Eduard Shirkovsky, the head of the Belarussian KGB, were summoned to the Supreme Council. They had the blame pinned on them for the international humiliation and were sacked, although the operation was led by the Prosecutor-General, Vasily Sholodonov. The then-Chairman of the Supreme Council, Stanislav Shushkevich, kept his post, albeit not for long. Three years later, future Belarussian President Alexander Lukashenka found another pretext to oust him – a box of nails that Shushkevich had allegedly forgotten to pay for. In a hungry society back then such a crime seemed more important than the tarnished dignity.

Neither the supporters of the then-debauched democracy, nor its opponents, managed to prove that Burokevičius' and Jermalavičius' handover was greenlit personally by Stanislav Shushkevich. The transcripts of the controversial Supreme Council sessions paint the following picture: Lithuanian prosecutors, fueled by the urge of revenge, demanded the extradition of the Communist Party ex-leaders. The brigades of investigators freely roamed Belarus and Russia and bombarded their prosecutors' offices with letters. Finally, the Belarussian Prosecutor-General conceded and asked his colleague, the Interior Minister, to aid the cause. Yegorov agreed, not being aware that he would make it into the history books thanks to this transcript that will outweigh all his previous and future professional accomplishments. To his credit, General-Colonel Vladimir Yegorov didn't turn down the interview, though he understood perfectly what he was going to be asked about and shamed for.

"We, Apparently, Are Not that Nation…"

Sapozhnikova: *Is it true that in early 90s you vehemently refused to crack down on an opposition rally in Minsk?*

Yegorov: The situation was phenomenally desperate, with outcomes that would have led to a lot of bloodshed. My name would have been damned by my compatriots. True, there were 100 thousand people rallying on the square. It was demanded that I disperse it. The members of the Bureau of the Central Committee of the Communist Party and all of the government gathered in the Council of Ministers President's cabinet and pointed at me, saying, "Look, what is happening – the protesters have climbed up on the Lenin monument, breeched the police lines, while you, a minister, are inactive." They tossed me a paper to write a resignation report. I told them, "No, I won't write anything, I know how it ended in other republics." We, apparently, are not a nation that would agree that it is better to use force and kill, let's say, 10-15 people, rather than to allow massive pogroms, riots and a much larger number of casualties. Later another situation took place: on Yakub Kolas Square one protester set up a tent and threated to cause an explosion. And there was going to be a giant rally of the Popular Front the next day. If we had started to tear down the tent and to use force, he would only have to light a match to burn it down. Can you imagine what the crowd would do in that case? Late at night, I sent a car to get the opposition leader Zianon Pozniak and said, "We won't remove the tent, but under one condition. If at least one shop window is broken down the avenue where you will be marching, I will use force..." And all went peacefully.

Sapozhnikova: *But afterwards you were suspected of harboring certain sympathies towards the opposition. Are you a committed democrat, or was it your police professionalism that told you that you shouldn't cross the line?*

Yegorov: I wasn't a committed democrat back then. But having worked as a Minister of Internal Affairs in Latvia, served in Afghanistan and travelled around the conflict zones, I understood how it all could end.

"It Was My Mistake"

Sapozhnikova: *In 1994, Belarus had already been independent for three years, right? Then why did secret services from Lithuania freely run around in your country, and you obediently arrested whomever they pointed at?*

Yegorov: You can't say that they ran around, but they visited. Especially when looking for Jermalavičius and Burokevičius. Our Prosecutor's Office maintained closest contact with the Lithuanian Prosecutor's Office. Lithuanians, as it turned out, arrived ten or more times and contacted officials on different levels, up to the Prosecutor-General. The Prosecutor's Office of Belarus set a goal for us to determine whether the people wanted by the Lithuanian authorities were actually located in Minsk. The Interior Ministry didn't have a treaty with Lithuania, but the Prosecutor's Office had.

Sapozhnikova: *But they were handed over under your personal consent? Or did Stanislav Shushkevich give you an order to do it?*

Yegorov: No one gave any orders. After the Lithuanian Prosecutor-General, Artūras Paulauskas, paid a visit to Minsk, an agreement was reached with the Belarussian Prosecutor-General, Vasily Sholodonov, to apprehend Burokevičius and Jermalavičius. Here is where my mistake happened. I should have requested a written order. I had good working relations with Sholodonov. I gave an order to apprehend him. It was just in the days of Bill Clinton's visit.

Sapozhnikova: *How is this connected?*

Yegorov: Maybe, the operation was timed to coincide with this moment. The Interior Minister didn't have time to take care of small matters when a US President arrived for a visit. We should have thought through the details. Naturally, I handled only that. Jermalavičius and Burokevičius were apprehended and taken to a city police station. The department head telephoned the Prosecutor-

General, who confirmed his consent to the extradition. We drove to the border, stayed there for four hours because Jermalavičius had no passport. The then-head of the border troops, Bocharov, yielded consent to let the detainees pass without a passport. Under the police regulations, the fact of an extradition isn't a big deal. But it appeared to be a good pretext to sack an Interior Minister and a KGB Chairman in one stroke, because just right before that we sent a petition to the Supreme Council and the Council of Ministers concerning some aspects of the political composition of Belarus, so we and the Council of Minister fell under attack.

Sapozhnikova: *How did the society find out about the handover? Who incited the scandal?*

Yegorov: The then-Supreme Council of Belarus had a strong pro-communist group.

Sapozhnikova: *Did you yourself feel worried for the communists? Your fate resolved well – in six months you took the seat of the Chairman of the KGB. While the poor Lithuanians spent 12 and 8 years in jail...*

Yegorov: But it wasn't us who sentenced them, not our court! It is not for me to comment on their trial.

Sapozhnikova: *Was the Burokevičius and Jermalavičius handover the sole and main blunder of your career? Or you don't consider it a blunder at all?*

Yegorov: No, it was a blunder. Prosecutor Sholodonov is a smart man. We knew each other, trusted each other, went to sauna together, worked together. How could I have told him "Vasily, go to hell..."? I didn't even think that I had to take a document from him. And I didn't treat it as some kind of a special operation. It would be wrong to say that I played a decisive role in the deal. In the end, the prosecutors would have arrested them anyway, and the Lithuanians would have taken and extracted them.

Sapozhnikova: *Did Lithuanians somehow thank you for the actions?*

Yegorov: No. I didn't think there would be such an outcry. I had to come back to this story, when I ran for parliament in Leninsky borough of the city of Brest. The constituents, communists and border guards, right on the spot posed a question about the Lithuanian communists. "Talk to them," a one party member advised me. 30-40 people were assembled and, I guess, pressed me for two hours. I took with me all excerpts and copies from the Supreme Council session's transcripts, where Sholodonov admitted that it was him, who gave consent to the handover of the Lithuanian communists, not me. And, you know what, I convinced them – I got elected!

* * *

This is the story that tied together four states at once – Lithuania, the US, Russia and Belarus. Only the Belarusians and Russians have apologized to these courageous old men, who went to jail as pensioners; these apologies were granted not on an official, but on societal level. Lithuanians, understanding that they had committed a low act, immediately sanctified and poeticized it, but on a state level. The Americans didn't even notice that they stepped on someone's foot. Or pretended that they didn't. And I thought, what did Bill Clinton have to do with it?

| Chapter Six |

THE LITHUANIAN UNDERGROUND

"Here is where I lived," Vladimir Sheyin showed me into a tiny shack on the first floor, whose main value was in having two entrances. "Let's say, someone rings a doorbell, and you go out through the window, and no one can catch you".

There was nothing romantic about that remark: in the early 90s, when Vladimir, just like other comrades participating in Communist Party activities, relocated from Lithuania to Minsk he had serious grounds to be afraid of any rustling sound.

"Why are you surprised?" another Vladimir – Antonov – chuckled at my reaction. "For several years we kept our bags packed on the balconies, and shook and shivered at every noise coming from the door."

It was an unbelievable experience, listening to how they and their associates, whose only crime was not wishing to dance on the grave of their own state, at the end of the 20th century lived in safehouses and were ready to run for the hills. But they felt it was better living this way—under false names, with signal "cranesbills pots" on window sills and expectations of being caught—than doing time in a Lithuanian jail. The majority of those awaiting repression from the new Lithuanian authorities left for Belarus, which pushed them away with one hand and petted them with the other. The state both betrayed and hid them at once – there was little logic in the murky times. You could say, all Lithuanian "underground activists" were saved by Mykolas Burokevičius and Juozas Jermalavičius. Apologizing for the old men handed over to Lithuania during the last days of Stanislaw Shushkevich's rule, Belarus dramatically changed its course and began aiding Lithuanian communists. As if the Belarusian officials remembered the traditions of their predecessors, who nearly a century ago hosted the inaugural congress of the Russian Social Democratic Labor Party...

This chapter will contain a few stories of the Lithuanian underground, no matter how pompous it would sound nowadays. People who were forced to flee Lithuania because of persecution by the Lithuanian secret services didn't intend to become underground activists.

VLADIMIR ANTONOV:
Former Secretary of the Communist Party Committee of the Vilnius Radio and Electronic Test Equipment Research Institute
and
VLADIMIR SHEYIN:
Former Secretary of the Communist Party Committee of the Interior Ministry of the Lithuanian SSR

"We Had no Idea that the Baltics Would Be Surrendered"

So, we have Vladimir Antonov, the former Secretary of the Communist Party Committee of the Vilnius Radio and Electronic Test Equipment Research Institute, and Vladimir Sheyin, the former Secretary of the Communist Party Committee of the Interior Ministry of the Lithuanian SSR. One of them arrived in Lithuania in childhood, by the will of his parents, the other stayed there after serving in the army. Despite being of the "wrong ethnicity", both made successful careers – unlike in previous times, in the multinational Vilnius of the late USSR, it was possible.

Sapozhnikova: *I will ask you both to go back to the early 80s. Is it memory that twists the pictures of the past, telling us that the USSR had no inter-ethnic problems? Or did you see certain initial disturbing signs back then?*

Antonov: We came to Lithuania in 1950, when I was 4 years old. I recall how my brother was struck by peritonitis, and he was rushed to the hospital. When we brought him in, a wounded chekist[1] was laying on a stretcher in a corridor, with two gunners standing nearby. Mom asked, "Why are you guarding him?" "Because we are waiting for a plane to Riga, where the district hospital is located," they replied. They didn't trust the Panevėžys medics to treat their own people. I remembered this event in January 1991. If the Alpha fighters hadn't handed over their comrade, Viktor Shatskikh, wounded on the night of 13 January, to the Lithuanian ambulance, but rather had sent him to the Vilnius Military Hospital, it would possibly have saved his life.

Many things were concealed from us during that period, we almost didn't know anything, for instance, about the existence of the nationalist gangs. But it all lived inside the Lithuanians and was passed along from generation to generation.

Later I learned from history, including how in 1941, Lithuanian bandits in Kaunas were massacring Jews and servicemen, when the Germans hadn't yet come, but our troops had already left. This is what we were afraid of in 1988-1989, that this history possibly might repeat itself. The only thing calming us down was the Soviet troops stationed here that protected themselves just like they did those who supported retaining the unity of the country. When the provocations were starting near the walls of Severny Gorodok (where the 107th Motor Rifle Division was stationed), the command was releasing its boys using belts as whips to drive away the instigators surrounding the army base.

Sheyin: I went to Lithuania during military service. I began as a policeman, a year later I was appointed local inspector, and moved on to become the Head of the Political and Morale Department of the Interior Ministry of the Lithuanian SSR, where I became acquainted with many participants in the future events. My roots are in Belgorod Uyezd, in the Sheyino village. We always knew that we are government-service people and that our ancestors were sent to Novorossiya to secure the home front. When the events in the Baltics started unfolding, Lithuanians told me, "How is that? You were born on the territory of the Ukrainian SSR, which means, you must be against the moskals,[2] moreover, your wife is Lithuanian..."

Sapozhnikova: *It is interesting, why did you choose one side over the other?*

Sheyin: I will tell you a story. In December 1989, a Congress of the Communist Party of Lithuania was underway, so the party conferences in the Interior Ministry were electing delegates. A former member of the anti-subversion battalion, who fought the nationalist underground resistance in the 50s, and at the time of the events headed the Political Department of the Interior Ministry of Lithuania, told us, "Guys, I was in Moscow, and we were instructed not to hustle, the Baltics will be surrendered." We were offered to relinquish the party membership cards and adopt the citizenship of Lithuania. One of the members of parliament told us that the Lithuanian authorities were reinstating the 1938 Constitution. It meant that Lithuania was to become a bourgeois state, and we would be serving under those who had served dictator, Smetona and Hitler! My mom was a Senior Lieutenant of the army medical corps. Together with my father, she had drawn a graffiti on the Reichstag building on 10 May 1945, and I was obliged to preserve the memory of my parents. I was sworn in as an officer—how was I going to break my oath?

Eleven people, led by the Minister of Interior Misiukonis, sided with Algirdas Brazauskas and discarded their party membership cards. And we, 7 people, led by Colonel Matuzanis and two heads of regional party departments, remained on the positions of the CPSU. Because of that we were referred to as "platformists" or "nighters", since everything happened in the night. But we were rather proud of it.

Sapozhnikova: *What did the Lithuanian national revival look like?*

Antonov: It wasn't a revival. Everything began from the visit to Vilnius of Alexander Yakovlev, one of the ideologues of the destruction of the country [the USSR]. Several papers were founded, which waged blatant nationalistic anti-Soviet propaganda. The official media stayed silent at first. As the sąjūdists' influence grew, they, too, got involved. The nationalist underground surfaced and gained momentum. Over time nationalists and separatists took over virtually all Lithuanian media. It naturally impacted common Lithuanians. I was shocked by the transition of one of my friends, with whom I had lived in a dormitory for five years, when studying in the city of Gorki. Our families were friends in Vilnius. And suddenly it turned out that he had always viewed me as an occupier's son and almost an enemy…

Sheyin: I, too, lost many of my good friends, for whom I put my life at stake on the job. One of my colleagues, for example, was a member of the USSR Olympic track team, and his wife was Russian. In August 1991, when I came to the transit police station, he shouted, "Hold him, he is an enemy!" And I had covered for him more than once, when he was hanging out with his mistress. I told the wife, "Everything is fine, the dude is on active duty…" Why did it turned out that way? I think the grandmas and grandpas passed on the germs of nationalism. For instance, I had the granddaughter of the revolutionary, Juozas Vareikis, working beside me in the investigative department. I had assumed that she was a Komsomol member, cherished grandpa's legacy and all that. But recently I saw her signature on the indictment that was sent from Lithuania to professor Lazutka… I couldn't believe my eyes!

The Script Was Written Jointly

Sapozhnikova: *Where had each of you been in January 1991, and what explanation of the events do you find genuine?*

Antonov: On the night of 13 January, one part of a militia was sent to the Radio and Television Committee building, the other part was sent to the TV tower. It was impossible to imagine a worse scenario. The troops behaved in accordance with their orders. We absolutely had no knowledge of the situation we were getting into. We were driven on the bus to the TV tower, already seized by the Alpha task force. The scene was, of course, gloomy: The airborne troops were firing blanks, surrounded by APCs that roamed the street, equipped with searchlights... According to the script, there would most likely have been casualties among us. But not all went just as planned for the screenwriter.

Sapozhnikova: *Who do you have in mind?*

Antonov: I believe the script was written by joint efforts. Judging by the interviews conducted later with Audrius Butkevičius, the head of the Department of National Defense, he had good contacts with the Chief of the General Staff of the Soviet Army, Mikhail Moiseyev. Butkevičius somehow was aware of when, where and how many troops were going to be deployed. The Lithuanian side knew all the plans of the army, and that is why it moved one step ahead of it. As far as I understood, in order to establish direct presidential rule in Lithuania, Alpha task force was prepared to seize the key spots, the Seimas and the Council of Ministers. But everything was changed at the last minute. Several days prior, it was possible to do all that with a single platoon of internal troops simply by ejecting everyone from the Seimas. But after 8 January, as the price hikes took hold, people were agitated to the maximum.

Sheyin: For 10-15 years I was a senior local police inspector in the same neighborhood, where the events were unfolding and where the house was located, from whose rooftops the snipers were shooting. At night, a special unit of our Interior Ministry was filming the area; it filmed everyone going up on the roofs – there was not one man present, but many – including those who shot using the Mosin-Nagant rifle. All the tapes mysteriously vanished from the criminal case file.

Sapozhnikova: *How did you live after the January tragedy and the August coup? Did you understand that everything was going downhill from there, or did you still hope to endure the challenges?*

Antonov: There was no way we could predict that Lithuania would be surrendered. Especially since several times we had conversations on that issue with Gorbachev in Moscow and in Vilnius, during his last trip. We positioned ourselves as people who would stand for the protection of the Russian-speaking population, living in Lithuania. The troops had to remain in the country for some long time, it seemed to us. A bank had already been established, with accounts set up for the Union [USSR]-controlled enterprises, which means that they wouldn't depend on the economy and the finances of the republic [of Lithuania] at all. An Association of Free Entrepreneurs with its own police force for protecting key institutions was created. But everything was brought down on 19 August.

Sheyin: We managed to create a force that was not under the command of the Lithuanian police. I was going to become the head of the Non-Departmental Security of all enterprises of Union importance – railroads, two ports in Klaipėda, the federal communications network, which at the time also split with one under command of Sąjūdis and one under command of Gorbachev. Did we have an opportunity to win? I am 99.9% sure that we had.

To Leave, Or Not to Leave?

Sapozhnikova: *When did you understand that was the last straw and you had to urgently leave Lithuania?*

Antonov: When on the last day of the August Coup the Central Committee of the Communist Party of Lithuania on the CPSU platform headquarters was surrounded by the Sąjūdis militias. The only person who took responsibility for saving the people remaining in the building happened to be the head of the police political department. At his own risk and peril, he had put those people who were in danger inside of the APCs and drove them to Severny Gorodok, from where they headed out however they could manage. I was a member of the Bureau of the Central Committee of the Communist Party of Lithuania and a member of the Central Control Commission of the CPSU Central Committee, therefore I wasn't going to wait for possible arrest and immediately left for Minsk. Earlier I had decided that a nationalistic Lithuania wasn't a place for my family. I knew several party committees' secretaries in Minsk, they helped me and a bunch of other folks to stay for a few days in the former hotel of the party regional committee. Later everyone had to take care of themselves; some rented apartments, others even moved to the Russian countryside. For instance, I formally divorced my wife. Why? Not long before that, the Second Secretary of the Party City Committee, Sergey Nagorny, attempted to privatize his own apartment. He was denied and was told that there was a decision not to allow communists, previously occupying leading posts, to do that. I passed all my rights to the apartment to my wife; after that we bought an apartment in Minsk. It took us about a year. During that time I was hiding here, while she stayed on high alert in Vilnius.

Sapozhnikova: *When you were crossing the border, did you have a bitter feeling in your heart that you were leaving Lithuania forever?*

Antonov: Not much held me back in Lithuania. I am a serviceman's son, since childhood I got accustomed to constant travel. South Sakhalin, Kharkiv, Panevėžys, Gorki, Tallinn, Minsk – this is the geography of myself and my family. The only thing I felt very sorry for was my job. It was clear that none of the more or less significant factories and plants would be preserved in Lithuania. And so it happened: factories and research institutes of Union importance perished. The Research Institute of Radio Test Equipment, where I had worked for 19 years, and the eponymous plant, manufacturing the equipment that we were designing, ceased to exist.

Sheyin: In Lithuania, I had criminal charges brought against me as an international criminal, despite that I was no longer a Party Committee Secretary of the Interior Ministry since 1 August 1991. I took a vacation, went to the Donetsk Region and returned only on the last day of the coup because there had been a problem in leaving the region. And when I came back, I understood that the situation wouldn't end well and that I couldn't stay there any longer. On 24 August, I had a meeting with one of the Interior Ministry top officials, who held beliefs similar to ours, and told me that the sąjūdists, apparently, had made a decision to arrest me. But since I was a former field agent myself and could invent legends, I didn't need those tales. I told my relative that I was leaving and, on 25 August, crossed the border to Belarus, assuming that the whole thing would last for two to three years.

Spiders in a Jar

Sapozhnikova: *There were more than 20 of you assembled in Belarus back then. Did you communicate? Did you have secret underground meetings in your apartments?*

Antonov: Up to the moment of Lukashenko coming to power, we felt uneasy, especially when Burokevičius and Jermalavičius got arrested. Without the assistance of the Belarusians, the Lithuanians couldn't have done anything. Professor Valentin Lazutka advised Burokevičius several times to prepare for us a base for retreat. But Burokevičius didn't listen, accused him of a defeatist attitude.

Sheyin: They offered to craft fake passports and change

Burokevičius to Burokevich, Jermalavičius to Yermalovich, both normal Belarusian last names. No, they said, those were criminal acts. They could have become citizens of the Russian Federation, but at that point didn't want to. One colleague of ours even gave them an offer to go to China. They flatly declined, saying, "We will be present near the events that will be unfolding any day now." They thought everything would change back to normal.

I also was one of those who were sure that in 2-3 years the government in Moscow would understand that it had made a big mistake. The Vilnius region was transferred to Lithuania by Stalin without a referendum, like the Belarusian lands between Neman and Poland, to appease the Lithuanians. According to the international agreements, the Eastern Prussia and the Memel Territory was acquired by the Soviet Union, not by Lithuania.

Antonov: For me, on the other hand, it was clear that matters were serious and were going to stay that way for a long time. After the January events, in February or March, a plenum of the CPSU Central Committee was taking place in Moscow. Along with Burokevičius, I was given the floor on the plenum. I gave a speech and read the statement of our council of the Vilnius party committees' secretaries, where all had been laid out point-by-point: demanding that the General Secretary of the Central Committee of the CPSU undertake measures to quell the armed groups, install a direct presidential rule in the republic and so on. Weak applause followed. During the break, the Deputy Prime Minister of the USSR, Yuri Maslyukov, walked up to me and said, "You did fine, but it is all in vain. Until those two spiders in a jar will resolve their issues" – meaning Gorbachev and Yeltsin – "nothing will change." Everyone understood it, but it was as if they were hypnotized, and couldn't do anything. There was not a single strong-minded man at the top.

***

VALENTIN LAZUTKA:
Professor of Philosophical Sciences

Among Strangers

By looking at him, you would have assumed that he was a hundred-percent Lithuanian, with light eyes and hair as blonde

Valentinas Lazutka's "crime" was that he knew for a fact that the Lithuanian Sąjūdis Perestroika movement was organized by a KGB order from Moscow.

as a harrier. While listening to him, you would get that he was a typical Siberian – certain distinctive words couldn't be cleansed from his speech, not even with decades of living in his historic homeland. His destiny had taken drastic twists: first the ancestors of Valentin Lazutka were drawn to Siberia in the 1880s by the generous promises of free land; later the parents were lured to post-war Lithuania by the tales of European living standards. And then it turned out that the new Lithuanian Republic didn't need Siberians, Lithuanians or clever folk, so as result, Doctor of Philosophical Sciences, Professor Valentin Lazutka, resides in Minsk.

Sapozhnikova: *When was your first encounter with Lithuania?*

Lazutka: On 12 June 1945, right after the war. Government officials came to us and campaigned for us to settle there. Since my three brothers served in the 16th Lithuanian Rifle Division, all our family signed up. And right after the war ended, we legally moved to Lithuania.

Sapozhnikova: *And what were your first impressions?*

Lazutka: We first arrived in Minsk; we had to wait for the train for a few hours. It was a horrifying picture – ruins everywhere. But in Vilnius everything was elegant! The most beautiful houses, Catholic churches. The only completely destroyed street was Muziejaus, called the Jewish Street at the time. There was a Jewish ghetto and the retreating Germans blew it up. Another detail: Vilnius was completely Polish. You would go to a hospital – everything was in the Polish language, you would go to a shop – everything was in Polish, you would go to a church – everything was in Polish... The first impressions of the country were the most positive. No thoughts of any possibility of an armed insurgency ever crossed my mind. It all was unveiled later. I and my brother lived in Vilnius, while our parents lived in Trakai. So, a relative on the wife's side visited my brother and said, "Our daddy's home was attacked by bandits, he and his wife began firing back, put up a defense, but he got wounded." It was the first encounter with Lithuanian guerillas. The second one happened in Trakai, where the First Secretary of the Party Committee, named Afonin, a commander of the Soviet partisan squad, and his son, only a few years older than me, were shot in the market in broad daylight. No one apprehended the bandits, they rode off on horseback.

"I Am Not Going to Create Sąjūdis!"

Sapozhnikova: *For how long did you manage to stay one among the Lithuanians? As long as you don't begin to tell your take on the events, you are impossible to be distinguished from a typical member of the Lithuanian nation.*

Lazutka: I was, naturally, always regarded as a Soviet man. I finished Russian schooling, later studied in Moscow, and my Lithuanian originally sounded like country talk. I was a Komsomol member in the Vilnius University. Once a Secretary of the Central Committee arrived and berated our secretary, "Why didn't you elect even a single Russian? Everyone is Lithuanian!" And he told him, "Well, we have Lazutka!" That is how, for the first time, I was openly called Russian... But, honestly, I regretted leaving Moscow. Of course, I suited Russian society more than Lithuanian.

Sapozhnikova: *Around what time in Vilnius did you understand that the ideological contradictions between two Lithuanians can be irresolvable?*

Lazutka: Almost as soon as I arrived. But I acknowledged the danger, unfortunately, only in 1986, when the protest rallies began. Aside from being the Director of the Institute of Philosophy, Sociology and Law, I also was the First Secretary of the Party Committee in the Lithuanian SSR Academy of Sciences, so I took the path of a robust struggle against anti-communism and anti-Sovietism. In the end, in the Academy of Sciences Party Committee, I became the only one who adhered to these positions.

I will tell you a story. On 3 June 1988, the head academic secretary phoned me and said that there would be a conference meeting at the Palace of Science. I arrived there and saw many familiar faces, CPL Central Committee Secretary for Ideology Lionginas Šepetys, Head Academic Secretary of the Lithuania SSR Academy of Sciences academic Eduardas Vilkas, and Academic Secretary of the Department of Societal Sciences Raimundas

Rajeckas. I assumed that we were going to speak about science, but the discussion was about how we needed to create a Lithuanian movement in support of Perestroika. A decision was passed that I and academic Vilkas would be responsible for its creation, while Šepetys, who was directly coordinating KGB activities, would be leading us. I decided – no, I am not going to create Sąjūdis. Besides, I had a good excuse – that day we had a panel awarding the Doctor of Sciences degrees scheduled, and I was the panel's president. So, to put it short, I didn't go anywhere. And for that I was almost expelled from the party.

That year, many foreigners appeared in the corridors of state institutions; Lithuania had suddenly attracted the great interest of the whole world. I asked our Central Committee KGB resident, "How many foreigners are there?" He replied, "About 400." And I had a thought, "Not a single one of them could have arrived without the authorization of the KGB." What – did they secretly move across the border or something? It meant that, with the KGB's approval and under its guidance, these aliens were operating in Lithuania with clearly hostile goals. Nobody impeded them, nobody took care of them. So, I filed a resignation letter to leave the post of the Director of the Institute of Philosophy and left the Academy of Sciences for the Vilnius Party School. That is how I ultimately severed ties with Sąjūdis.

"Damned" Presidency

Sapozhnikova: *You went into the same high party school, where the current president of Lithuania, Dalia Grybauskaitė, worked?*

Lazutka: She had ties with the party school president, Sigizmundas Šimkus, who wore the distinguished Chekist's badge on his jacket. You had to serve 25 years in the security services to earn it. Since I had good relations with the president, he confessed to me that he had been cooperating with the secret services since his school years and handing over his Forest Brethren friends. Then, he didn't really conceal it. He had his people, also connected with the

KGB. One of them was Dalia Grybauskaitė, a young woman, who had just come from Leningrad. In the High Party School she was an academic secretary. Unlike the Academy of Sciences, where an academic secretary is practically the second-in-command, a type of a "commissary" for the director, in the party school it is a purely technical figure who writes protocols of the academic council. She was rarely seen. She worked at the National Economy Department.

Sapozhnikova: *Was she a committed communist?*

Lazutka: Don't know. I had a feeling that she was very scared of me, like of some kind of wild beast. I even thought to myself that she was actually afraid of all men, and me in particular. She only befriended women, and ran from men. For some reason, a thought of marrying her had never occurred to anyone. Later, under the government's decision, the Vilnius High Party School was transferred to the Pedagogical Institute, and, to protect the Union property, the building was seized by the soldiers of the internal troops' division. Šimkus urgently checked himself into a hospital. And Dalia vanished. When the Bureau of the CPL Central Committee decided to shut down the Vilnius High Party School entirely and relieve Šimkus from the presidency, I was suddenly called by the First Secretary of the Communist Party of the CPSU platform Mykolas Burokevičius, who told me that it was decided to appoint me... as the president! And my damn presidency began, along with a fierce fighting within the party school. The teaching staff broke apart, so did the accounting department. Half of the staff recognized me, the other half didn't. It was 1990.

Sapozhnikova: *Where was Dalia going at that moment?*

Lazutka: She disappeared, just like all KGB people – they all went to Sąjūdis. She later appeared in the Academy of Sciences. As I understood, she joined her colleagues... She later came to actively play the role of a Lithuanian nationalist. She went to America, allegedly to the USSR embassy. As far as I am aware, she didn't stay there for long, because a campaign began against her as a former KGB operative. She became a persona non grata. But only several months later, she again appeared taking courses in one American university, where Lithuanian officials were trained. And upon returning, she immediately became actively involved with Sajūdis, went off to work in the Ministry of Finance and soon became a minister.

No Fear for Life

Sapozhnikova: *Do you have an explanation of her so aggressive attitude towards Russia? In essence, the center of European Russophobia is currently located in Vilnius.*

Lazutka: You want to look at Grybauskaitė as an independent politician, whose actions are based on her views, but that is not true: she has authority above her, she receives commands, she has a patron standing behind her, who will always protect her. And she tries very hard to play the part to the end. What else does she have left? What is going on in her soul is hard to imagine, because such a pivot is a trauma for any person. I have decided for myself that if I am to be executed by firing squad, I will stay true to the same position I stand on today. There is no other choice. This is not due to fear for my life, although I had grounds for it, since there was an attempt on my life, but my driver died instead of me.

Sapozhnikova: *When?*

Lazutka: In the fall of 1990. I was a Secretary of the Central Committee of CLP on the CPSU platform, and simultaneously held an unpaid position of the First Secretary of Vilnius Party City Committee. All members of the Bureau were about to take a train to Moscow. My driver was coming to get me. Suddenly the phone rang. An unknown voice said, "Wait, you are at home?" And the person dropped the phone. It was unclear who called. I thought it was strange, even more so since I was not in my apartment

The Lithuanian Underground 169

but at my mother-in-law's. Around, maybe, five minutes passed and another call came from the traffic police. They said, "A road accident has happened, your diver died." On the last railway signal post at the train station a fire truck had crashed into him. Everyone was searching for Lazutka, but Lazutka wasn't in the car... I called Gorbachev's aide Rymarenko, told him the story, and he said, "Don't go anywhere, stay at your house, the trip to Moscow for you is impossible." He called me back the next day, saying, "Everything is fine, nobody will touch you ever again..."

Sapozhnikova: *Who could have wanted you dead?*

Lazutka: They said, at Landsbergis' meeting it was decided that a provocation victim was required. And for the victim they chose a secretary of the Secretary of the Central Committee of CLP on the CPSU platform. Who personally? In one Lithuanian journalist's book, I much later read that I had been selected as the candidate.

Who Was the Scapegoat?

Sapozhnikova: *After the events of January 1991, did you feel the desire to tell Mikhail Gorbachev everything you thought about him? You studied together with Gorbachev's wife, Raisa, and were well acquainted with her, right?*

Lazutka: After 13 January, I firmly decided not to have any relations with Gorbachev ever again. Even if some conferences had been arranged, I wouldn't have attended them. Everything became clear to me, especially since it has become known what our president was negotiating about with Ronald Reagan in Reykjavik. Everything was clear – Gorbachev was a traitor, and absolutely nothing depended on us. And God forbid, it would have happened just like generals Varennikov and Achalov wanted, when they were calling me on the night of the January events and asking me to send out the workers on a protest rally. Why did they need it? I believe they had understood that they were going to be made scapegoats. They needed to point at the "guilty ones". And we were most suited for that role. That was their logic.

Sapozhnikova: *So you blame the military for what happened in Vilnius?*

Lazutka: No, the provocation was absolutely certainly staged by the Landsbergists together with the Moscow top officials headed by Gorbachev and Kryuchkov. Technically, all was organized by the head of the Department of National Defense, Butkevičius. He later bragged in his interviews that he had managed to convince the head of General Staff to deploy the Alpha task force. I was, as I recall, surprised, because the Alpha task force was under the command of the KGB, not the General Staff. So the Alpha task force was simply framed.

I was in Moscow just before the events in Vilnius, on 7 January 1991. Gorbachev, apparently, had wanted to talk to us, but in the end didn't meet us. His aide put it bluntly – we were to act only if there had been, either in Gorbachev's televised address, or in the decision of the Council of Federation, a statement that an anti-Soviet coup had taken place and that the fight to restore Soviet authority was underway. "The Council of Federation has decided against it, there will be no direct presidential rule", the aide told us over the phone when we got back to Vilnius. Together with Burokevičius I said, "Well, thank God!", and declared Saturday and Sunday days off. Next morning I went to the countryside, got back at 5 PM, and my mother-in-law told me that Burokevičius' secretary had called and said that he was urgently waiting for me. I drove to the Central Committee office, waited for five minutes, then ten... No one was there. I stood up to leave, and then four unknown young men appeared, standing in front of the door. And I sat in the office for several hours, like an idiot, mentally cursing Burokevičius. At the same time, all party officials were sitting in a conference room for several hours in the same fashion – they were told that I had ordered them to be gathered there. While Burokevičius himself, as it turned out later, was isolated the same way, just like me.

Sapozhnikova: *Where exactly were you during the assault on the TV tower and the TV and radio center?*

Lazutka: Just as I have told you: I was sitting in Burokevičius' cabinet lobby... Then suddenly the tanks started firing. I called the military base staff. Colonel Maskhadov, who was in command of an artillery division, responded, "This is a provocation, don't do anything." I would like to note that it wasn't the only provocation that night. The information of snipers firing from the rooftops and dead bodies being shot while lying up on the tables became available to me next morning. Two families, parents with daughters, visited my cabinet. And the girls told me how they had been pushed under cars, pushed in a stampede and shot at from somewhere on the side... I even thought, "Could it have been possible that the army had managed to deploy soldiers that were firing at the crowd?" For someone to fire from our side – it was totally impossible! Which means, the shots came from the opposite side...

British journalist David Pryce-Jones wrote later in his book that in the morning of 14 January, along with his friend, an ex-Sąjūdis supporter Arvydas Juozaitis, he visited Landsbergis and bluntly asked, "Who needed those casualties and why?" He replied that blood was required for freedom and the dead "sacrificed their lives for motherland and its liberty." Even the Brit was shocked by this cynical response, writing, "Nerves of steel. But they also convey the frightening inner world of this man."

"We Were Betrayed, and It Was a Coup"

Sapozhnikova: *After what happened, did you have a feeling that you will be forced to leave Lithuania?*

Lazutka: I went to Burokevičius with this question and offered to purchase a house for all of us in Belarus. "No", he argued. "That is panicking thinking". On 19 August 1991, I was in Sochi, came to the sea and heard two women talking about Moscow and Gorbachev. I came out of the water, told my wife, "Pack your bags, we are going home." We flew to Vilnius at 1 PM. By 3 PM I was already at Burokevičius' office. I asked, "What is going on?" He said, "The same as 13 January, a provocation." Were there any instructions from Moscow? "Absolutely nothing. We have been betrayed, and this is a coup." The same day we assembled the Central Committee Bureau and discussed what to do. I posed a question, would we be going underground? Burokevičius replied, "No, there won't be any underground..." He called Brazauskas (leader of the breakaway Communist Party of Lithuania Central Committee, the future President of the Lithuanian Republic); the latter informed him that a Seimas session took place that decided to ban the Communist Party. In other words, "Take off where you want, because you can get murdered here..." We started acting on Brazauskas' advice. I had a visa and a ticket to Germany where two of my sons lived. When the whole ordeal began, one of my sons got expelled from the university because of his father, the other son started having problems on his job, and they left. "Well, fine", I thought. "I will move there for a week." I went to Osnabrück. From there I called my secretary, and she told me, "Everyone left, no one is here. There is nowhere to return to." Then I called my brother, he was a university professor. He said, "Don't even think of coming back here, you will be killed right on the border." An article came out in the Lithuanian press, with my last name in it, saying that communists' apartments were searched, including mine, where some weapons were found. Obviously, my home wasn't searched, but the message of the piece was that dangerous armed communists are walking around the country, so they should be shot. Until 2001, I had to stay in Germany. The aid, allocated to political refugees, was quite enough to survive, so I didn't suffer from financial burdens. I became a chess coach, participated in tournaments, occasionally won.

Sapozhnikova: *Then why are we having this conversation now in Minsk, not in Berlin?*

Lazutka: I had decided to return quite long ago. But my Soviet passport was invalid. With the German document issued to me, as an asylum seeker, I couldn't cross the border. I didn't get Lithuanian citizenship, so I got Russian citizenship instead. I notified the German officials that I desired to leave the country, and everyone suddenly got agitated, started running around. I couldn't understand: why all of a sudden did I become such a valuable asset? As it turned out, Lithuania had already appealed to Germany two times, demanding my extradition. The Germans didn't know what to do – break the law or damage political relations with Lithuania? On 2 January 2001, the police arrived at my place, drove me to the airport and escorted me to the plane. I flew to Minsk; no one even asked any questions.

Sapozhnikova: *Did things end up well for you in Belarus?*

Lazutka: I was given a residency permit and a pension. The court case about the organization of a coup with the intent to seize power, which is being brought against me in Lithuania, according to which I allegedly attacked the students, attempted to take over a railway and threatened to shut down the Ingalina Nuclear Power Plant, is still pending as of today. It is an obvious stupidity – there was no other legal authority in 1991 except the Soviets, I was a USSR citizen, and Lithuania was a Soviet republic, one of fifteen others.

*

Lithuania caught up to professor Lazutka one more time and spat on his back. In the fall of 2014, Valentin's beloved wife Anna went to Vilnius to see her son and didn't return due to a fatal stroke... Valentin spent her funeral day alone, gazing at a church from the window of their Minsk apartment. If the 82-year-old professor had gone to pay his last respects to his spouse and mourn her passing, he would have been arrested on the Lithuanian border.

***

STALISLAVA JUONIENĖ:
Former newspaper editor

"My homeland doesn't exist anymore"

"Fools, they thought they would be given stockings and sausages... That they would have democracy...", grumbled the former editor of the *Tarybų Lietuva ("Soviet Lithuania")* newspaper, Stalislava Juonienė, while setting the table. The conversation took place in Belarus – such talk would have been impossible in contemporary Lithuania because problems with freedom of speech and the hunt for journalists began there not today, but 25 years ago, during the times of glasnost. Stalislava's colleague, the former editor-in-chief of the radio station bearing the same name, *Tarybų Lietuva*, Stanislovas Mickevičius, was tried by the Lithuanian court in the late 90s, but avoided punishment, wisely leaving the Lithuanian Republic's territory on the day before the ruling. Stalislava Juonienė has been in defense mode for the last quarter of a century and has declined to give interviews with her colleagues even when Lithuania demanded her extradition. She and General Vladimir Uskhopchik serve as the best possible parallel of the pen and bayonet metaphor, which was so revolutionarily enacted by Lithuania...

So I decided to be bold and simply rang her doorbell, without a prior arrangement for the interview, knowing that she would have declined it anyway. Four different cats were suspiciously looking at my voice recorder as I was getting to know their owner, a still beautiful and striking woman, who deliberately emphasized her unwillingness to dig deep in the past. Cats and stuffed toys were the wall behind which Stalislava Juonienė had decided to hide away from the world that had disappointed her.

Sapozhnikova: *This is what I can't understand: who in the early 90s had convinced us, idealist journalists, that absolutely all of Lithuania wanted only one thing – independence?*

Juonienė: No way! ALL of Lithuania never wanted it. Normal people, even poorly-educated ones, understood what was going on – the sale of the country, its values and people.

Sapozhnikova: *We were inexperienced in terms of waging a psychological war, and so we couldn't resist the information onslaught? Or were we stopped by curiosity about the yet-undiscovered capitalist future?*

Juonienė: For many years, in the Soviet Union, the work was carried out to destroy socialism, the USSR, the foundations of the life we lived. And that is why everyone was staring at America with their mouths wide open. Everyone thought that they would be free. But should we ask them now, what freedom is, they won't answer.

A Cloud of Discord

Sapozhnikova: *Were your views influenced by the opinions of your family members? Being a hundred-percent Lithuanian and living in Lithuania, you could have grown up a totally different person...*

Juonienė: I grew up as myself. My parents were peasants, normal, smart people. No one spoke of politics back then. I was born in Kaunas, but when the war started, my parents went to live in the countryside. I finished school there and went to Vilnius, got enrolled in a university, and never returned to my home.

Sapozhnikova: *Did discord arise between your relatives or friends?*

Juonienė: I was divorced. The main reason for our divorce was that we were different people. I was an eternal communist, while he was an eternal anti-communist. He passed away and, thank God, had time to acknowledge what was really going on. He actively supported Sąjūdis. He attended their events where everyone held hands. He stood for freedom and independence. He agreed that "those Russians" were bad. And later he saw what had happened in reality and screamed, "Idiots and crooks came to Lithuania!" That was an absolutely fair definition. Later, he wrote me letters, saying, "It is so good that you have left Lithuania because you couldn't have lived here. You couldn't have accepted the betrayal of the Lithuanian nation that happened." He even came to visit me with his new woman to talk about how Lithuania was destroyed. So, all normal people understood where it all led.

Sapozhnikova: *When I met Gene Sharp in America, I was astonished by his story of how he completely openly taught the agents from the Baltic republics how to dismantle the Soviet Union from the inside, giving lectures in Moscow. Which means, absolutely everyone knew what was being prepared and couldn't confront it?*

Juonienė: But could Lithuania have stopped it? All was organized by the West. To dismantle the Soviet Union, they began to organize the events first in Fergana, Baku and Tbilisi. No matter how the Asians were shooting each other, the Europeans and Americans sat calmly and watched. They probably thought, "Let the apes shoot each other." Later, they decided to cause a commotion in the Baltic republics, especially in Lithuania, because they had worked there for a long time. And everything unfolded from there on...

On Fools and Christmas Toys

Sapozhnikova: *Where were you on the night of 13 January 1991?*

Juonienė: I was sitting in the kitchen and recording everything said on the radio. No one was shooting yet, but the radio was shouting that medical assistance was required and there were casualties.

Sapozhnikova: *Why did Gene Sharp's techniques, such as having coffins passed around above the crowds, vigil lights, the* *poetization of death, work on some people, but didn't work on you personally?*

Juonienė: Well, only fools didn't understand that everything was organized by their own people, who killed each other. It is sad that there are so many fools in Lithuania. Even our neighbors – the husband worked in the factory, the wife worked at the Central Committee of the Lithuanian Communist Party – also rushed to the TV and radio building and the TV tower because everyone was called to go there. My son was scoffed at, people told him, "Your mom was among those who were shooting the people..." Though, later they apologized a thousand times. Up to this day, when they see Gintaras, they beg for forgiveness for "saying bad things about his mom." What had actually happened near the Radio and Television Committee building and the TV tower was later told to us by the ordinary people from the countryside, who were assembled beforehand, put on buses and driven to the center of events. They sent us many letters about which positions they were put in and from where they were fired upon. Everything got published in the *Tarybų Lietuva* paper.

Sapozhnikova:- *If now you had a chance to meet Mikhail Gorbachev, what would you say to him?*

Juonienė: Everything was already said. One time a story happened: I went to Mykolas Burokevičius' office (recently deceased Secretary of the Communist Part of Lithuania on the CPSU platform) and told him, "If Gorbachev was to be hanged on the Red Square, I would walk to Moscow on foot." He looked at me and looked, and said, "You are a con artist..."

I have another interesting memory about this case. When, in January 1990, Gorbachev came to Lithuania and decided to make a speech for the party staff, only Russians were given an opportunity to speak. We deliberately wanted to show him that a nationalist process was underway, not any other process. Finally Vladimir Antonov asked to speak and instead of a speech he said,

"I want you to listen to Stalislava Juonienė..." After a long silence I was finally given the floor. I read the letters of Lithuanians who protested against the so-called Perestroika. It was a blast! Because ordinary normal people were writing about the destruction of our political system and our life... I gave Gorbachev those letters.

Only fools failed to see what was going on. The colleague, who went to Moscow, told us that the issue of the factories of Union importance located in the Baltic states didn't interest anyone. The factories' conversion was underway, the plants working for the defense industry were recommended to produce Christmas toys. Everything was being sold out, it was all transparent... There were many fools, but also there were traitors. Both were sent to the top.

"I Don't Resort to Nostalgia"

Sapozhnikova: *When and how did you leave Lithuania?*

Juonienė: In 1991. A colleague drove me away in his car, using side routes. Back then I was called Valentina Zhukovskaya.

Sapozhnikova: *How so?*

Juonienė: I worked in the paper and, not to annoy Belarusians with my weird last name, which no one could pronounce, introduced myself as Zhukovskaya. It was the last name of a woman who housed me.

Sapozhnikova: *Since what time was there a hunt for you going on in Lithuania?*

Juonienė: All became clear after the August Coup happened. There were calls, threats. Boleslav Makutynovich (an OMON ex-commander) rescued me—he sent men over to help me quickly pack my stuff. For two first weeks I lived in the paper's office, then at my friends' place. One woman had sheltered me, she was a Soviet-minded, normal person.

Sapozhnikova: *What did you do underground?*

Juonienė: We made brochures, released 7 or 8 editions, dedicated to what was actually going on. And we printed *Tarybų Lietuva* in the Russian and English languages.

Sapozhnikova: *Did the authorities in Lithuania look for you for a long time to hold you responsible?*

Juonienė: For a long time, yes. They asked for me everywhere, including questioning the children. When the Lithuanian authorities came to power, the pressure was strong... They had no moral boundaries. They even prepared lists of undesirable persons, who needed to be eliminated.

Sapozhnikova: *What was the basis of that hatred? Do you, as a Lithuanian and a former high school educator, see the roots of this phenomenon?*

Juonienė: The general logic goes like this: Russian occupiers taught Lithuanians to drink, curse and to work poorly – the Russians are, well, villains... Belarusians, too, are scum. Poland for Lithuanians has always been displayed as a bad state, with Poles as thieves and scammers. The basis for hatred is nationalism. A normal person doesn't degrade others, he doesn't need to prove his superiority. While a loser always says everything is rotten – this wife has a dumb husband, that husband has a lousy wife, that man has bad feet and so on... Lithuania currently holds the first place for alcohol consumption per capita in the world, and is leading in suicides, while everybody blamed the Russians.

"We Got Sold Out Beforehand"

Sapozhnikova: *For the last 25 years, you have never once been to Lithuania?*

Juonienė: I went there for my mother's funeral in 1993. We quit making trips there after Ivan Kucherov was arrested.

Sapozhnikova: *Separation from your own country – how would you describe it? What is it? Dreams, grudges, the desire for revenge, or the need to tell the truth?*

Juonienė: Well, my homeland got destroyed! My homeland is no more... I don't want to see such a homeland, it doesn't interest me. It is not a pity – there were bigger world empires that have collapsed. By the word "homeland" I don't mean Lithuania, I am referring to the Soviet Union and socialism. I am a representative of scientific communism, a Candidate of Sciences. And I, by the way, not only taught, but also led a department in a construction engineering institute.

Sapozhnikova: *Rewinding time, can you recall a moment in the late 80s when everything could still be stopped and history could have been changed?*

Juonienė: Of course not! If we couldn't save such a great country as the Soviet Union, what was there to talk about in small Estonia, Latvia and Lithuania? Those were global events. Global.

Sapozhnikova: *Are cats a certain curtain, behind which you have deliberately hidden yourself from the past?*

Juonienė: Yes. I laugh at the people who held political office, acting all important and thinking that they mean something in this life. I have passed many stages in my life. And right now I am just a cat lady. I won't write memoirs. This is how much everything is clear about this world...

Sapozhnikova: *Do you, along with your associates, feel like victims or losers?*

Juonienė: Neither. We didn't imitate the struggle, we fought for real. The fact that we failed is a different issue. We failed because we were set up. We were set up, get it? What happened in Lithuania held no meaning, because the most important thing was the Soviet Union... We have nothing to regret, we did all we could. But it wasn't us who lost – the world lost.

***

ČESLAVS VISOCKIS:
Secretary, underground CLP Central Committee

"I lived underground, because Lithuania didn't stop its attempts to catch me."

"I am a communist, the Secretary of the underground CLP Central Committee." An elderly but energetic man shook my hand with a business fashion, inviting me to his "palace", a two-room apartment in a nursery home for veterans of war and labor. Among paintings and wooden trinkets hanging on the walls of an improvised home museum, three pictures stood out – the portraits of the First Secretary of the CPL, Mykolas Burokevičius, the leader

Political refugee Česlav Visockis says that instead of trying him for treason of the motherland, they must put Mikhail Gorbachev on trial.

of Russian communists Gennady Zyuganov, and the President of Belarus, Alexander Lukashenko. This combo would seem weird, if you weren't familiar with the biography of the speaker...

Sapozhnikova: *You have a Polish name. What is your nationality?*

Visockis: My mother is Lithuanian, my father is Polish. And I am an internationalist, in the full sense of the word. I was born in Lithuania, in the Vilnius District, in the Novy Gai village. I was born in 1934, practically near Poland, in a family of farm laborers. Mom and dad worked at a fish farm under the Polish landlord Kostelkowski. And I am proud that I come from a worker family. I finished school and studied at a pedagogical college. Then, thanks to the Soviet authority, I graduated from three institutes for free, plus I graduated from the high party school in Russia. After that I taught Polish in Trakai and was a school principal. Later I was transferred to the Šalčininkai District, where I became a Secretary of the Party Regional Committee and the Chairman of the Regional Council of the People's Deputies.

Sapozhnikova: *Let's remember 1985-1986, when the Soviet Union hadn't yet fallen into the abyss and the troubles seemed temporary. When and how did you sense that something was boiling up in Lithuanian society?*

Visockis: As Poland, by the design of the CIA, became a trampoline for the dismantlement of the socialist bloc, Lithuania became a trampoline for the dismantlement of the Soviet Union. The politicians were saying one thing and were doing completely the opposite. Bribes became a norm. The cooperatives' movement was blooming, the state property was given away to private persons almost for free. Later an epoch of the inflating of nationalism started. The problem of the national minorities arose.

With my colleagues, every week I was reporting to Kryuchkov and Gorbachev that Lithuania was seceding from the Union. We were travelling to Belarus and from there we were delivering the information to Moscow. We had been doing it for a whole year. It became clear that if no drastic measures were to be applied at the top level of the Union, Lithuania would secede from the USSR. But we didn't know that the decision about the Baltic states' secession from Union had been already adopted...

"The Red District"

Visockis: We looked for opportunities to gain ground. Our Šalčininkai District and the neighboring Vilnius District were mostly inhabited by Poles. And those districts were the most underdeveloped. We calculated that they had 4-5 times fewer doctors than other Lithuanian districts, as well as schools and kindergartens. The same could be said for industry. So we, knowing that Lithuania was going to leave the Union, began to look for opportunities to keep those districts in the Soviet Union. We came up with the idea of Polish autonomy, although I was against it. I said, "Let's rather call it an international autonomy." But my colleagues objected, "Well, we are going to have an autonomy, it should have a certain name." The autonomy couldn't be Lithuanian because only 9% of Lithuanians lived there. And so we had decided to create a Polish territorial unit in the Lithuanian SSR where only the USSR Constitution would have power.

Sapozhnikova: *Why didn't you want independence?*

Visockis: Because we had seen rampant unfairness. We understood that the new rules of the game were demeaning our district. Besides, we were the supporters of the Soviet Union. I spoke at the 28th Congress of the CPSU in Moscow and was the only one who said, "We must elect a new General Secretary – not Gorbachev." Everyone began stomping their feet, screaming, "Remove this provocateur!" Sazhi Umalatova had jumped up to a microphone after me and put it even more bluntly, "Traitors!" Yeltsin threw away his party card. And that was when I said, "The Soviet Union will be gone. Gorbachev had sold it out and the one throwing the party card away will finish it off..."

Sapozhnikova: *What was your autonomy like?*

Visockis: We decided that we would have three state languages – Polish, Lithuanian and Russian. The languages would be used in the press, in schools, and on street and road signs. We adopted a flag and a coat of arms. And we ruled that we would only follow the Constitution of the USSR and wouldn't follow the Constitution of the Lithuanian SSR. I got summoned to the Supreme Council of the Republic. I said, "You, the deputies, have adopted an illegal act of the secession from the USSR. The legal way is having a referendum, therefore I won't follow your rulings." I stood up and left.

And it began – the authorities were erecting border signs and poles on the borders, while I was giving orders to remove them. Vilnius decided to disrupt the draft to the Soviet army; we, on the other hand, gathered 400 conscripts. We were the only district on the territory of the Baltic states where the conscription law functioned. I even reached the Chairman of the Council of Ministers and struck a deal that the supply of the district will be done through Belarus. Petroleum, its products and other industrial goods were going from Moscow to Lida; we were retrieving them from there. Lithuania was viewing itself as a different state, while we for two and a half years continued to live in the Soviet Union, in an international "red" district.

"I Won't Trade My Wife for Opinions"

Sapozhnikova: *After the events of 13 January 1991, or to be more precise – after the way they were covered by the media – the sympathies for you among the common people surely faded? Did your life become more complicated afterwards?*

Visockis: Nothing became more complicated for us! The party grew in size. All institutions functioned properly – the KGB, the police – everything we had was Soviet. We were getting many letters, hundreds… To be fair, some of them targeted me. People wrote, "You are a Lithuanian and you have betrayed Lithuania, aren't you ashamed?"

Sapozhnikova: *With whom did your numbers grow? With Lithuanians, Russians or Poles?*

Visockis: There were no Lithuanians in those areas before the war – 80% of the territory's population was Polish. I will tell you a little known fact. When we declared a Polish territorial national unit, top officials from Poland came to visit us and officially came to my home to talk to me as the chairman of the regional council. They offered, "We can make a great deal. No, not even great, but a unique deal! Do you see what is happening in the Soviet Union right now? It has a very weak army. And, in Poland, we have 400 thousand servicemen in the military. Poles live in Lithuania, Belarus and Ukraine. There is an opportunity to unite the national districts and make them Polish territory, from the Baltic Sea to the Black Sea, if you will support us." I told them, "We are not going to fall for this provocation, because we are internationalists." The stakes were very high.

Sapozhnikova: *Can we say that the half of Lithuania was against leaving the Soviet Union?*

Visockis: Probably, even more than a half was for the Soviet Union. In our district, 93,9% has voted for the Union on the referendum. By the way, I was the Deputy Chairman of the Committee for Conducting the Referendum of 27 March 1991, which was officially banned in Lithuania.

Sapozhnikova: *When the TV began running Swan Lake, did you understand the ramifications of it all?*

Visockis: The smart men in Moscow immediately told us, "Don't cheer on, don't get involved anywhere, because it is just set dressing." Most likely, everyone already knew that is was just a show to put the last nail in the coffin of the Union. That evening friends told me, "Leave quickly." I left, and three minutes later my house was surrounded by the prosecutor of the republic, the district prosecutor and a lot of sajūdists with machine guns. I took only a shirt with me, left everything and fled.

Sapozhnikova: *What about your family?*

Visockis: Our family was considered exemplary. My wife joined the Popular Front, while I was a communist and said, "I am not trading my wife for opinions." To this very day I have no complaints regarding her. But our opinions are totally different. We had seven families of top officials broken up and filing for divorce because of that. It may be very hard for you to process, but imagine this: my wife carries a Sąjūdis flag, while I am walking next to a red banner...

"As If We Are Living Under Communism!"

Sapozhnikova: *Where did you hide in Belarus after the coup? What did you do and how did you make the ends meet?*

Visockis: I arrived at Svislach District. My friend was the Second Secretary of the Regional Party Committee there. I told him, "I have nowhere to stay and nowhere to work." The kolkhoz chairman said, "All my shepherds got drunk, I have no shepherds left." I replied, "Count me in!" And for two years I was a shepherd in the village of Kornad, Svislach District. I was living underground, living in a mud hut, because Lithuania didn't cease trying to catch me. I was living under a different name, Ivan Voytkevich, and wrote that I had only primary education, although I actually had three university degrees. There was a funny incident once. The farm manager assembled the cattle-raisers. Pay attention, she said, Ivan Voytkevich doesn't drink, works well, but look – he had already lived most of his life and has no car and no house, all because he has only primary education. While I, she continued, have finished technical college and work as a farm manager. So study, she concluded, and don'tbe like Ivan! It was sad and funny at the same time...

Once an ex-OMON commander, Boleslav Makutynovich, whom I met in Moscow during a plenum, gave me an envelope with 100 dollars inside. I tried to vehemently decline the gift, but he insisted. For me, it was a large sum. I mean, there were times when I used to live off merely 4 dollars a month. Having exchanged them for Belarusian rubles, I bought clothes, shoes, and spent the remaining money on food enough for a whole year, and even managed to buy butter, a loaf of bread and herring meat. It was the first time since 1991, when for a week I ate wheat bread with butter, just like in the Soviet times.

Sapozhnikova: *When did you leave underground?*

Visockis: There was a Central Committee plenum and the Svisloch Communist Party Secretary suggested I join. So I joined the party. Communists called Zyuganov and Air Force General Kopyshev and told them that there was a communist that had nowhere to stay. We wrote a letter to Lukashenko. I was summoned to the police station. I was afraid of the KGB and the police because, in 1994, Belarus had extradited Burokevičius and Jermalavičius. Only when Lukashenko came to power, did it become a safe environment. But all turned out well, I was issued a passport and granted asylum. So now I am not afraid of anything or anyone, and I am living under the last name Visockis, not Voytkevich. My current pension is as if I had been a bum, it is the lowest available, because Lithuanian authorities didn't return my documents – my employment record book was left in Lithuania. Instead, I was provided with two rooms in a nursing home for free. Here I get clothes, shoes, medical treatment. It is like we are living under communism!

I have an incredibly tight schedule here. I have articles to write, a poetry book to complete, another painting to finish, I'm taking someone to the cafeteria. We had one man named Roman Zaytsev. It happened that he went blind. His wife dumped him. And he cried, "I will hang myself here." I said, "No, I will rather assist you to walk everywhere before death." So I saved him, and he later worked as our lecturer! Now I assist two women and one man. For free.

"The Soviet Union Could Have Been Saved."

Sapozhnikova: *Did Lithuania track you for a long time?*

Visockis: It still does! Till this day I remain on the wanted list. In 1997, I went to the Central Committee plenum in Moscow, and suddenly I was handcuffed. Three men in civilian clothes said that they were policemen and demanded that I immediately follow them as if I were a criminal, who had committed a crime on the territory of Lithuania. They told me that there was a bilateral treaty between Russia and Lithuania for the extradition of criminals, in accordance with which I was to be arrested to be handed over to the Lithuanian authorities. Good thing that it was all going down in the Izmailovo hotel, where the plenum was. Delegates and foreign guests were beginning to gather in the corridor. Zyuganov had been informed about the incident. We called Lukashenko and got in touch with the Interior Minister. For two days I was held handcuffed and later released. Dalia Grybauskaitė had already sent two letters to Lukashenko, asking for me to be handed over and tried. But Lukashenko gave a reply, saying, "No, Visockis is innocent, and we won't hand him over." And when Lukashenko came to our nursing home, I gave him my painting as gift and said, "Thank you for saving my life…" And that is why I can fall on my knees in front of him.

Sapozhnikova: *What do you regret in your life?*

Visockis: I left many things half-done. I should have rung the alarm when I saw that the Soviet Union was collapsing. It could have been saved. The associates still come to visit me, but they are scared so much of everything in Lithuania that they ask me, "Only don't tell our last names." I will never tell them. But I believe that the truth will prevail!

Sapozhnikova: *When?*

Visockis: I won't live to that moment, but it will happen. My daughter wrote to me in the last letter, "Daddy, I am a Soviet Lithuanian!" And I am happy. I don't need anything else.

*

What had happened to the activists of the Šalčininkai Districts, who, unlike Česlavs Visockis, stayed in Lithuania after the coup? They were convicted. Convicted for the referendum, for the autonomy and for recognizing three equally official state languages. In August 1997, a criminal case was opened against Visockis and his comrades. In legal terms, the charges were brought for "an active participation of the leadership of the district in conducting a coup d'état in August 1991, participation in the activities of a foreign organization of another state (USSR), a foreign organization (CPSU) and its branches in Lithuania." Three of the defendants (Leonas Jankelevičius, Alfredas Aliukas, Janis Jurolait) were sentenced to various terms in prison, one defendant (Ivan Kutsevich) was acquitted due to the absence of a crime. "The trial of the Šalčininkai saboteurs has ended," reported the newspaper, employing the familiar lexicon from the school history books. The only difference is that those were not Stalin's, but Lithuanian times.

You are Indeed the Best German

Three years after the collapse of the Soviet Union, Česlavs Visockis wrote an open letter to Mikhail Gorbachev:

> Up to 22 August 1991, in Lithuania, I worked as the Chairman of the Šalčininkai Regional Council of Deputies and the Secretary of the Party Regional Committee. This district was the only one in the Baltic sates that remained Soviet for a year and a

half after Lithuania's exit from the USSR. In it, the Constitution of the USSR kept functioning. In August 1991, the Lithuanian authorities declared me an enemy of the Lithuanian nation for treason against the homeland. I was "guilty" of defending the Soviet regime, the CPSU, the USSR. Right now I am in the underground, without a job and a roof over my head. I was put on the international wanted list. But I don't lose my spirit and don't complain about my fate. Currently I serve as the Secretary of the Communist Party of Lithuania that continues to operate underground.

I strongly believed in you; with earnestness and integrity I followed the decision of the Congress of the People's Deputies of the USSR. On a joint meeting of the members of the CPL Central Committee Bureau you had assured us that Lithuania will remain in the USSR, while the efforts directed at maintaining the Soviet authority will be supported. That time I didn't believe you and bluntly told this to you.

…You completely fulfilled the West's order. You betrayed your comrades, you unleashed a human massacre and drenched our soil with blood, you devastated our rich and mighty country. You turned honest men into pariahs. You deliberately let the mafia, crooks and villains accede to power, you were carrying out the orders of the CIA, and for that you were awarded with the Nobel Peace Prize. But it was not a peace prize; you got the prize for treason.

You turned out to be a friend amongst enemies and an enemy amongst friends.

You are indeed the best German.

There is no need for traitors of the nation. In time of war, such a person, that took an oath of his army and later sold himself to the enemies, would be executed by firing squad. Now is not a time of war.

But you must be tried for treason against the homeland, so I make a proposition to bring M. Gorbachev to trial at a public tribunal, strip him of Russian citizenship and offer him the opportunity to leave Russia to any state, which shall desire to accept him.

You are a traitor, a criminal, a murderer. I damn you!

I believe in your disgraceful end, fit for Judas.

With the deepest contempt,

Česlavs Visockis, a Distinguished Worker of Culture of the Lithuanian SSR.

| Chapter Seven |

HOMELAND OR DEATH?

There is a magic word, which in the early 90s Baltics could paralyze anyone. And that word is "OMON."[1] A bullet word, a burn word, a gunshot word...

However the life of the Vilnius OMON, as well as the one in Riga, Latvia, was so fleeting that not many managed to figure out who fought for what and just who were those men in fatigues, who stood up for the then unpopular principles, stubbornly repeating, "We defend our right to think differently and act like our duty and oath dictate."

At the time, the 10-minute clip "Nashi", ("Our own" in Russian) made by Alexander Nevzorov for his TV program 600 Seconds felt like a slap in the face. The OMON officers themselves seemed like dangerous retrogrades, who got hold of some weapons. That was of course not everyone's opinion; a different part of the impoverished, morally defeated and absolutely confused Soviet society saw them as their protectors. In days of uncertainty, they had to believe in someone...

Rewatching the Nevzorov shorts today is shameful and scary: turns out were laughing at the truth and didn't realize who were our own and who were the enemy. "We are fighting the Baltic fascism!" says one "hero" into the camera in all seriousness. Back then it seemed like an out-of-line statement. However, after 25 years, this has become a reality: we are really struggling with Baltic fascism...

On the screen – the burning letters so familiar from the '90s and Winter Vilnius. Barricades. Chaotic shooting. We see the Soviet Union falling apart in front of us, like a weak piece of a cliff on a precipice.

"And what would comrade Nevzorov advise that we do in this situation?" asked the Vilnius OMON commander, Boleslav Makutynovich, of the film's author.

"Stand!" said the journalist with a flame in his eye.

And the OMON officers stood there, still unaware that they can't keep the country together. Unaware that Lithuanians will view their loyalty to their oath as crimes against humanity. And that both sides of the Lithuania-Russia border will eventually accept that.

"Create lists of the opposing side, their addresses and mark the apartments," Alexander Nevzorov was almost growling into the microphone when he outlined the nationalists' plans. This clashed with the beautiful tricolor ribbons and candles that used to be associated with the words "Lithuania and Lithuanians" up to a certain moment in time! Just 8 months later and this will be true – there will be leaflets on the streets with pictures of the commander with a star on the forehead and holes on the eyes. And the newspapers published a list of people suspected of treason… The most infamous Soviet and Russian reporter of the early 90s turned out to be the one with the most foresight.

By his own admission, this happened as a fluke of fate.

"I accidentally ended up on the side of truth," said Alexander Nevzorov in Winter 2012 interviews, before he became an ardent member of the opposition once again. Homeland or death, the Soviet Union or demise, "ours" or enemies: the man who made this choice 25 ago was rude and original and definitely didn't fit in political landscape of the time. With his current anti-government scandalous behavior,[2] he probably wishes he could edit that moment of his journalistic career. But alas, you can only do that in the movies and not in real life.

***

ALEXANDER NEVZOROV
Journalist

"The Assault on the USSR Was Rehearsed and Staged"

Sapozhnikova: So how did you manage to beat the other journalists to the scoop and hit the jackpot?

Nevzorov: I was on my way to Vilnius, pumped full of the Soviet propaganda of the time. I was electrified with the media stories about our tanks rolling over free-spirited Lithuanians. The first body I got to see in the morgue had clear and obvious signs of Zhiguli car tires. I knew how a body run over by tank would look like, because I have been through the Karabakh and the first stage of the Azerbaijani war. I saw gunshot wounds that were clearly not from army issue weapons, because you can easily tell the 12 gauge [hunting rounds – G.S.] apart from the others. The biggest misconception is that a sniper is someone who shoots from a hiding place. You don't have to demonize anyone and imagine mysterious ninjas prowling on the rooftops. It was people from the crowd, who shot hunting weapons and sawed-off rifles. A man from Sąjūdis just stood back and fired away...

These events were a colossal surprise for our Defense Ministry. The wondrous Dmitry Yazov was the Defense Minister at the time. A frontline veteran who shot lots of Germans, he was deathly afraid of being branded a killer of his own. And all of the army tip-toed around him, being categorically forbidden not just to shoot, but even to think about it! And the Lithuanians were definitely **our own.** The Vilnius OMON, the only battle-ready Soviet unit in Lithuania, was already paralyzed by then. Look at the tapes from that time, their guns don't have any magazines in them!

Sapozhnikova: Also, how did it happen that at the right place and the right time a lot of foreign journalists were there on the spot, while none of our press was there?

Nevzorov: The press was invited by the producers, directors and main actors. And we were given the role of the audience. A humiliated audience.

Sapozhnikova: *At which point did you realize it was staged?*

Nevzorov: When I saw the magazines of those lads. I was accidentally on the side of truth. It happened only because I had to choose between my sympathies, either the screaming, squealing hysteria or those devoted to their countrymen, like the illustrious commander of the Vilnius OMON, Boleslav Makutynovich, and the Pskov paratroopers. I chose THEM.

Stars and Swastikas

Sapozhnikova: *Is it true that after your film, Nashi, someone drew swastikas on your St. Petersburg office?*

Nevzorov: Yes they did. They were pressuring us in any way they could imagine. Starting with collective letters – because that was the main genre for the Soviet and Russian intelligentsia. The letters were signed by everyone rather hysterically: that all of Nashi is a hideous set-up, lies and insinuation. They demanded I be banished, my show cancelled and they made up debunking articles. A less cynical man would probably not withstand all of that. Don't forget, I was plucked from the territory of absolute glory, the subscribers loved me like their own son. And then I go to Vilnius and instead of the anticipated story on "Soviet aggression" I do THAT… There were no rumors about me being bribed. You should know Dmitry Yazov and the Soviet system at the time: they just didn't have the agency to do the bribing. I can't say I was a martyr for truth. First, that is not my role. Second, there was a counterbalance – I got completely wonderful letters and telegrams from all over the country from those who weren't the artistic intelligentsia. Pilots send their flight helmets with "Our own" and a surviving war veteran from the Berlin Air Squadron sent over an order which enlisted me into its ranks. I can't say that I wouldn't have made it without the support. But it felt damn fine. As you know, I didn't just film Nashi, I bluntly took that stand and held it for 20 years: we didn't kill anyone, it was all set up, it was treachery, an attempt to tear the country apart. I stood my ground, that it was all a lie. The only one in all of the Soviet press.

Sapozhnikova: *Then explain what was with the others? Was everyone blind?*

Nevzorov: It is impossible to suspect that 99.9% of the them were bribed by the West, because it wasn't commonplace back then, there were no bank cards. The country was completely overtaken by the new ideology, new demagogy, shining in all of its splendor as presented by Anatoly Sobchak and Sergey Stankevich well before he was a grump. It was all well-made, goddamnit! The approach against the Soviet Union was rehearsed and directed very well, as I can now see. And concerning the willingness to believe... What is belief? The absence of knowledge. You believe in the sanctity of Lithuania and sins of Yazov and Kryuchkov. There was no other knowledge so I can't give it to you. I only gave it to those who knew that our people wouldn't go shooting into a crowd, even if it was raving stupid. That neither Yazov, nor Kryuchkov, were incapable of shooting their own.

Sapozhnikova: *Then why didn't you say "B" after saying "A"? And why didn't you follow the lives of the Riga and Vilnius OMON officers later, with Lithuania and Latvia now hunting them all over the world?*

Nevzorov: Don't forget that I was already afflicted by then. Not only in Lithuania, but in all of the Soviet press, my name lost all respect. Precisely thanks to the Nashi film.
You can't mend destinies, can't bring back the country. We could seem farsighted 25 years later as much as we want, but it won't change the fate of the Vilnius OMON commander

Boleslav Makutynovich [who died in November 2015 – G.S.], nor the Alpha officer, Viktor Shatskikh. The Lithuanians will stick to their myth and keep preaching it further; they even built a government ideology on it, because they have nothing except the January events.

*

...This chapter is about the OMON officers who fought windmills and how they survived once they found out that no one needed them.

The Atlas Who Couldn't Keep the Sky from Falling

It was hard gathering them together, even though they live in one apartment complex on the outskirts of Moscow. After many years of hard work, the former leader of the Vilnius OMON, Boleslav Makutynovich, had finally managed to secure a few apartments for his fighters and move them in together.

Not all of them decided to convene, and there were reasons for that. Some agreed, and as they went over to Viktor Roschin's apartment in their indoor slippers, they laughed: "When we moved in, the precinct cop dropped by and asked whether we were wanted for alimony or something. And we joked, yeah, all of us at once..."

Our meeting was supposed to look completely different. The commander would line them up just like in the Nevzorov short and tell them in his unmistakable voice, "Squad! Here is your combat order!" And then these atlases would sit down and tell me how they tried to hold up the USSR sky on their stone arms...

Alas: Boleslav Makutynovich passed away without saying his final word. He turned down interviews for years, not wanting to make excuses or clear his reputation. Which is why his story and the story of the squad will be told by others: head of emergency response Viktor Roschin, analyst department officer

Yuri Rakhman. The 25 years that passed from the most important and glorious events in their lives have obviously left their mark. It is not about the gray hairs, it is about them finally leaving their illusions. To some of them Lithuania is still the homeland they see in their sleep. For the others it is a thorn in their side, which they would rather pull out and forget. They are united by one thing – they are hated by that same homeland; it is better to welcome the devil, than a Vilnius OMON officer.

"There are genuine, pure Lithuanian OMON officers in our house. I won't say their names, because they have relatives in Lithuania. And I can speak freely because my mother died last year. There is nothing they can do to me now," said Viktor Roschin openly. The others are listening intently. Every one of them is ready to stand for their words, but in order not to lose the thread of logic and make the answer collective.

VICTOR ROSCHIN:
Former OMON Head of Emergency Response

"Gathering Weapons From all of Lithuania"

Sapozhnikova: *Who had the idea to organize the OMON?*

Roschin: It was an order from Moscow. OMONs were being created in all of the republics, local center cities and cities with a population over a million, in order to combat. They needed units that could counter mass riots and group hooliganism. The backbone of the Vilnius OMON was made up of the Vilnius Patrol and Checkpoint Service (PPS), which was considered to be one of the best in the Union. The OMON was made up of athletic people, who had done police service. We received information from operative channels that the Department of National Defense was trying to get weapons. They were gathering weapons from all of Lithuania, from hunting clubs, sports sections and school primary military education classes. When all of the nationalistic bedlam started, many were eyeing the police weapon stock. But the PPS was considered "red", so they decided not to go there. And when the orders to hand in our weapons came in, me and my crew, in accordance with the USSR Interior Ministry, gathered the 40 assault rifles and gave them to the OMON, where they should have been. And that is what has the Lithuanian prosecutor's office chasing him for 25 years, rather than the events of 13 January 1991. None of the four was even in the OMON at that point.

Sapozhnikova: *What do you think was really behind all of those events?*

Roschin: On 8 January, the Lithuanian government suddenly more than doubled the prices on food products. In addition to the atmosphere: the tension was in the air, with open calls to take over Russian-speaking schools and kindergartens. There was a big protest meeting in front of the Supreme Council and representatives of the labor groups tried to get inside. The Vilnius OMON hadn't split at that point and they saw what was happening in the building itself. There were a lot of armed men inside. Even the old nationalists crawled out into the sun, wearing their uniforms and fascist crosses. Many had German rifles from WW2 times.

Sapozhnikova: *What do you think about the theory of some "third power", which provoked the tragedy?*

Roschin: That power was probably the Department of National Defense and Sąjūdis. According to our intel, the people were most likely also shot by members of the criminal investigation unit of Lithuania's Interior Ministry, from assault rifles with shortened barrels, chambered at 5.45. They rolled in kids from orphanages to the TV tower and TV center. Restaurants and cafes were told to prepare food and deliver it to the Supreme Council, the TV center and the TV tower. Overall, it was everything that later happened on the Kiev Maidan, only with fewer casualties. Right now people are used to it, and 10, 20 or 30 killed doesn't surprise anyone. Back then it was insane if even one person died... One of us served in the forensics expert department of the Interior Ministry and his work took him to the morgue quite a lot. Well, hear this: the local workers said that the next morning, when they were counting the casualties, they had bodies in the morgue that could not be categorized as victims in any way. As if they were gathered from all of the accidents around Vilnius for the past 24 hours and driven to one spot. All of these details were passed on to the Lithuania prosecutor's office.

Aurora on the Neris

Sapozhnikova: *You joined the OMON. It was past its glory days, in May 1991, when it was already clear that the situation was far from pleasant. And, nevertheless, you joined.*

Roschin: We were hoping it would all sort itself out. The country is big and we thought that its end couldn't be like THIS. Even during the first day of the coup we were sure that everything would end well. On the second day we busted out the vodka...

Sapozhnikova: *What was it like, living as rogues for these few months before the coup? Were they scared of you in Lithuania?*

Roschin: They respected us. They knew that we look out for our own. Some gave us bread and apples, others spit at our backs. We were heroes to some and outcasts to others. We were all young and hot-headed, we thought that the sea was knee deep and were fearless. Our photographs were hung on the fence in an attempt to threaten us, but there was such a feeling of brotherhood that nothing seemed too scary! The Lithuanian government was of course very scared of us. We could just ride the BTR a kilometer and a half away from the Supreme Council, and they would get all of the armed forces on high alert. We were just testing the motor and drove to the TV tower and back, in order to keep the BTRs in service, you need to warm them up on occasion. And they would just jump into a panic: "they are storming, they are storming"...

Can I tell you about an anecdotal situation? We needed to deliver an overview report to the military department of the CPL Central Committee and there were some traffic police on the way there. We knew each other face to face, having been part of the same operations. We exit the car and say: "We will put rails here and there... Fellas, are there any machinists among you?" "No, why?" "We are building a path for an armored train and there aren't enough machinists for it." And you wouldn't believe it, the next day the TV reported that an armored train would storm the Supreme Council... We then made a hoax for the papers, that the *Aurora* from St. Petersburg will approach the Supreme Council via the Neris river. They bought that joke as well.

Sapozhnikova: *After 13 January, logically, there should have been some fear of a man with a gun among the people...*

Roschin: No, it was more similar to a game. But it was all a novelty. Somebody was playing independence, somebody was protecting his country.

"Why Did You Abandon Us?"

Sapozhnikova: *So, on the first day of the August coup you watched TV and on the second you had vodka...?*

Roschin: No, on the first day we restored Soviet power! When the coup started, a man from the first platoon ran in with news: he said that the military was storming the parliament. Everyone was happy: we thought that our guys would roll in and put everything in place! And then it turns out that it wasn't in Vilnius, but in Moscow. And a sort of confusion settled in... We were waiting for order to be established, and even more disorder came out.

There was an order to disarm us. And we didn't want to disarm, because we knew that as soon as we would turn our guns in, they would just shoot us. It was even downright silly: the Pskov troopers were told that the OMON is attacking the internal forces and if they try to protect the OMON then the tanks will shoot you. Severny Gorodok, where the division was situated, was told that we were being attacked by the troopers. They were trying to sic us onto each other. But they failed. The officers of Severny Gorodok called us and told us to come on over, they would give us some more ammunition. We asked: "Aren't you going to attack us?" and they replied: "Why would you even think that? Why would we harm anyone for you!" When we arrived, they almost picked us up and carried us triumphantly. At that moment, the internal troops division, to which we were formally answering, denied us food and communications. They turned their backs on us and we were in their command. And a completely different military regiment gave us bread and rations. On the third day of the coup, Lithuanian prosecutor Artūras Paulauskas and Interior Minister Marijonas Misiukonis came to our squad. They were trying to prove to us that an oath can be taken multiple times... Proposed that we turn our commander in. And that is when we got the feeling that the end was near...

It is noteworthy how we were relocated to the military unit ground. We loaded all of our belongings unto a BTR, raised the banner of the Lithuanian SSR Interior Ministry, which we still have to this day, and rode to Severny Gorodok. People stood on the side of the road and watched us off. No curses – just flowers and apples... You wouldn't believe it, but it wasn't just from the Russian-speaking people, but also native Lithuanians, who were close to the Soviet power and they said: "Why are you abandoning us? We fought the Forest Brethren and now you are leaving us to be gutted by them?" The lads were crying from those words... And the Supreme Council was on alert. They said that the OMON was once again going to storm them.

No one wanted to leave, everyone insisted that the squad could be relocated as a whole. But they tricked us and multiple times, even after they moved us to the military unit grounds: first they forbade us from walking around with weapons and when we went to the cafeteria, the weapons were taken away. And we were no one without weapons...

A part of us quit and remained in Lithuania and a part went to serve in the army, the others flew to Moscow. Boris Pugo was no longer alive at that moment, but they still called in the Interior Minister's airplane for us. We were delivered to the Vilnius airfield by military cars. The USSR Interior Ministry commission was supposed to be flying with us, but its head, Mr. Demidov, got scared after we joked about hijacking the plane to go abroad, so he didn't fly with us. Officers of the 107th Division lined up on the landing strip and saluted us. The future Chechen president, Aslan Maskhadov, was always among them, saluting! At that moment he was decidedly a Soviet officer, the president of the Officer Assembly of the whole garrison. So we know him from a slightly different perspective than the rest.

Sapozhnikova: *What was on your mind when the plane took off?*

Roschin: I was hoping it wouldn't land back in Vilnius... As we flew we made grim jokes about whether the landing is already secured. Because we were told that we were being taken to the Dzerzhinsky division for house arrest. We left the plane and some colonel approached us, asking where we were from. We said we were from Vilnius. He asked "Where were you a few days ago? You would have helped preserve Soviet power..."

We were all seen as ardent coup supporters. Our "reconnaissance" reported that there was an unspoken directive to not hire us, fire us at the first opportunity and categorically stop us from working in Moscow, Leningrad and the surrounding areas. Even a few years later, when we had wandered around the country and waited through the hard times, many of us decided to reclaim our positions in the police, and whenever they heard we were from the Vilnius OMON they would just say no. We went to the Defense Ministry. We said that we are officers, we want to serve and the war in Chechnya had just started. But wherever we would settle in, it would end with a response of "your service is not needed."

Starting from Scratch

Sapozhnikova: *What jobs did you end up with?*

Roschin: Some were guards, some were drivers. Many of us had to abandon our dreams and forsake our skills. So we had make our lives into something we never expected to be doing. Nobody wanted us in law enforcement anymore. There were exceptions for specific people. But not as former officers, they had to enlist anew. From scratch. As soon as you mention in the papers that you are from the Vilnius OMON, you get shut down instantly...

Fifteen people drove to the Minsk Police School. And there as well, they told us that we were not needed. And then some guy in a corridor asks us: "Lads, where are you from?" We were all dressed in uniform or fatigues. We tell him that we are from Vilnius, they assigned us to Belarus, but they won't have us. "Why don't you come and serve with me in the city of Borisov, I am the chief of the local police precinct." That was Colonel Shibalko. A month later, he saved us again – warning us that a special brigade had arrived in Borisov to arrest us. If he is still alive, then I wish him many good years! If not – then a fond memory...

We had no idea what to do. Three of our guys arrived, the ones who flew to Tyumen along with the Riga OMON and proposed we go to the Riga squad! We arrived and then we were shocked to learn that just now they had arrested the Deputy Commander of the Riga OMON, Sergey Parfenof. He was called by the Internal Affairs Directorate chief and as he entered the office, the Latvians apprehended him and took him to Riga.

The Tyumen police chiefs treated us well, but still wouldn't hire us. They proposed to make us militiamen temporarily... We had about 100-150 rubles left, and a kilo of macaroni cost around 100. And then one of us sold the winter camouflage kit to the shift guys and we got tickets to Moscow.

Sapozhnikova: *Were you hunted during this time?*

Roschin: Officially, only three names were listed as wanted by Interpol: Roschin, Rasvodov and Makutynovich. But they were hunting for everyone. The wanted lists are quite vague and the Lithuanian prosecutors constantly shift them. Tell me, when did the tank crew member Yuri Mel get on that list? Only AFTER he was apprehended, right? That is what I'm talking about...

* * *

I pull out my camera to take a photo. They glance at each other: "So should we put on our berets?" They put them on and are immediately recognizable as those very OMON officers from the early 90s, who were used to scare the people on TV. "Hey, Roschin, you are renovating your apartment soon, right?" they ask the owner of the apartment, looking at the white wallpaper: "Let's write 'We will be back' on the wall and send the photo to Vilnius? Come on?"

... In order to avoid any incidents, they decided against ruining the wall. So it wouldn't be like that armored car or the Aurora cruiser...

On the Right Side of History

In June 2015, Lithuanians suddenly heard the voice of reason, when judge Audrius Cininas unexpectedly acquitted the former Vilnius OMON commander, Boleslav Makutynovich and HQ chief Vladimir Razvodov, who were tried in absentia. "From an accusatory standpoint, there was no state of war declared, no armed conflict, no occupation, therefore, there was no basis for the Geneva Convention to be in effect," said the judge in his decision, admitting the obvious: making the detained into war criminals is legal nonsense.

Makutynovich would never know how the trial ended. His "accomplice," Vladimir Razvodov, will face a lot of trouble from the Lithuanian prosecution though -- they do have to do something to make up for 25 years of work with no results. Aside from the endless blank spots around the 13 January tragedy, Lithuanian history has another unsolved conundrum – the murder of the border control officers in Medininkai, in the early morning of 31 July 1991, on the exact day that George Bush Sr. visits Moscow. I should remind you that the old communists Burokevičius and Jarmalavičius were taken from Minsk on the day Bill Clinton flew in. It appears that was the... political fad at the time. The official "scapegoat" for the border post shootout had already been found and given a life sentence. Despite the lack of evidence, that sentence was given to former Riga OMON fighter Konstantin Nikulin-Mikhailov. But sentencing one man is clearly not enough for the "crime of the century." So the Lithuanian prosecution was hard at work to find him some decent company. The former head of the Vilnius OMON HQ, Vladimir Razvodov, was a nice pick.

No matter how you try to change your fate, he couldn't avoid encountering the OMON. Trooper, candidate master at sambo, who served in the internal troops and had command of a special forces company – what side could he be on in 1991 if not this one? When the turbulent times began, there were two options: either become a bandit or someone who combats them. At first the OMON was viewed just like that – crimefighters. Theoretically, the people's sympathies should have been with them, because everyone, no matter the nationality, was suffering from the crime wave. But it turned out differently.

VLADIMIR RAZVODOV
Former OMON HQ Chief

"Us and Not Us"

Sapozhnikova: *How did you turn from friends of the people into enemies?*

Razvodov[3]**:** The divide into "us and not us" began for everyone. In 1990, when Vytautas Landsbergis came to power, there were protests, which quickly developed into mass riots. And the specialization I got in the special school was called just that: "Combating mass insubordination and mass rioting." The Lithuanian SSR OMON was responsible for the security at all of the state institutions – the Supreme Council, the Minister Council, the Interior Ministry. 7 November 1990, a crowd of thousands of Russians and Poles rushed the Supreme Council in order to engage with the government. We, 30 OMON officers, were set up as a live shield between the people and the Supreme Council. We were called every curse word and had everything thrown at us… We led two people inside in order to explain why we weren't letting them in: inside there were pro-Sąjūdis fighters, armed not only with knives and crowbars, but also real firearms and were just waiting for a chance to turn the crowd to mincemeat. After that, the protesters themselves started helping to keep the crowd back. But the "internal fighters" inside the building started provoking the people over our heads. Somebody grabbed a fire-hose with hot water and started spraying the crowd. They howled… Truth be told, it was hard holding the people back from confrontation then.

Sapozhnikova: *You knew about the weapons with absolute certainty?*

Razvodov: Of course. I saw the pistols, Nagants, Mosin rifles and TOZovkas [small caliber sport rifles] with my own eyes.

Sapozhnikova: *…which were used, possibly, a few months later by unknown snipers while shooting from the roofs on that night of the January tragedy? How did a group of professionals such as yourselves miss the provocation in preparation?*

Razvodov: We sent materials and reports to our superiors. But as long as the Vilnius OMON had the nationalist, Erikas Kaliačius, among its chiefs, it was all for nothing.

Sapozhnikova: *So the squad fell apart due to national reasons?*

Razvodov: Not quite. The Vilnius OMON was multinational, with Lithuanians, Poles, Russians and Armenians serving with us. Most disagreed with what was happening in the republic, but there were Sąjūdis supporters as well. On New Year's night, when we were on alert because there were attacks on restaurants and stores, we were almost fighting each other in the units as well: Lithuanians were attacking Russians and Poles while the Poles and Russians were attacking the Lithuanians. On the night between 11 and 12 January 1991, the final divide in the Vilnius OMON happened mostly on political grounds. Some remained loyal to the Soviet Union, and some to Lithuania. We took all of the weapons and vehicles with us and relocated to the police school, which was fairly close to our base. At first a lot of lads went with us, but later, people started going away – some had families, others had Lithuanian relatives. In the end, we had only 12 people. Honestly, I had a real feeling of numbness... The nationalists were starting to surround us. We mobilized everyone, set up posts and Boleslav Makutynovich started calling the military commandant of the city, Colonel Belogorodov, saying that he needs help and protection. And he replied, saying that they were also surrounded and trying to contact the troopers. And the troopers from Alytus [a city 100 km from Vilnius, location of the 97th Guard Paratrooper Regiment] came to our aid – they rallied the special battalion, entered Vilnius and gave us a platoon with BMDs.[4] For four hours, as if they had wings! We were grateful like all hell. Then everything stabilized a bit, the people started slowly returning and, by the end of the month, the squad had around 80 people. So we couldn't be part of the 13 January 1991 events even if we had wanted to – we were blocked at our own base by a gang of angry people, who were screaming out that we were the enemy... Back then I pointed out the duplicity of his news story to Nevzorov, which made it seem like we were heroically shooting back from the Vilnius TV tower and he waved it off, saying that it was just a clip on TV and that people will figure it out on their own... The people didn't figure it out: there has been almost 25 years now of us always having to prove that we weren't there.

The Age of Aggression

Sapozhnikova: *Have the Lithuanian people changed since then? As a general rule, people become more humane in face of desolation and shock...*

Razvodov: On the contrary, there was more aggression. This is best seen among the members of my generation and those younger. Middle-aged and older people reacted differently, because they knew what the Soviet Union was and what normal human life was. When everything settled down more or less, we started letting the guys go home to visit their families. I went to visit mine as well. I exit my apartment and see a neighbor going up the stairs, Algis was his name, he served in the Department of National Defense and lived directly across from us. He and his wife were very hostile towards us, to the point where if we met them on the staircase, I had a shiver run up my spine. Then my wife was visited by Algis' father, who apologized and said: "Tell your husband so he won't come here so openly, because my son gave an order to set up an ambush here." He was a great man! I even asked him to look after my family if what – because the doors was set on fire and the windows were broken at times... But not everyone did that – other Lithuanians supported us. Strangers gathered money and food for us, because Boris Gromov, who was the First Deputy of the Interior Minister at the time, attached us to the 42nd division. And then we had uniforms, supplies and proper food. And more people. There were truly priceless additions to our OMON squad, like, say, the criminal detective major, Alexey Antonenko, who headed the squads operative department. Later on, we saved a lot of people thanks to him.

Playing War

Sapozhnikova: *In 1991, the Riga OMON was more in the news spotlight than the Vilnius one.*

Razvodov: Purely thanks to the commander of the Riga OMON, Česlavs Mļiņņiks. I am a man of the military and I don't tolerate those police tricks. I always said: a combat unit must act with precision and by the code. And Makutynovich and Mļiņņiks are policemen –one was a political officer and the other was a beat cop – to them this was just bravado, playing war. That is why they made friends with Nevzorov and made a ton of movies with him. Me and Alexey Antonenko sighed: circus clowns, they were definitely going to get bitten in the ass by it! Boleslav was directly warned – if he would take the spotlight, he would be wishing he didn't, later. "No, we must be on the cover" he said in response...

Sapozhnikova: *And they were – especially when they started enthusiastically attacking border posts. Was that an order or just fulfilling your duty in such a way?*

Razvodov: In actuality, these painted wagons with the traffic control barriers on the nonexistent border, with "border control" written on them in Lithuanian, were there only to rob the people. People went to complain to us *en masse*. We reported to Moscow. And the reply was a clear and direct order: there are to be no border posts there, because this is territory of the Soviet Union. Not a problem: we went around to the posts in small groups and cleared them out. Later they tried to accuse us of beating people, but we had it all recorded, we are no fools... We recorded every step on film, because we knew what it might have been spun into. It looked something like this: we took the border control's weapons, tore down the insignia and told them to run along, or else we would whack them. And those who resisted got a more harsh response. The wagons were burned down and the territory was freed. We received complaints about the Medininkai post as well, reports that drivers were being stripped of all valuables. We developed an operation, sent men out there with video cameras. And that was it! We later handed the cassettes to the prosecutions, but they disappeared from the criminal case.

Homeland or Death? 211

Sapozhnikova: *Do you remember the night of the "border guard" killings?*

Razvodov: I arrive at work and the shift guard reports: a post was shot out in Medininkai, but all of our men were in place, no one had left to go anywhere. I was shocked... I went to the commander and he was shocked too. The first thought in my head was they would blame it all on us. And that is exactly how it turned out: the very first speech accused the OMON of everything. Apparently, the witness lost all memory of the incident, but managed to recognize Razvodov, Makutynovich, Nikulin-Mikhailov and another group of Riga OMON operatives by our voices in conversation... What nonsense! Does that guy at least know himself? He and I have never seen each other, and how could he recognize me by a conversation? I was at home that night. Want to confirm it? Go ahead and ask my warden and neighbor, the head of the Department of National Defense, where I was that night. He later confirmed and I checked, Razvodov was home. The backlash was huge! No one understood anything. Did the OMON guys attack the border posts before? Yes they did. And then suddenly – bam! A murder... And go and prove that that two plus two isn't five. As I understand it, Landsbergis and company needed to rile up the people, so the accusations against us just kept flowing.

Sapozhnikova: *When and why did the shadow of the Riga OMON appear in this situation?*

Razvodov: We kept in touch, visited each other – we had to exchange experiences and I am from Latvia originally. Maybe they just staked it out and reported at one point that the Riga OMON spent the night at our base? We had a number of the so-called "spies" in our squad. We found four of them, and how many went uncaught?

I know that it wasn't done by the OMON. We had information on smugglers – apparently Belarussians bandits wanted to get a large shipment of fur over the border and a

Lithuanian crew wanted to move a shipment of drugs and they didn't see eye to eye. According to photos and videos made right after the murder on the border, we could say for sure – that was not how we operate. We would have gone in, dragged the border guards to the back yard, face down to the ground and left. Yes, I know my lads well – they would have demolished everything. And there, according to the photos, even a bottle of vodka with untouched snacks remained, and the border guards were carefully lined up on the ground, with bullet holes in the backs of their heads.

"The Police Were After Us Like We Were Criminals"

Sapozhnikova: *There were mere weeks before the Vilnius OMON was disbanded. How were the last days of the squad in Lithuania?*

Razvodov: In late August, after the failed coup, we started getting visits from big bosses. Instead of General Uskhopchik, Colonel Frolov came to Severny Gorodok to lead the motorized rifle division. He came to the squad a few times and set some ultimatums, telling us to hand in our guns and leave the base grounds. I tolerated that for a while and then said: "Colonel, go away and never come back!" We had a shouting match with him. Deputy Interior Minister General-Major Demidov came from Moscow. The question was whether to extract the squad or disband it. Frolov said that it needed to be disbanded, because the OMON officers are criminals… And Severny Gorodok had an Officer Assembly, which was led by Maskhadov. You know the one. I later fought him in Chechnya. Later still, we drank vodka together. A great man and a terrific officer. They were all in support of the Soviet Union, all in unison. And he said that if we needed help, then Severny Gorodok territory was at our disposal. We gathered up, loaded onto the cars and relocated all of the gear and vehicles there. The squad was eventually disbanded. The main bulk of it – around 89 people – were flown to Moscow by plane. The vehicles and weapons were given to Lithuania.

Sapozhnikova: *How did the homeland greet you?*

Razvodov: That is another topic altogether. When we returned, we were far from heroes. Most of us hailed from the Baltics and had never lived in Russia until then. I was assigned to the Internal Affairs Academy. Sometime later, the rector called me to his officer and whispered: "Careful, your compatriots have arrived." I went "What compatriots?" and he goes, "Lithuanians from the prosecutor's officer." I enter to see an officer and there are two of them there, greeting me in Lithuanian... Investigators, one of them knew me personally and was there specifically to identify me. And the rector tells me: "Comrade major, you should go to Lithuania and give a testimony to lift the suspicions off you." And I asked him, "You do understand that there would be no returning?" "What do you mean there will be no returning?" he asked, being more a scientist, he didn't quite understand... I stepped out to the corridor and saw three black Volga cars and six lads in plainclothes, with three more patrolling the first floor. I jumped out the bathroom window on the second floor, went to the dorms via the back entrance, changed clothes and left quickly. Later Alexey Antonenko told me that 70 men were sent to Moscow from Lithuania to catch us all. And in addition to the Lithuanians, the Moscow police were after us, as if we were criminals.

Early in 1992, to give credit where credit is due, Yeltsin gave the order to restore our officer ranks, because we wanted to continue serving Russia. I was invited to the Novosibirsk OMON. Then I had an emissary ask that I help Abkhazia. They formed a squad from Vilnius and Riga operatives and we joined. There we were betrayed again and driven to a mine field. Many died that day. I received a serious concussion.

I transferred to St. Petersburg, served in FSIN (Federal Penitentiary Service) and was Deputy Commander of the Typhoon squad (an internal forces special unit). Two tours of duty in Chechnya, Rapid Response unit, and finally retirement – the concussion played in. Everything was fine until someone called from Interpol and said I was locked down. If I go out of the country, I would be apprehended. That is how I found out about the absentia trial.

Leave No One Behind?

Razvodov: It would be untactful to call it an international circus. A political farce! They are trying to make us out to be war criminals or murders – and that is just nonsense. Almost 25 years after, now I receive papers about my extradition. A few times, I have had the police drop by and tell me that I must leave, as a citizen of Lithuania. I tell them that I am a police lieutenant-colonel in retirement, served in Russia – why am I a Lithuanian citizen suddenly? They look at my passport in surprise, they apologize and leave. I was at the Prosecutor-General's office and the chief of the extradition office told me that we don't give up our own. It was quiet for a few years. Then another political wave started apparently and again... Recently, at 6 am, someone knocked at the door. Three men, boys around 22-23, court officers. They tell me that there is a presiding judge's order to get me to Kirov district court and they try to neutralize me. I tell them: "Lads, don't do anything stupid and don't let my old age fool you, I can throw you out of here along with the doors and set a precedent. Let's settle this in peace!" Long story short, I had to kick them out. We agreed that I would go to court myself. But my wife, scared for my safety, called my former colleagues. When they arrived, there was a whole squad of former OMON guys there... The deputy presiding judge was apologizing for a long while.

I haven't done anything illegal. I was fulfilling my oath, specific orders, set up by the leaders. If the leaders renounce it, then let it be on their conscience. I still view my lads as boys, whom I would protect like a mountain. The eldest was 27 at the time. And now they are all gray-haired...

ALEXEY ANTONENKO
Former Deputy Commander of Operative Work of the Vilnius OMON

Soviet-Brew Robin Hood.

It is just 12 kilometers from this house to the Lithuanian border: it is almost like you could reach Lithuania, but you can't. It is dangerous.

This hamlet on the edge of an old Belarussian village was hastily completed by former Deputy Commander of Operative Work of the Vilnius OMON, Alexey Antonenko, in Summer 1991, as if he felt they he would have to leave Lithuania soon. He thought that he could hide here, along with his squad mates, if anything happened. The place is sturdy, secluded from prying eyes: if not for the local Ksiądz (Polish catholic priest) we would never have found him in the maze of forest roads.

It is raining, the men exit the minivan first, the windows are tinted – a very worrying image for someone who has lived many years in the crosshairs. The head of the house's eyes are aimed at us, and they burn like lightning.

Antonenko: I was born in Vilnius, my mother is a Pole, my father is a Ukrainian. When I was 16 and I had to choose a nationality, I said I wanted to be Russian. And they told me: "No, you must pick one from your parents." Had to write myself as a Pole. How did my father get to the Baltics? When Lithuania was liberated in 1944, Antanas Sniečkus, the First Secretary of the CPL, asked Russia for help – they needed specialists, because all of the engineers fled to the West. So first my brother went there to check things out, he had just finished college on refrigerating machinery, and he wrote to my father saying that he could settle here.

I have worked within the Vilnius law enforcement for 20 years. The criminal investigation department was a predominantly Russian organization, the Lithuanians mostly worked in the OBKhSS (Department for Combating Theft of Socialist Property and Speculation) or the Ministry – where the seats are comfier. And the Russians were given the dirty work. From the very start, we knew that we were second-rate people to them. But we didn't take it to heart. Somewhere around 1987, when everyone stopped adoring Gorbachev, Lithuanians started whispering behind our backs. Before this, we got along fine, but now they avoided conversation. Sąjūdis slogans of democracy and freedom attracted multiple people; only ardent communists saw it as a revolt, the others were interested in where this would lead. There was this belief that even if Lithuania did leave the Soviet Union, you could still live and work there. After all, criminal investigation isn't going anywhere, any type of regime has crime. It was completely clear where we were heading in Autumn 1989, when Sąjūdis has its first convention in the Sport Palace, with delegates from all over Lithuania, and the events were broadcast over all of the Lithuanian TV channels. And that was when I heard how they were planning to decide our fate, it was all clear.

A Creeping Genocide

Sapozhnikova: *You realized that you can't wait this one out in the trenches and you will have to fight anyway?*

Antonenko: Around 1987 I started paying closer attention to everything happening around me and thinking about a possible alternative. Because it was clear that if Gorbachev is not a traitor, then he is a fool. We were used to trusting our leaders and here we have this... Everything just keeps picking up speed, and now Lithuanians refuse to speak to you. Previously, my former colleagues just ignored me, but now they asked caringly whether I was going to leave Lithuania or not? I told them that I had nowhere to go. I was born here, this is my hometown. When they said that Lithuania would have only the Lithuanian language and adopted many different laws, on the next day, the bus stop signs still had the Lithuanian names, but the Russian ones were whittled off. It looked so crude... You are just walking down the street, you walk up to a bus stop and you see it as if it spat at your face. You wipe your face and keep moving, but 200 meters later there is another stop and another shot at your face... I remember, on 9 May, me and my friends wanted to join the march in commemoration of Victory Day through Gediminas street, which was Lenin street earlier. We joined the military column, which is marching and a woman shouts "parasites" at us. And I was so surprised by this... We go further and a crowd of students drop in, screaming "Geda, geda, geda!" (shame in Lithuanian). And they were almost spitting at us.

Sapozhnikova: *This beast of nationalism within the Lithuanians, that was awakened in the late 80s, did it emerge on its own or did someone help it?*

Antonenko: The people were hyped up by the media. And it was indirect. I would call it a "creeping genocide." Even criminals were divided into ours and foreign ones. The TV always pointed out the nationality of the criminal – Russian, Polish or Lithuanian. In search of an alternative, I started going to protests. I really liked Valery Ivanov's idea about solving the national issue. The same way they did in the Soviet Unions: if the percentage of Lithuanians and non-Lithuanians in Vilnius is 50/50, then all officials, elected posts and ministers must also hold these posts in that proportion. And the Lithuanians protested when I told them this idea. They told me, "Where would you find so many smart Russian speakers?"

And you see it snowballing... And then January 1991 came. I was highly opposed to Sąjūdis at that point and stood with the crowd in the yard of the Supreme Council when Landsbergis peeked from the second floor window in fear. Maybe if the people stormed inside and killed this regime in the crib, everything would have been different. But it didn't turn out like that. The unarmed did not go to face the armed.

"Who Was Robbing the Border Posts?"

Sapozhnikova: *You transferred to the OMON after it all* *happened: the 13 January events and the squad's divide. Why did you almost wait until May?*

Antonenko: I wanted to transfer earlier as a regular fighter, but they refused. Said that I had a great opportunity to help them, because I was in the center of the events. I gave lots of valuable information to the squad.

For example, how in May 1991, Belarussian police captain Alexandr Fiyas' was murdered on the Belarus-Lithuania border, something Lithuania doesn't like to recall.

He was on his way to Vilnius via car with his wife and children. There was a border wagon, he didn't comply with the imposters and drove up to the crossing barrier. And there was a secret post in the bushes, armed with a shotgun and someone shot him in the back. The shooter was arrested and put into pre-trial, and I was part of developing leads from the cells at that point. I gave him a very "good" cellmate - planted a smart guy who later told us the "what and why" of it all. Then the republican prosecutors showed up and told him what to say. The case was clear, but the press wrote everywhere that Fiyas' was the first one to draw a weapon... The shooter was later acquitted due to following instructions correctly.

Sapozhnikova: *Could the murder of the border guards in Medininkai two months later have been foreseen?*

Antonenko: Just before it, we were planning an operation of our own. The thing is, we had received intel that the border guards were robbing people in broad daylight. That post was considered to be the main one, because it had the most traffic go through it – cars, trucks – and the border guards got a toll from all of them. At the end of the shift, they went to someone's country house, stored the loot and divided it amongst them. According to our intel, the same kind of robbery was also happening at the airport customs. An operative promised to plant our guy there, with a video camera to capture all of the events. And we decided that if there was a chance, then we needed to film Medininkai as well, in order to show it on "Caspervision" later – that is what we called Burokevičius' TV. And that is why on 29 July 1991, we went to the spot with a colleague, a police major as well, who worked in OBKhSS before. The plan was this: across from the border post, a bit lower, there were some bushes and aspen trees – we wanted to place two guys there from our unit, which were on outside surveillance earlier. And on the Belarussian side, we found a spot for a HQ car with a powerful antenna where our engineer and surveillance crew is. The outside surveillance team would spot someone getting robbed, tell us the code word and we would stop the car and interview the passengers.

Sapozhnikova: *Did someone do it before you did? Or was your plan leaked?*

Antonenko: I don't think it was leaked. I don't know… We reported to Makutynovich. In his office, he had a chalkboard, where I drew up the plan and everything. And I went home to rest. When I arrived the next day, the news from Medininkai came out of nowhere…

Sapozhnikova: *Did you immediately realize it was a trap?*

Antonenko: No, I didn't see it like that. We were used to them blaming everything on us. On daily basis, people would walk to the base, teachers would bring their students and shout similarly to how they do in Ukraine now: "Down with the commies!" and the orphans would chant: "OMON go home! OMON is AIDS on the body of Lithuania!"… And before I joined the unit, the lads went to stop the illegal border control posts, then later Moscow forbade us to do so. Completely! And they didn't just forbid it, the also sent their emissary – a lieutenant-colonel from USSR Interior Ministry department of maintaining public order – who lived on our base and sat in for Makutynovich. Somebody continued robbing them. All of the OMON weapons were locked up by then, so there were no questions about us.

"I Love the USSR"

Sapozhnikova: *As a former detective, do you have your own theory on these events?*

Antonenko: Well, you could theorize about pretty much anything. We thought that it was the Department of National Defense doing it in order to discredit the OMON. The most we could do to them was make the border guards do 10 push-ups and say, "I love the USSR" and send them to Vilnius on foot. And here it was all done, in a way, to show off...

During the investigation carried out by ourselves, the Interior Ministry, the KGB and the Lithuanian prosecution, we had multiple theories. The prosecutors also examined a theory that it was people from the official Lithuanian forces. I and the investigation crew couldn't confirm a connection, but it was established that the people were killed in a building different from the one they were found in. Because there were no bullet holes in the floor or the walls, just blood. Among the killed border guards, four were armed – two with assault rifles from the APAC [Lithuanian anti-terrorist police unit – G.S.] and the other two were from the traffic police, who were no slouches either and could have easily drawn their weapons if the situation called for it. But for some reason no one resisted. What does that mean? It means that the operation was meticulously planned.

Around a week after the events in Medininkai, there was another provocation not many people know about. There were a few days of mourning declared in the republic. Landsbergis was throwing fits over the radio and TV about how the OMON needs to be ended, because they are killers and he called for the people to come to a three-day protest at our base. We received word of the planned operation, "Storm". The point was to gather as many people as they could at the protest, start a riot, shoot a few people and blame it all on us. The crowd was supposed to surround the building and try to enter it and then the OMON would be forced to vacate the base. That version was offered to the people.

We understood that we would lose either way and addressed the population on TV, telling them that a provocation was planned. We phoned the Moscow and Leningrad newspapers. We did not get a lot of journalists though. But when the protest started, a few people – reporters and OMON operatives with cameras – were on the rooftops.

The second day of the protest was the most dramatic. At 5 pm they told us that two crew moved out from the Department of National Defense, carrying a crate of weapons. At 5:30 pm we are told that there was a drive-by shooting of the internal troops division HQ by an unknown party. At 5:55 pm we suddenly lost all radio connection. It was clear that they were preparing… And at 6 pm sharp, young men started surrounding us from all sides, but they weren't the protestors. The protesters were mostly aggressive old ladies. Then there was a burst fired over the heads of those on the roof, but no one was harmed. They either didn't want to hit anyone or missed. The commander gave the order to all posts to immediately hide in the base building. I ran to the protesters and shouted: "For God's sake, go away! We were just shot from the forest, now they will start shooting you to make another 13 January!"

"You are the ones who shot yourselves!" shouted the old ladies.

The deputy chief of the traffic police was standing right there, already in the new Lithuanian police uniform.

"Please, you explain it to them, maybe they will listen to you!" I asked him.

And yes, after his words, half of the crowd dispersed, and the others quieted down. No other shots were fired from the forest. By the third day, they had all dispersed.

…And concerning Medininkai – there was a lot of theories about it, I have a whole archive of them over the years. Later they recruited a lot of people from those who chose to remain in Lithuania, even among former OMON guys – it wasn't hard to apply some pressure to them, especially those with residence permits. Since you have to extend them each year, you either cooperate or you can't stay. Many of them probably had to compromise in order to be left alone.

So it is not surprising, that many years later, these new witnesses showed up in that story. They are brought into the light when the prosecution needs to exonerate themselves. That is how Konstantin Nikulin-Mikhailov, formerly of the Riga OMON, came to be imprisoned without any evidence. There is a whole campaign in Lithuania in his defense. We also received donations at one point; people didn't think we were still receiving our salaries. Grannies gathered it up, handed us canned goods. People in Lithuania were convinced that the OMON were like Robin Hoods of sorts. I was surprised, when I received 400+ rubles from an absolutely pro-Lithuanian village in the Kaunas region, which was a lot at the time. There was even a list of contributors in the letter. And Nikulin right now is helped by former dissident Nijolė Sadūnaitė, who handled the printing of the chronicle of Catholic life in Lithuania during the Soviet times. The KGB were tripping over themselves, trying to shut down that printing. And now it is suddenly revealed that Sadūnaitė is part of some order of monks, has a modest pension and uses it to buy and send packages to prison...

"We Were Ready to Die for Our Country"

Sapozhnikova: *How do you remember the August Coup?*

Antonenko: A few days earlier, we were approached for advice by Česlav Visockis, the president of district executive committee of Šalčininkai district. The issue was that they had the first stage of the convention of all MPs of all levels and agreed to have the second stage – discussing breaking away from the Lithuanian republic like Transnistria[5] had done. He asked us to be the base of the future army. For a starter we were to handle the protection of the convention, where they were to accept the Constitution. We took the job, not with enthusiasm, but with curiosity. He talked to us on 15 August and said that the convention would to be in a week. And on the 19 August, the coup happened.

Our first reaction was: "Hooray! Thank God!" After lunch, people from the Alytus troop regiment showed up: they were tasked with taking the Supreme Council. They tried to do some reconnaissance and encountered difficulties – the streets were blocked by formidable concrete guardhouses. Moreover, the Viliya [the Belarussian name for the river Neris. – t.n.] Riverwalk was rigged with mines, along with all of the lawns and approaches to the Supreme Council building. They asked us, as locals who knew the grounds, to look for loopholes. We drove there, found a proper spot to break through the main barricade. But instead of going along with that plan, we got an order from the Interior Minister to seize the Republican communications junction and then hand it over under army protection. We seized the building. Later in the day, a recon battalion from Severny Gorodok arrives. Later it turned out that neither the junction [a communications unit in the army] nor the recon guys were needed at all and they had to leave. That was it. The coup ended.

Sapozhnikova: *When did you realize that you would have to leave Lithuania?*

Antonenko: When they started pulling the army out. On 19 September, the order came through to make me a major. I, as the chief of the squad's operative department, had lots of confidants, agents, and at that moment, I was still in the OMON. And now all of those people were kind of unutilized, but were still keeping in touch and giving me valuable information. At the moment, I was most interested in opportunities to ensure the safety of the Vilnius OMON officers. So I managed to warn Vladimir Razvodov twice about 70 people having photos of him and out to catch him. I also managed to warn Roschin. Despite my phone being under surveillance, I still managed to get some things done. All of it led to their just deciding to take me out of Lithuania in May 1992. First, the police called me in for interrogation. They asked if I had a service weapon and did I carry it with me? When they knew I was armed, they decided not to mess with me and do it differently.

My brother Andrey's adopted daughter was being married and her fiancé spoke somewhere that there would be "wedding general" at the wedding like me. And the higher-ups made a quick decision.

The police were very corrupt and possibly just had an agreement with the criminals. During the wedding there was a rumor that the fiancé went missing. We walked outside and see that there are 8 thugs outside, and all of them are staring at me... They beat and stomped and I only heard my ribcage crack. The last thought in my head was: why are they beating me this hard, they are liable to kill me?! And I still didn't realize that I was "the objective", I thought they were just hooligans.

Sapozhnikova: *And was not being in Lithuania any more the right choice?*

Antonenko: No, what "right choices" are there? Heavens no. I was a healthy man and two months later I was back on my feet. I went to work, the campaign of getting the Division out of Lithuania was well underway. Then I was in Leningrad and then in Abkhazia. Before that I was also in Transnistria a bit. Sadly they didn't put us on the KGB watch list as part of operative surveillance. Looking at it clearly, we were rebels, albeit legal ones. We all had a feeling of not being understood. We were ready to die for our country! And it turns out that we were unneeded. So the people who went to fight in Donbass in 2014, I understand those...

Here's what his wife, **Lyubov**, said when her husband didn't hear.

Lyubov: You can't imagine how hard it was to leave. My husband just told you that he was back on his feet in two months. He just couldn't remember anything in the hospital – when I went to his command, when I got everyone to visit him and got them all on their feet, demanding that they give medical attention to a Russian citizen. He doesn't remember a man in the police who said: "I was an intern of your husband, if you want him to live, then get him out of the hospital and hide away immediately." And me, my friends and relatives brought him to this house, in an empty field, where there was nothing, no windows, no heating – and we used clay to patch up the holes in the wall to survive the winter.

Brought him home, pale as chalk, no blood in the face. And after an open trauma of the head 14 cm wide, he also had to go to all these Abkhazias, Leningrads and Transnistrias, because he couldn't abandon his lads…

He has his own life tragedy – the family torn apart. His eldest son remained in Vilnius, married to a Lithuanian, his grandson doesn't speak a lick of Russian. The youngest lives in Belarus, with his own thoughts and convictions and his children don't speak Lithuanian at all. They can't communicate.

| Chapter Eight |

AND IF YOU RUN OUT OF ENEMIES...

For Lithuania's ideologues, life with the lack of an official enemy was unbearable: they couldn't scare people anymore with Soviet monster, which had been immobilized by the August Coup; the army was about to be pulled back any day; the OMON flew off without saying goodbye; and the local communists hid underground in the neighboring states... How can a state exist, where the number of those willing to repress vastly surpasses the number of potential victims?

If you run out of enemies, you should think up new ones.

And in the same fall of 1991, Lithuania began to vehemently forge a myth of the armed underground resistance, which actually didn't exist. Having created a verdict, the state started to adamantly attach it to anybody it could get its hands on.

The initial idea was to evoke an image of vicious traitors against the homeland, who planned to derail trains and blow up bridges. But no such people were found. Then the state decided to track down those who had publicly expressed frustration over the price hike at the 8 January 1991 rally. That failed too, because, by the time of the public reading of the verdict, all defendants were Russian citizens, so the "treason against the homeland" charge couldn't be applied. Moreover, some of them, like, for instance, Alexander Bobylev, an engineer at the Vilnius Electronic Test Equipment Research Institute, were in the Supreme Council building, meeting the members of the government, by their own invitation. You won't put a man in jail for publicly refusing to shake the Deputy Prime Minister's hand...

But! They carried a petition not of their own, but at the request of the CPL of the CPSU platform leadership! Thus, as judge V. Višinskis ruled, "they participated in the activity of the said party, whose goal was to undermine the state and the society framework." That is saying that the existing government was engaged in anti-government actions!

He wasn't the worst judge in the world, by the way, despite his last name (which was often compared to the infamous USSR Prosecutor-General, Andrey Vyshinsky, his namesake), because he didn't allow Lithuania to become a world laughing stock and dismissed the most absurd arguments of the state. The majority of the charges in this notable criminal case of the Lithuanian SSR officials, which saw the verdict delivered on 29 April 1994, were found to be inconsistent: the diverse tally of defendants, including a conscript doing military service, a bunch of engineers, a Knowledge Society lecturer, a city party committee staffer and one telephone operator, didn't, in fact, organize rallies with several hundred participants, didn't destroy the property of the Supreme Council and didn't "deliberately organize a criminal entity with the purpose to overthrow the state authority of the Lithuanian Republic".

Glory to the October Revolution!

...I don't know what astonishes me the most in this story – the arrogance of those who manufactured the sentence, or the naïveté, bordering on stupidity, of those who were defendants in the case, which ended with a sentence of 3 to 8 years in prison.

The episodes bore no connection to each other whatsoever. How was the petition about the price hikes, which was delivered by the protesters to the Supreme Council on January 1991, related to the armed skirmish on the border post near the city of Shumsk that took place ten months later? The Lithuanian justice system didn't care for such "literary" nuances: the two totally unconnected stories went hand in hand like train cars, separated by a comma. The mentioned arithmetic led to a gang, comprised of 8 persons. It was almost a solid terrorist organization!

Just read the charges: in Autumn of 1991, several men, whose heart and soul stayed Soviet, decided to make a radio broadcast to congratulate the Lithuanian people on the 74th anniversary of the October Revolution from the territory of Belarus... Currently it sounds unbelievably silly, but back then, in conditions of a total ban on everything communist, including Soviet holidays, you couldn't imagine anything other than this.

The operation to eliminate the last remnants of the Soviet regime sympathizers was a tremendous success; the future defendants took the bait in full – the Soviet Union was truly an incubator for the naïve. Twenty-five years later, this "gallant feat" looks like cheap romantics, inspired by a school course of Soviet literature and essays about the Young Guard resistance movement. But for the people, who in 1991 tried to undertake the said project and drove on bumpy village roads to adjust the transmitter, everything was real.

Those who thought up a role in this play for the "new partisans", obviously, weren't smart as well, but did the most important thing – besides the questionable idea, they managed to attach a compromising file with a guaranteed "foul" story inside for the perpetrators, and rolled out some popcorn, while awaiting in the bushes for the theatrics finale. Nothing surprising – along with Soviet troops leaving the Baltic states, a lot of military hardware remained and was sold practically via newspaper adverts; the stock included everything one could wish for, from rockets to RPGs.

So, imagine: on 6 November 1991, four men, members of the neighborhood watch – Alexander Smotkin and Vladimir Shorokhov, a former serviceman, Hetag Dzagoyev and a civic activist, Viktor Orlov – went off to the Belarusian region near the city of Shumsk, neighboring with Lithuania, to adjust the radio broadcast. "Our true goal was the following," wrote the latter of them from jail. "We wanted to congratulate everyone who cherished the ideals of the socialist homeland, on the Great October Socialist Revolution holiday. We didn't see another way to do it in a democratic and free Lithuania. So, in November 1991, we went in three cars to Belarus, which at the time still remained in the USSR, and, acting in the moral right as USSR citizens, who by the wicked will of the politicians were rendered pariahs in our own land, did a test broadcast, checking the transmitter's operation. On the way back from Belarus to Lithuania, we were apprehended by the Department of Nation Defense servicemen."

All was going according to plan, but the "loaded gun", which, as the famous saying by Anton Chekhov goes, must fire in the final act, discharged at the most unsuitable moment: Alexander Smotkin let the nerves get the best of him, and, fleeing, he threw a grenade... Everybody, thank God, survived, but that circumstance foiled the Department of Nation Defense plans to capture the "red activists". It took them several years to exploit that episode to the maximum.

A prominent trial of the "terrorists" was supposed to strengthen the new regime, then existing in a state of euphoria. It wasn't like the "Killer Doctors' Trial" during the Stalin times, obviously, but it looked fancy nonetheless.

ALEXANDER BOBYLEV
Pro- Soviet Activist

Thorns for Wounds

Bobylev: "...I am not the man I was 16 months ago; I got so charged up with hatred, with the desire to jump into the fight, that I am awaiting the trial with passion. Not all, but the majority of us holds the belief that we should not defend ourselves in court, dodging hits, BUT WE MUST FIGHT LIKE MEN. It is not a kangaroo court that we will meet, but a trial exposing all foulness and the inner essence of the provocation, which struck the nation,

For organizing a referendum for saving the USSR, Alexander Bobylev was imprisoned for three years.

the country and us personally. I am trying to collect all tiny pieces of information, how, under the auspices of a certain M. Gorbachev, the whole process was elaborated and set in motion. It is time to open people's eyes, or else we will be late again, and these bastards will avoid responsibility. They wanted a political process, so be it. That is how Georgy Dimitrov acted, hitting them with their own weapons, poking their faces into their own shit.

It is a joy to be on the frontline. Being gone missing in action is what is difficult, frightening. We simply got too used to living peacefully and well. I used to read about war and think, how was it possible to sit in dugout shelters, to eat and drink inside them. It seemed to me that every minute you had to shoot, cut the Germans' throats...

...How could it happen that a nation with such history would be subjected to such challenge?! I read A. Tolstoy's *Russian Character*. It is striking how our nation is resilient in the face of an external enemy, but childishly naïve and weak in the face of the wile of a domestic enemy. We are gullible; it is our national trait, too. But you can't eject from us the sense of Motherland, the feeling of love for OUR Soviet regime; we managed to experience it all too well, just like the repulsive stench that is being offered to replace it. Oh, what wonderful letters and post cards were sent to us on the New Year's Eve and 23 February by our SOVIET people! It is with this crystal clear love for Motherland and the unyielding, undying pride we triumph; it isn't sold or bought for cash. We were simply dumbfounded by the insolence, suddenness and Goebbels-style hubris of the beast appearing before us. It is fine, we are already resurging. With a communist hello…"

*

If several years ago someone would have said to Alexander Bobylev that he will land in jail for writing such "communist hellos" from the slammer, he wouldn't have believed it. Up to a particular point, he was indifferent towards politics, and joined the Communist Party right when everyone was fleeing from it. "I assumed, that since various shit resurfaced, I had to act as a replacement in the party and somehow strengthen it," he explained the logic of his decision of join the CPL just right after its split. "Back when there were eloquent speeches about independence, sovereignty and the national revival, I perfectly understood that they were talking about the breakup of the Soviet Union. It was only a tool to alter the social structure. In no way could I have agreed to that."

It didn't take the results long to arrive: Bobylev landed in jail, because such thoughts didn't fit in the standards of independent Lithuania, neither back then, nor now. Its hysterical attitude towards any free thought must have some kind of roots, and they do exist: in 1991, when no one paid attention to Lithuania. Everyone praised the Lithuanian authorities for granting citizenship to all its residents, but they had another reason to do it – all dissenters were given citizenship and then tried for treason.

They Wanted Revenge

Sapozhnikova: *What type of gang were you framed as?*

Bobylev: It was, essentially, the first group of people in Lithuania convicted of political offense. Before us, only one person got convicted under this section (Article 70, anti-state activities), Sergey Reznik, because he stepped in as the head of the CLP publishing office, which was transferred under the control of the CPSU. So, he was convicted first, in summer of 1993, then was our group's turn. How did the authorities form it?

Valery Ivanov was under surveillance as the leader of Venibe-Edinstvo-Ednost, which was a very powerful, determined claim to start an international movement confronting nationalism in Lithuania. He had no connections to other defendants in court, other than participating in petitioning the government. The authorities attached me to him merely due to my future wife's last name, which was identical to Ivanov's – they decided that we were related. When they discovered that it wasn't true, they made me an active member of Venibe-Edinstvo-Ednost, though I never was. Viktor Orlov and Hetag Dzagoyev had absolutely no relation to politics, Venibe-Edinstvo-Ednost or the civil militias; both were a separate group of civic activists with their own positions. We all got glued together in a single case. The authorities assembled a gang out of us and smacked us with a sentence.

First they charged us under the Article 62 of the Lithuanian Soviet Criminal Code with treason against the homeland. But we were Russian citizens – what treason? They really wanted to convict us just like their ancestors were once tried under the Article 58 of the Soviet Criminal Code for political crimes; they wanted revenge! They were itching to do it, understand, for 50 years they were itching to do it! And they still itch... And the more time passes, the stronger the itch gets. In the end, there were two charges: anti-state activity and illegal possession of firearms, because during the arrest I had a handgun that I got after serving several weeks in the OMON and couldn't surrender it due to the turmoil with the evacuation of the team. I got three years in prison.

Party's Battle Squad

Sapozhnikova: *Could you imagine that a Lithuanian Singing Revolution would end up with such a grimace? Or did you still have hope for its somewhat peaceful resolution?*

Bobylev: During the last days prior to 13 January, the hope was almost gone. It was clear that the situation wouldn't unfold peacefully, but everyone hoped to avoid casualties. There was rally after rally, provocation after provocation. There were several attempts to vandalize Lenin's monument standing in the center of Vilnius – it was doused with paint and flammable liquid. At least two times we went to guard it. After being punched badly in a street fight with nationalists, I came to enlist myself in a workers' militia.

Sapozhnikova: *Who were the militias and where did they come from?*

Bobylev: This is a crucial question. The militia was never a battle organization; we had no weapons and no aim to apply force. The people's militias in the Soviet Union existed in every city and town. They were ordinary neighborhood patrols together with the police to uphold public safety. Later, when the rallies began, ours and Lithuanians', which were followed by numerous provocations, the Party City Committee appealed to the heads of the primary squads of militias in the factories and asked us to join in. We had no special equipment, aside from red armbands. But since fights constantly broke out at rallies, we started taking physical training courses to at least acquire elementary self-defense skills. While in court, we were portrayed as a secret militarized organization. I guess, the guys from the Lithuanian secret services thus wanted to prop up their importance – look, we have captured scary spies! They persistently tried to depict us as the party's elite battle squad to emphasize that we were an organization with a structure, leadership, common plan and goals.

"I Won't Shake Your Hand..."

Sapozhnikova: *What was the turning point, after which the situation in Vilnius became completely derailed?*

Bobylev: On 8 January, prices were hiked dramatically, and the food became three-four times more expensive. Women rushed to the stores and came back all freaked out, with watery eyes, saying, "Have you seen the prices?!" The institute radio reported that the fuel factory workers were going to hold a protest rally in front of the Supreme Council. And we came too. At first the rally was quite peaceful, but at some point a group of young men aged 25-35 began agitating the crowd. The crowd moved back and forth, and went on to storm the building. We approached the doors from the side, and there I met with Vladimir Razvodov, because the OMON, still holding together, formed a cordon. A giant, well-built man stood by, and I came up to him and said, "Hey, Captain, what is with your uniform? It looks like a Soviet policeman, but the buttons are new, Lithuanian, with knights on them?" He went ballistic, tore off all the buttons and threw them away, saying, "Here you go, they're driving me mad already!" We talked for a bit and understood that we, apparently, weren't really enemies... And the assault began. The crowd got startled. I got knocked down onto the ground. Someone delivered news that the Supreme Council of Deputies had asked us to organize an official group so we would formulate our demands. We entered the building; there were 12 of us. The Deputy Prime Minister Romualdas Ozolas, a well-known Nazi, who declared that Lithuania was allegedly in a state of war with the USSR, went down to greet us one by one. He came up to me, extended his hand, and I told him, "Sorry, I won't shake your hand..."

Sapozhnikova: *Did you think that only 4 days later you along with other militias would go there again?*

Bobylev: On 12 January, we were assembled in the Party City Committee and were told that the situation was very tense, so it was quite possible that there would be a need to arrange patrolling of the city. The workers of several Vilnius factories formulated a petition to the Lithuanian government stating that it carried out policies harmful to the people. The petition was to be delivered to the Council of Ministers and the Supreme Council. We got separated into two parts – one group went to the Supreme Council, the other headed to the Council of Ministers. I have an impression that, within both sides, someone knew the whole script quite well, at least the Lithuanian side for sure was aware. Skirmishes occurred; we didn't manage to deliver a petition. We returned to the Party City Committee. Returning, we saw the armored vehicles moving towards the TV tower.

As soon as we started entering the conference hall, we had to urgently drive to the TV and Radio Committee building. We didn't witness the assault itself. The shots were heard, something was exploding here and there –the glass from the nine-story building was falling down like decorations from a Christmas tree. We formed a human chain behind the soldiers' backs and stood like this till morning. When we were finally let into the TV station, everything there was already broken and trashed beyond repair; the windows were smashed, so it was chilling inside.

We were asked to clean up the mess, provided with nails, hammers, and we were mending windows in the semi-basement. I came out only on 18 January. I came to my father and said, "Finally we will have an opportunity to deliver accurate information, we have drove the Nazis out from their propaganda speaker!" And he said, "You can pack your bags, soon you will be driven out from Lithuania, just like a cork from the champagne bottle." He understood by then, how everything would end. We didn't.

Flawed Cases

Sapozhnikova: *Can I ask you to restore the picture of what you saw as if you were making a documentary?*

Bobylev: The corpses were already removed when I arrived. Only a pool of blood on the porch was left from Alvydas Kanapinskas, in whose hands an explosive device went off. We were asked to wash away the traces; we cleaned them with mops and buckets. We talked to the soldiers, and they told us that many protesters had explosives. The Moscow court files contained testimonies of our soldiers who saw how civilians were rushing against the armored column and tried to toss explosives on the trucks with troops inside. At least twice or three times the devices went off in their hands. While in prison, I have read through the court files and seen a series of photographs of Kanapinskas. It was a standard procedure of a forensic-medical examination of the corpse: the body was lying on a tile floor, then it was undressed; everything was photographed in the process. The first photo: the man was lying in a coat, whose sides were turned inside out by the explosion. he next photo: he was in a sweater, then in a sailor vest, while the pieces of the fabric were stuck inside of the wound. When I was given an opportunity to look at the files for a second time, the photos were missing. A year ago, I was passing by the porch of the TV and Radio Committee building and saw a plaque with a sign, "A hero Kanapinskas died here"... Well, maybe, he was, in fact, a hero: we came there to defend our country, and he came to defend his. How would he have known what type of explosives Audrius Butkevičius gave him? That man, as everyone knows, is prone to vanity and hubris – one Lithuanian paper had an article, in which he told how a year before the events of 1991 he created a workshop near Kaunas, where he made homemade bombs. Kanapinskas detonated the device, holding it under his armpit or was simply pinned down in the crowd.

Next morning we were allowed to enter the new TV and Radio Committee building. The lobby on the first floor had an entrance to the cafeteria. Near the entrance, there was a table covered with a dark yellow plush curtain. The curtain was fully drenched in blood, and a pool of blood was underneath the table. I was told that the Alpha Group serviceman, Viktor Shatskikh was laid there. I personally removed the curtain and cleaned the floor. My hands were all covered with his blood...

When we were given the first look on the court files, the Shatskikh file was attached to them. It was a whole volume: a forensic report made in Minsk, numerous documents and photos. The files stated that a bullet entered through the back plate of the bulletproof vest from a 45 degree angle upwards, pierced the lung, ricocheted off the chest bone and, on the way back, damaged the spleen and liver. And with this wound he kept on running in the human chain and told his commanding officer that he felt a burn in the back... Afterwards all this vanished from the court files; it was missing during my second reading of the case, along with the photos of Kanapinskas. In any decent state, it would have led to criminal cases opened against the judges and investigators.

Not a single high-profile criminal case concerning the 1991 events in Lithuania has substantial evidential grounds. Each has a plethora of inconsistencies and lost documents, not to mention the lost gun of the dead customs officer in the criminal case of the Medininkai shooting. Well, fine, a videotape or some police documents were lost, but how could a weapon get lost? The Soviet Criminal Code contained responsibility of judges and investigators for unlawful prosecution or unlawful conviction. In Lithuania, such acts aren't considered offenses, therefore, the authorities abuse the law.

Either We Lied, or They Did

Sapozhnikova: *In one interview, you said that, by putting you to prison, the authorities "took the revenge" on you for "the referendum". What did you mean?*

Bobylev: I was the Chairman of the Vilnius District Commission for the Preparation of the 17 March 1991 Referendum. For the referendum, I received 25 thousand rubles, a large sum of money at the time. Being a frugal man that I am, I managed to organize everything while spending 6 thousand rubles, and the spared 19 thousand I gave to Boleslav Makutynovich, because the OMON troops were basically stationery, surrounded and barely eating due to the fact they weren't receiving their salaries. We carried out the referendum fairly. Its main result was that, in Vilnius District, there was a large discrepancy between our referendum results and the data of the poll, which the Sąjūdists later portrayed as a plebiscite. So, either we lied, or they did. But I can vouch for our results. It is another Sąjūdist lie that can resurface one day.

Sapozhnikova: *Up to some point, we were living in the Soviet Union, not remembering old national problems or not noticing, due to naivety, that our neighbors had grudges against us. The high pace at which the Balts have changed their attitudes towards their neighbors in apartment blocks and friends from the same yard, is a topic for a separate research. In prison, how did you manage to tell friends from foes?*

Bobylev: When I was brought to prison, all correctional officers still strolled around the territory in Soviet uniforms. An officer was sitting in front of you, and you couldn't tell how to treat him, as a friend or an enemy? Then they changed to Lithuanian uniforms, and it became a lot easier. But it was interesting, too: let's say, I got summoned by an officer not with little stars on the shoulder marks, but with little cubes on them, just like the Germans have, and I felt that he was sincerely sympathizing with me... Or the opposite.

Nazism is a thing that can infect even a healthy man. For many years, I went fishing with a wonderful Lithuanian family. We had become friends long ago; I grew very close to those peasants. And later, one of their sons told me to never set a foot in their place again. After leaving prison, I still came to them. Their daughter opened the gate. "Aldona," I said. "Forgive me that I came to see you. Algis told me to never set a foot here." And she practically cried out, "Sasha, stop it, we understood everything long ago and are happy to see you..."

Two tumors poison the relations between Russia and Lithuania today: the January events and the Medininkai murders. If something happens, a trump card is thrown on the table, saying, "Do you remember how the Russians are? They made 13 January happen, they killed the customs officers." This issue is popping up and buzzing over and over again; every time nails are being placed into the wound so it would keep on bleeding. And until we uncover the true circumstances of those stories completely, blood will be shed all the time.

VIKTOR ORLOV:
Twenty-six-year-old Political Prisoner

Happy Holidays...

How exactly this letter made its way out of prison, I will leave a mystery. The most important thing is that it got preserved on the sheets of cheap yellow paper, although the color lost its brightness in some places. It would have been a sin to cut its content because the style, the language and, most importantly, the public stance of the author, Viktor Orlov, who was a 26-year-old political prisoner at the time, were so good that it makes sense to publish it almost unredacted:

> I was apprehended on 6 November 1991 on the Shumsk checkpoint by the operatives of the Department of National Defense of the Lithuanian Republic. During the inspection, a weapon was found in the car, which was kept in case of a criminal attack on us (it was unsafe to travel on Lithuanian roads in a car from Finland with a foreign license plate and an expensive radio station on board, because lately instances of robbers' attacks on foreign-registered vehicles became more frequent). During nightfall, on a high road, crossing the forest...
>
> The incoming group, composed of the Department of National Defense (DND) officers, ambushed me and my comrade Hetag Dzagoyev, and began gun-butting us. Then we were put facing a road sign with our hands up. We heard them chamber rounds. From the shouting in Russian and Lithuanian, I understood that we were about to be shot. Shots were fired. A burst of rounds went over our heads. I turned around and saw that one of the DND officers was holding his colleague's gun barrel upward. Apparently, it saved our lives.

They searched me, not finding anything except personal documents. We were ordered to get in an army truck. Every time I tried to get in the back of the truck, I was gun-butted and saw that Hetag was beaten too. After I finally managed to get in the vehicle, I was thrown on the floor, ordered to hold my hands over my head and to lie face down. One of the convoy guards put his leg on my back and held the barrel of a gun close to the back of my neck, saying, "Move and I will shoot you, scum."

I heard Hetag panting near me. The vehicle was shaking and moving side to side while hitting road bumps, and, I guess, only God knew, which of my involuntary movements the guard could have viewed as an escape attempt.

We were taken to the Supreme Council of the Lithuanian Republic, where Hetag and I were handcuffed and, pushed by gun barrels, were led inside of the building.

In one of the offices, at the time belonging to the top government officials, including head of the Department of National Defense Audrius Butkevičius and acting Interior Minister Algirdas Matonis, we were handed over to the Interior Ministry agencies. The first thing that caught my sight was several men in the Soviet Army officers' uniform, but with the collar patches torn off. "Traitors!" was the thought that pierced my mind like an electric shock. The soldier stood and smiled, looking at us, dirty and beat up, in handcuffs.

I was separated from Hetag and led to a room, where three ministry officials began questioning sessions, which went on for almost 24 hours during the next two and a half days. Only at the very end of the second day, I was laid on the floor, handcuffed to the table leg and was allowed to "rest" for a few hours.

I was dragged from a cabinet to cabinet, while being constantly in tracker handcuffs. Even in the bathroom I wasn't allowed to take off the "bracelets". All the people were expressing hatred and enmity towards everything Soviet, everything I was inseparably related to in my life. And it couldn't have been otherwise, because I didn't live on Mars or the Moon. Everything I lived through is my life! To some extent, it was also their former life. I was born and grew up in a state called USSR. And I was proud of being a Soviet citizen. I studied and worked for the sake of my Motherland. In the military, I took an oath to be faithful to my country and my nation, and I couldn't back down from it.

From the moment of my arrest and the beginning of the investigation, I was blown away by the familiarity and the measures, undertaken to spy on and apprehend the dissenters, ordinary Soviet people, who by the will of the rulers suddenly became foreigners in their own republics, which only yesterday had been an inseparable part of the Soviet Union, whose citizens we all were. More than a hundred searches were conducted on one night of 12 November 1991 in apartments of citizens caught actively supporting the Soviet authority. From the very beginning, I clearly understood that the investigative bodies were following a precisely set goal to accuse me of ties with the outlawed Communist Party of Lithuania and other socialist-oriented organizations.

...I was thrown into a cell with hardline criminals, who were provided with the information that I might have been an OMON trooper. I think, it is obvious how I was met by inmates, who have viewed me as a policeman, although I have never served in the Interior Ministry's bodies. The cell was crowded; for a long time I was forced to sleep on the concrete floor. During the time spent in a pre-trail detention center, I was forced to remain in custody with murderers, rapists and repeat offenders. I was constantly subjected to moral and physical terror. It was like I was forgotten – for four months after I was indicted, an investigator never summoned me. Apparently, the reasoning behind this move was simple: to immerse me in an environment where I would break down. That was how they wanted to turn me into material that could have been molded into anything, at the investigation's desire.

When the Prosecutor-General's Office of the Lithuanian Republic had tried to maintain the myth it, itself, created that there are no political prisoners in the republic prosecuted for their beliefs, I was sitting in a cell, designed for two, together with 8-10 other inmates. There were unsanitary conditions, mice, rats, lice, itchiness, absence of a sauna... All that made being in a detention cell an inhumane challenge.

Meanwhile, Lithuania was preparing for the new Seimas election. In the summer of 1992, I was presented with an act saying that our so-called Shumsk Case was joined with the case of Valery Ivanov (Venibe-Edinstvo-Ednost leader), a part of the 13 January 1991 events in Vilnius case, and the case of an ex-OMON trooper, A. Bobylev, charged with illegal firearms possession. I could only guess what the investigators were thinking, while adopting a decision to bring the cases together. Most likely, they were following a political order to utilize the process in the election campaign. We became hostages of a political calculation. The calculation became evident, when, in early October, 1992, we were charged with organizing a coup. What, was there a coup unfolding in Shumsk? Albeit absurd, the charges were very serious, though along with my comrades I just wanted to congratulate people with a holiday...

On my appeals describing the violations of my civil rights (I was repeatedly subjected to verbal insults with foul language from the guards and other detention center officials) I got an answer, which was verbatim: "Be happy that you are enjoying this type of conditions and this crowd, because we can transfer you to such a cell that will make you crawl the walls and bite the bars!"

...They are following a single goal – humiliating, degrading a man to a cattle-like state, so he himself would understand how "puny and worthless" he is, while they are the masters of his fate! They are afraid of men with inner strength; for them, such people are a living blow to the whole system of suppression and humiliation.

I and my comrades are studying the court files right now, all forty-six volumes! The Prosecutor-General's Office workers themselves tell us that the charges will, most certainly, be revoked in court. Then why press them? Why accuse me of creating a criminal group with the intent to overthrow the state authority of the Lithuanian Republic? Why join together the cases, unconnected to one another? Do authorities really need a trial, on which they wish to singlehandedly quell political opposition?
Viktor Orlov,
26 y.o.,
cell 271,
pre-trial detention center inmate,
Lukiškės Prison, Vilnius,
December 1992."

Political prisoners of new Europe. Photo from the archives of the book's heroes. Author unknown.

Mug of Vodka on the Table

The most difficult interview in the book is this one, because it had to be conducted via Skype, carefully bypassing the "minefields" in the form of the obligatory – given the contemporary Lithuanian Republic – phone tapping of avoiding sensitive issues. Viktor Orlov had stayed living in Vilnius, and it is quite telling... Where else would he run? Lithuania is his homeland, not only by the place of birth, but by blood too: his Lithuanian great-grandfather, the First Commissioner of the Baltic Railway, Major-General Vaclav Kadziulus, lived here.

But most surprising is the other thing: in 1991, Orlov, a young man, not burdened with a communist past, could have been on the completely other side of the barricades. For some reason he chose this one...

"I felt myself a different man. I mean, I felt responsible for our country. And I sacrificed everything," he pompously explained.

Honestly, his answer was vague. Practically every character of the *Lithuanian Hunt* had a certain tipping point, determining his further destiny. This person didn't...

Orlov: The rudeness of neighbors, treason, or other disturbances didn't push me; I simply reached an understanding that we must stand in defense of our homeland. In 1991, I was a citizen of the USSR. And with my late father-in-law I wrote a telegram to Gorbachev, saying that we wanted to stop the breakup of the Union. It was already impossible to send such a text from Lithuania, so we went to Belarus, to the city of Lida, and mailed the letter via state courier post to Kremlin, Moscow, Gorbachev.

Sapozhnikova: *Is it true – the mock execution that you wrote about in prison? In no way do I idealize the methods of the Soviet police, but the things I read about in your case files shocked me...*

Orlov: Only thanks to the fact that the Lithuanian officers weren't insane, I and Hetag weren't shot on the spot near the road sign, with our hands up. In our harsh century, where violence on the TV screen happens every day, our suffering looks petty. But in 1991, people were more democratically inclined and didn't accept violence.

Sapozhnikova: *What was Hetag Dzagoyev like, as a man, as a person? (he passed away several years ago)*

Orlov: An ordinary sergeant, a conscript, who was given a last task before demobilization: "Hey, you will help the boys to set up a transmission and then will go home."

He didn't know any Lithuanian secrets at all, because he was from South Ossetia. He even had a ticket purchased on a plane to Vladikavkaz. All conceivable and inconceivable norms were violated in our case. The things authorities tried to tie us to! Just imagine: two years later I was suddenly brought to the prison warden in for questioning, who had a Radio Liberty reporter sitting in the office, and was told, "You are being accused of the murder of the Medininkai customs officers." I was shown a chart, allegedly depicting that I shot everybody... Later they backtracked and said, "No, of course, not. Orlov bears no relation to it."

There were also fun things: On every 23 February, for instance, the guards opened a food delivery hatch and passed in a mug of vodka. And I drank it down. Once, along with my inmates, we bought a radio set for 500 coupons, and listened to everything what was going on in October 1993 in Moscow. And we thought, "Finally!" But it didn't work out. And we were left alone again...

We were completely betrayed to enforce the theory of an armed underground resistance that was preparing to topple the new Lithuanian authority. That was the reason why Bobylev, Hetag and I, and even the cases of the CPL on the CPSU platform Central Committee secretaries got joined together as well. Because there wouldn't have been a common case, if everything was brought before the court as separate episodes. And Burokevičius would have nothing to go to jail for. And here you had a leader and perpetrators with guns. And even the terrorist Smotkin who threw a grenade.

The Department for Protecting the Peaceful Atom

After we were released from prison, I returned home. I was almost immediately summoned to the migration service, allegedly for documents check, but once I arrived, I had a residence permit taken away and was told that I was staying on Lithuanian territory illegally. But prior to going to the migration service, I had gone to a notary office and made a copy of my residence permit.

Afterwards, all our team, which had been left in Lithuania after the release, called a press conference and told the journalists about the upcoming deportation, because we received an order, signed by the Director of the Migration Department and the Interior Ministry, to leave the Lithuanian territory within 48 hours, despite us having families, parents and children here.

Then the authorities back-peddled; the Department Director was fired and a new one installed. He summoned me, gave me a new residence permit, but obliged me to make a written pledge not to come closer than 50 kilometers to the Ingalina Nuclear Power Plant. The violations of this rule would be considered a pretext to deport me.

Sapozhnikova: *What do you regret the most?*

Orlov: I have no regrets. It is just that, apparently, my upbringing wasn't right. This is not a jab at my parents; it is my inner protest, it began in the 70s-80s, when we were maturing as men. If I had initially taken the position in life that I embraced after 1989-1991, then, maybe – all that happened to USSR – we wouldn't let it happen.
We are guilty of what had happened to our county. We are.

ALEXANDER SMOTKIN
A Man With a Rifle

"Believe me, for ten years after the ambush I had the very same dream – I am running away and being captured. And all these memories are coming back. It is hard for me; out of everyone, I have spent the most time in jail. Well, only Burokevičius and Jermalavičius spent more."

The man, now generously sharing his newspaper archive with me, was harsh in judgments and very blunt. He was not in the mood for sentiments. For him, Lithuania was a dagger in the back, a symbol of treason. Not for the 8 years spent in prison. Physical pain can be forgotten, while scars from spiritual traumas don't go away. You carry them your whole life like a tattoo, whose blue color shines through any clothes.

Smotkin: I was born in Vilnius, in 1949. My name is Alexander Smotkin. My father is a Great Patriotic War veteran. During the assault on Berlin he was the commanding officer of the 293rd Field Artillery Regiment. My father came from the Yukhnovichi village, Rasony District of the Byelorussian SSR. In February,

1942, all his relatives were savagely murdered by the Germans, the Latvian Police Battalions and Belarusian traitors. All relatives were exterminated... In 1963, I was 14 years old, and father took me to Belarus for the first time. Before that I didn't know that he was born there; he kept it secret. His partisan friends wrote him a letter, saying that a former policeman, who killed my grandfather, had arrived in the village, so father came to look into his eyes. I had seen that scary scene, when father grabbed him by the neck. The whole street rushed to stare, and everyone began shouting, "You have no right! He spent 25 years in prison. The authorities have forgiven him!" And father said, "I didn't." The crowd barely managed to separate the two... That was how I first found out about the tragedy of my family.

So when an issue arose that Belarus was about to hand me over to Lithuania, father, who was suffering from cancer by that point, had made the following decision – he took a hunting rifle and told the local authorities in the city of Hlybokaye, "Tell everyone, I have taken up defense at a railway station, and, if the Lithuanians dare to come here, I will open fire. I won't allow you to take my son." But I was arrested anyway.

Over all of Lithuania, the Sky Is Clear

Smotkin: It all began unexpectedly. At the time, I was working at a telephone station. We were speaking in a mixture of languages – Vilnius was an absolutely non-Lithuanian city. Suddenly our Lithuanians ran over to me and shouted, "Go, learn Lithuanian. Who doesn't speak Lithuanian, won't work with us." I asked, "Since when are you imposing Lithuanian on us? Don't you know how you got Vilnius? So let me remind you: on 10 October, 1939, Stalin and your President Smetona conducted the Molotov-Škirpa Treaty. Under the treaty, bourgeois Lithuania received the Vilnius Region. When Lithuanians got the city to themselves, they immediately sent the president of the Polish University Górski to a concentration camp, gathered the Poles and the Jews on the Soviet-Lithuanian border and handed them over to our border guards, saying that they had allegedly fled from Belarus, and, at the hands of the NKVD,[1] sent them to Siberia. Thus, the city was Lithuanized. As a result, in June, 1940, Vilnius met the Red Army with flowers. The Poles and the Jews were shouting, "Better you, than Lithuanians!"

Sapozhnikova: *Are you saying that from the first second you had no illusions about the outcomes of the national Lithuanian revival?*

Smotkin: Yes. I found out that the director of the radio equipment factory [Hero of Socialist Labour October Osipovich Burdenko – G.S.] had convened the party committee and invited communists from all factories to deliver a speech. The Vienybė-Yedinstvo-Jedność Organization was created during the meeting. The first thing we did, on 12 February, 1989, was organize a spectacular rally against Lithuania's secession from the USSR and against the persecution of the Russian language. We adopted a decision that, if the Lithuanian nationalists wouldn't cease to impose their views on the citizens of other nationalities, we would declare a political strike. I got hurt the most, because, during my speech at the rally, I said, "Let's remember 1936 Spain, when a code phrase – *Above all of Spain, the sky is clear* - was broadcast on the radio, and the fascists went on the offensive on Madrid. Right now we have a cloudless sky above Vilnius. First we will be thrown out from Lithuania with the chants – *Suitcase! Train station! Russia*! – and then we will lose the Soviet Union." After that my mom, while riding on a trolley bus, was attacked by a Lithuanian, who injured her spine with a metal baton, wrapped in a newspaper. My brother, who paid absolutely no interest to politics, ran up to me, called me to go outside of the factory gates and punched me in the face. "What are you saying, you politician?! Mom is now on the hospital bed…"

"We Assumed Everyone Was an Enemy"

Sapozhnikova:- *Do you recall how the year 1991 started for you?*

Smotkin: We initiated a political strike. All of Vilnius shut down. The Chairman of the Presidium of the Supreme Council of the Lithuanian SSR Vytautas Astrauskas invited a delegation from our movement over, promising to restore order in the republic. We fell for this lie, called off the strike. In the end, our movement was completely crushed. In January, 1991, the situation became critical, so the tanks were deployed to Vilnius under the order from Moscow. And we didn't even know what was about to go down. We protested. Three days of protests and no reaction... Trains didn't go to Vilnius. Foreigners came to complain, "What are you doing? In passenger cars, even the bathrooms are closed!" We said, "You are supporting the nationalists, so go in their flats and ask them to provide you bathrooms. We don't want to get separated from the Soviet Union, so you go and get separated with them!" On the fourth day of the strike – it was precisely on the night of 13 January – we went to the Party City Committee and were told, "Get into two buses, 50 men in each. One group will drive to the TV and Radio Committee, the other group will head to the TV tower. These buildings are occupied by crowds of nationalists armed with metal batons, which had been gathered from all across Lithuania and taken here. Several soldiers have been beaten. Only officers have guns. Be warned – you might get killed. But we, the members of the Party City Committee, will be the first to move out..."

We thanked God that our bus was directed to the TV and Radio Committee building and not to the TV tower, where people got shot. When the militias approached the nationalist crowd, shouts were heard, "Death to Russian murderers!" The Secretary of the Sovetsky Regional Party Committees, Izya Butrimovich, was the first to meet them. He was viciously beaten...

The workers tried to rescue him and rushed ahead, but he had all his ribs broken so badly that three days later we, all our sad Communist Party, were at his funeral in the Jewish cemetery. The rabbi said, "In Vilnius' existence, I have never seen so many non-Jews burying one Jew..."

It was less tense near the TV and Radio Committee. Our bus was only shot up – by friendly fire. The column was led by a

CPL Central Committee staffer, Romas Juhnevičius. Some soldier gun-butted him. He screamed, "I am a communist! Can't you see the red armband?" The officer said, "For the first time this night I have seen Vilnius residents who support us. We assumed, everyone here were enemies to us." We asked him about the casualties. He said that Captain Gavrilov had a heel torn off by an explosive charge. The Alpha Force was also injured – nationalists shot a fighter in the back from close range; he was rushed to the hospital. One of our militias, a former paramedic, screamed, "You have sent him to die! Lithuanian doctors declared that they won't treat Russians!" It turned out to be true...

Meanwhile, something horrible was unfolding near the TV tower. By the account of a machine factory worker, their flag-bearer was deliberately gunned down and killed to demonstrate that the Russians were firing. The protection rampart, encircling the TV tower perimeter, was covered with a grill fence. The officer screamed from the armored vehicle, "Citizens, the center is taken under the control of the USSR armed forces. We ask you to calm down to avoid casualties." Our militias saw how the Lithuanians grabbed Loreta Asanavičiūtė and threw her on the fence, and the armored vehicle pinned her down, due to its own momentum. She was alive and died only during surgery. While Lithuanians screamed that she was crushed deliberately.

In a Single Formation

Smotkin: After the liberation of the TV tower and the TV center, the specialists, who could work instead of the escaping nationalists, were invited to work on TV. I was maintaining the communications in the building, while others handled the transmitters. In August, 1991, when the coup happened, we were ordered to leave immediately, because the building was surrounded by the Sąjūdists. We ran to the Central Committee office to get the employment record books. We arrived and saw how people were being dragged out of the office and loaded into cars at gunpoint. The Soviet police was nowhere to be found, while the Department of National Defense fighters were doing all the action. Where were our documents? They were taken to the Vilnius Radio Technical College. We went there. An officer carried them out and told, "Guys, I can't take you under my protection. We received an order from Moscow not to interfere." We, several men, stood still and didn't know what to do. Someone said, "Makutynovich and Razvodov locked themselves up in the OMON base, and said that they don't recognize this rotten authority and will defend their country." We went there.

Initially, they didn't give us weapons, but later decided to arm us, because armed squads of nationalists were located nearby. When the troops stood in formation, one of the officers said, "Since you took up arms, stand in the formation with us." A lieutenant-colonel of the USSR Interior Ministry arrived, pale as sour cream, saying, "Why do you have armed civilians? Comrade Makutynovich, can you explain?" He told him, "People came who had taken an oath to serve the Soviet Army. They found out that you have betrayed the Soviet homeland, and your Deputy Minister of the Interior Demidov issued an order to the division commander to eliminate us with fire, because right now we are the separatists, an illegal military group that hampers the restoring of the order in the democratic Lithuanian Republic."

Everyone stood silent. And suddenly one of the OMON fighters shouted, "The Lieutenant-colonel has already pissed on the red flag, while we will die for it!" The lieutenant-colonel got into the car and quickly left. Sometime later Makutynovich explained that General Uskhopchik had called and said that he would bombard with artillery shells anyone who would to kill Soviet citizens. And one OMON trooper said, "In Moscow, they got scared of the precedent that in the Soviet Union one military unit spat on this whole democracy and decided to die for the Soviet homeland…"

"We Will Both Die Now!"

Smotkin: After that I went to Polotsk. I was employed at the

Polotsk Communications Center. My superior tasked me to go to Vilnius to terminate the resident registration permit. Then I received a letter from Pavel Vasilenko – he was the head of staff of the people's militia at the Party City Committee – which said, "Come here, we have to make a certain radio broadcast." I arrived and on the street "incidentally" met other "accomplices". I thought that they had deliberately waited for me. We loaded an assault rifle, given to us by Vasilenko, into the car and drove to Belarus.

The ones, who were waiting to ambush us, of course, knew that that rifle was "marked". They wanted to frame the OMON, but once they saw that a choleric like Smotkin was running around, they decided that it would be even better to use us. The plan was devised by somebody within our ranks; it was clear because no ordinary man could have brought "bad" rifles to the OMON and said, "Take the weapons of the killed." Which means that someone had come in, shown an ID card and said, "Let this temporarily be with you." I had two grenades with me. No one knew about them.

Sapozhnikova: *Where did you, a civilian, get them?*

Smotkin: During the same trip to Vilnius, I met an OMON trooper in plain clothes on the trolley bus stop. That guy told me that the OMON servicemen were being hunted down across Lithuania. To avoid arrest, the remaining squad members took grenades from the box and went, in groups or alone, to Moscow. If they would be arrested, they would blow themselves up. I asked him to give me a grenade, convincing him that, to blow himself up, one was enough. The second one was given to me by Hetag Dzagoyev; they had a lot of them in the military.

You could say that those grenades saved me from death.

I threw the first grenade, which led to no fatalities, since I tossed it into a ditch. And when a customs officer pointed a rifle at me and wanted to shoot me, I screamed, "We will both die!", and tossed a grenade. He managed to jump away. It stopped them from aiming at me, so I ran to the forest.

On foot I reached the Shumsk train station, which was still Lithuanian territory, boarded the train and rode to Minsk. There I was turned in by one traitor, whom I had met before on some party congress in Leningrad.

He said, "Move to Polotsk, no one will touch you." And there I was captured. Lieutenant-Colonel O. Dragun, the Deputy Chief of the Polotsk City Police Station, arrived and said, "We know what you did, so don't worry – we will get you to Vitebsk." But instead four armed Lithuanians came over. One of them was Adiklis, the senior Lithuanian police officer from the organized crime unit; he was later convicted by a Lithuanian court of murder during questioning. Dragun put his dress uniform on, stood in front of the Lithuanians, like a collaborationist policeman in front of the Gestapo, and handed me over to their disposal. Him handing me over wasn't the thing that caused the most outrage in me – it was the fact that he stood in front of them in a subordinate fashion...

When escorted away, I bowed down to all of them and told one of the policemen, "Thank you, Captain, for handing me over to the Lithuanian fascists." I met him many years later on a Polotsk bus – he apologized and nearly sobbed...

"Turn Your Back"

Smotkin: They beat me in the car during the whole ride to Vilnius. Investigator Adiklis stuck a handgun into my stomach and was imposing the idea on me that I had taken the weapon from the OMON myself. I spat in his face and hit the windshield with my feet to cause an accident. Near the Lithuanian Ministry of Interior building I decided to provoke them to shoot me and hit the rifleman Vasiliauskas in the groin. But he didn't get an order to shoot, so he broke my three ribs with a gun stock. Then I was thrown into a cell for death row inmates; up till 1993, in Lithuania criminals were executed by firing squad. The cells were cold, up to 12 degrees without heating. I was prohibited from sleeping during the daytime. I spent some time in a prison mental institution in the city of Utena. There the officials were trying to convince me to make a written statement that communists were the ones who ordered me to throw the grenade. I was saved by the head of that institution who was a Jew. She didn't allow them to sedate me with seduxen and sent me to a city hospital to have the broken ribs documented. This led to this institution's police commissioner, a Lithuanian, being fired for sympathizing with communists.

I was confined separately from everyone in the block with enhanced security so I wouldn't corrupt inmates with political talk, and given one-hour walks in the inner yard, where I saw the sky only through the bars.

I was saved by Kostas, a Lithuanian gypsy and former Lithuanian SSR boxing champion – he was a prison gang leader. He gave an instruction not to touch the political prisoner. So we survived.

Sapozhnikova: *For what exactly did you get such a long term in prison?*

Smotkin: For "attempting to murder state officials of the Lithuanian Republic, who were in the line of duty." I spent eight years in prison, then, escorted by men with rifles, I was driven to the border and handed over to Belarus. One of the Russian embassy officials, a very good man, drove me. To another good man, Sergey Zagryadsky, to whom I owe my life, because, in 1992, he took a passport of a Russian citizen, went to the detention center, putting his career at risk, found a Russian-speaking officer, told him "turn your back" and gave me the passport so I could sign it. He gave me a passport and to all the other political prisoners present there. Then the following happened: our lawyers told the prosecutor Gaudutis, "How can you put a foreign national on trial for treason against Lithuania?" Gaudutis then stated that the Russian consul, Zagryadsky, had deceptively entered the detention center and given the criminals passports to sign. The Russian Federation received a diplomatic protest note, and the consul was recalled to Moscow. Such a selfless man he was...

Sapozhnikova: *Does the reemerging interest to the 25-year-old story surprise you?*

Smotkin: I didn't change my convictions. All these years Russia practically didn't notice what happened to us and didn't do anything. Russia now is taking the Soviet Union's path; it is being hated just like the USSR was hated during its days. Russia – no matter how it is, tsarist, Soviet, or capitalist – isn't supposed to exist – that is what the West thinks. And people try to do the same thing with it, just like they did with the Soviet Union. That is why I got interested in the issue, how the USSR was sold out via wholesale or retail? And who are the traitors who are going to do the same to Russia?

Last Words

More than twenty years later, Alexander Smotkin found out two important things. The operation he accidentally foiled due to his temperament was called *The Bag*. According to the plan, all "radio guys" who were trying to congratulate the Lithuanian people for the October Revolution, were supposed to be shot on the spot, in the forest. It was to be the resolution of an issue: the Medininkai crime was yet unsolved, but suddenly there would have been a success – a group of "red" activists with weapons from the murdered border guards... But Smotkin, having escaped, foiled the plans. Because presenting those romantically-minded "simpletons" with burning hearts as professional killers was simply hilarious.

And so the Lithuanian authorities began forging a story that the murder of the customs officers was done by the Riga OMON troops. This was the first thing.

The second thing became a bitter discovery for Aleander Smotkin, and not without my help. In my archive, I found a clipping from the *Pravda* newspaper, which Aleander Smotkin didn't know about, that said, "I am dying. Allow be to say goodbye to my son." In the article, his terminally ill father, Roman, lying on a bed in the department of oncology of a Belarusian regional hospital, was asking the Lithuanian President and the former communist leader, Algirdas Brazauskas, to let his son say goodbye to his still alive father:

> I am the father of the political suspect Alexander Smotkin, who for more than 15 months is confined in the Lukiškės Prison. I ask you to release him without bail, because neither I, nor him, have the means to pay it. I swear that my son won't dishonor my last word, given before death, and will appear before court if there will be a trial. He, just like all his comrades, is a victim of political intrigues and provocations of the regime, directed against its own people.

Naturally, no answer followed.

"I don't know any letter from my father to this traitor!" Smotkin Jr. erupted in rage, when I told him about it, with the same anger as he had when he once threw a grenade in the forest. No wonder – he was sitting in a Lithuanian prison, where you couldn't get *Pravda*...

Father and son weren't allowed to say goodbye to each other – Smotkin Sr. passed away in December, 1994, while his son still had five years to spend in jail.

Create Fighting Squads on Your Own and Protect Your Factory on Your Own

Lithuanian prosecutors didn't succeed in proving this people's association with either the coup organization, or the murder of the customs officers, no matter how hard they tried.

The maximum of what the court could establish didn't sound so scary:

> The summation of the aforementioned evidence demonstrates that the defendants have partaken in an active participation in the activities of the

CPL (CPSU), an organization, whose goal was to undermine the state and society structure, based on the Constitution, to limit the rights of the sovereign Lithuanian state.

What was left was the radio broadcast, although even the Lithuanian court didn't manage to convert into a criminal charge the fact that CPL ex-First Secretary Mykolas Burokevičius' voice was supposed to deliver the congratulation.

"The majority of the text, prepared for the radio broadcast, is flagrantly hostile to the Lithuanian Republic, yet propaganda of such kind doesn't constitute a criminal responsibility under the existing law," the court admitted, duly adding that the song *Goodbye, Comrade!* by Boris Gunko, which was planned to be broadcast, and which calls for armed resistance ("Create armed squads by yourself, defend your factory by yourself"), can't be considered a public call for violation of the sovereignty of Lithuania.

To avoid the rumors, I will quote the song's lyrics in full:

> Слушай, товарищ, буржуй наступает, душат народ палачи,
> Родину-мать как хотят, унижают, что ж ты сидишь на печи?
> Кооператор и приватизатор хитрые сети плетут,
> Коль не проснешься сегодня, то завтра будет на шее хомут!
> Право на труд, на леченье, на отдых будешь ещё вспоминать,
> Кровью добытое даром ты отдал, предал ты Родину-мать!
> Чёрная стая бандитов отпетых правят твоею судьбой.
> Гордость и совесть рабочая, где ты, что же случилось с тобой?
> Ведь ни Чубайс, ни пахан его Ельцин,

выжить тебе не дадут,
Оба они к униженью и смерти нас на арканах ведут!
Нету в правительстве доброго дяди, все подалися в воры.
Время настало, детей своих ради, в руку винтовку бери!
Сам создавай боевые отряды, сам защищай свой завод
Есть голова, есть товарищи рядом – целый советский народ!
В чёрную ночку конец одиночке, много ли сможешь один?
Только в сплочённости сила рабочих, вместе всегда победим!
Брось же к собачьим чертям телевизор, трёп бесполезный, вино, огород.
В эти часы избивают Отчизну, битва за правду идёт.
Слушай, товарищ, великая сила в нас, если мы не скоты,
Кто же ещё выйдет в бой за Россию, если не я и не ты!

Listen, comrade, the bourgeois attack, the butchers are strangling the people,
They humiliate the Motherland as they please, why do you sit on the stove?
The Cooperator and the Privatizer weave their trickster plots,
If you don't wake up today, come tomorrow, there will be a collar on you!
The rights to labor, healthcare, vacation, all will be distant memories,
Giving away for free, that which you gained with blood, betraying the Motherland!

> A black pack of outright bandits now rule your fate.
> Worker's pride and conscience, where art thou, what happened to you?
> Because nor Chubais, nor his overlord Yeltsin will let you survive,
> Both of them lead us to shame and death with their nooses!
> Not a single good man in all of the government, all of them becoming thieves.
> The time has come, for the sake of your children, take the rifle in hand!
> By yourself create battle squads, by yourself protect that factory.
> You have a head, you have a comrade beside you – the whole Soviet nation!
> In the dark of the night, don't go in alone, how much can you do on your own?
> Only assembled together the workers are strong, together we will ever prevail!
> Cast to hell that TV, the useless banter, the wine and even your garden.
> In this hour, the Fatherland is beaten, the battle for truth is at hand.
> Listen, comrade, a great power is within us, if we are not livestock,
> Who would come out and fight for Russia, if not I and not you!

...A very decent poet he was, by the way. Many of his poems in the early 90s seemed archaic. And now they seem prophetic.

| Chapter Nine |

WITHOUT A HOMELAND

The hatred that sparked against foreigners was predictable and clear. It was easy to set it ablaze – you only needed the spark of nationalism and it was burning with a steady flame, which easily jumped from Ivanov to Kucherov, from Sholokhov to Orlov or from Dzagoev to Smotkin.

Overall, the victors, once "free of the imperial shackles," did not care who they hated, because it was about the Russian world.

A completely different thing – hating their own – those Lithuanians who were better and more successful in the system called the Soviet Union.

Under different circumstances, the people in this chapter could have been the pride and glory of the small Baltic country, which already was short on big names.

But they weren't.

The punishment selected for them was to take their homeland away.

EDMUNDAS KASPERAVIČIUS
Soviet Army Colonel, host of "red" Lithuanian TV

Now Watching "Kaspervision"

If we had to pick someone who took the most of the hit, then it was Soviet Army colonel Edmundas Kasperavičius, who wasn't afraid to become the host of "red" Lithuanian TV, which started broadcasting from the liberated rooms of the TV and radio center, mere days after the 13 January 1991 events and remained on the air for months until the August Coup. It is hard to imagine how many people cursed at their TVs each evening when this man was on screen. But still, with a purely Lithuanian stubbornness, he sat in the host chair. His due reward – the programming created by him was called "kaspervision."

The Geometry of Destiny

Kasperavičius: I tell everyone that I was "planned" in honor of Lithuania's liberation from the Germans. My father married my mother, who worked as a maid to a much richer grandma, the mother of my father, and lived in the local village. She went to the forest where father hid, brought him food. And when it was clear that the war was over – they got married. In March 1945, I was born. A year before my birth, my paternal grandfather was shot by the Germans. My dad became a POW during the first night of the war – Lithuanians, as dependable people, were used to skim through the forest and protect bridges. Virtually, my father served the Germans. But when, as a prisoner, he found out that his father was shot, he managed to be allowed home to pay respects. And after finding out that he was shot for nothing, due to slander, he did not return to the Germans. He hid in the forest from then on, until in 1944, when Lithuania was liberated by the Soviet Army.

Sapozhnikova: *So who were the heroes in your family history – the Forest Brethren or the Soviet soldiers?*

Kasperavičius: I think my father himself didn't know who was right and who was wrong. It was a very arduous time! I didn't know any of that either, because I was a child.

Sapozhnikova: *How did you end up in the Soviet Army then? Your family didn't have any fondness for it.*

Kasperavičius: If replying with a dash of humor, then there are two reasons. First, because my father's heart was softer than the heart of my neighbor. Second, because on 10 April 1961, on a Tuesday, I didn't know geometry. Jokes aside, it was like this: a small accordion was being sold in our village, so me and my friend went to convince our parents to buy it. I convinced my father to do it faster than my friend did his. And we bought the accordion for five rubles, I learned to play it and compose music. This was heard by the composer Balsys and I made my parents send me to a music school in Tauragė. That is how I got into the city. If I hadn't, I wouldn't have known about the military commission. This one time in 11th grade, I knew that the teacher would ask me a question, so I was looking for a reason to skip out geometry. And suddenly, my desk mate Almutas Dumčius said that he was going to the military commission, saying that everyone who wants to go the military academy is invited to attend. I jumped at the solution! I ran to my class teacher. She asked if I was a fool. But I still ran off, ready to sit the lesson out in the bushes and then I suddenly bump into the principal. What are you doing here? Going to the military commission? Well then, go! And I had to go because the officer wrote my name down. I started passing exams without even knowing Russian fairly well. And they still say that there was russification... No, we studied every subject in Lithuanian, and I, as a Lithuanian, was allowed to pass the mathematics exam in my native language.

Who Is Lying and Who Isn't?

Kasperavičius: I always aimed for the Baltics. On my first year, I already made it a goal to finish the academy with honors, in order to have a right to serve in Lithuania. And that was how it turned out, but they didn't send me to Lithuania, but to Sovetsk, which was 37 km from Tauragė. Which was basically sending me back home. But sometime later, it started heating up on the Chinese border and I was dropped off there. Then they brought me back to Riga. Then they suddenly needed a man in Afghanistan. After the war, I was begging them to send me only to the Baltics. I came back and Sąjūdis was afoot...

Sapozhnikova: *Were you sent here with some mission or was this purely your request?*

Kasperavičius: I decided that I wouldn't fight in another war after Afghan. I was 43 with 30 years of service. I had enough stored up to retire. In Afghanistan, I had no time to think about what was happening within the Soviet Union. I only remember that after another Party Convention, I sat down to take notes from the Secretary-General's speech... and found nothing to write down. A flow of words...Due to that, there was no position for me in Lithuania. I was sent to be a political officer in the civil defense HQ. I wanted to relax in my last years of service, and then protests started... Only then I started looking into what was happening. Arriving in Lithuania, I didn't know the situation at all. Essentially, it was the second time in my life where I had to seriously choose who did I want to be with. The majority of Lithuanians knew clearly – to be with Sąjūdis. And I was contemplating for a while – all of 1988 and 1989.

Sapozhnikova: *What was the deciding factor for you?*

Kasperavičius: The answer to the question of: Who is lying and who isn't? Right now, those who led Sąjūdis are made out to be heroes and the communists are painted black as the enemies. And I knew them to be very honest people. If they said that Russia and Lithuania are brothers, then that was what they truly believe in. I tried to understand the Molotov-Ribbentrop pact – probably wasted six months. And finally joined those, who were telling the truth in my opinion, not wanting anything to do with those who were devious and crooked.

"We Are Already Here"

Sapozhnikova: *When did you arrive in Vilnius?*

Kasperavičius: August 1989. Assumed my position. And that is when the protests started, the communist party split, and in March 1990, the Supreme Council of Lithuania declared independence. I was still working at the civil defense. And one time, a journalist friend of mine asked me: "Hey, you fought in Afghanistan, right? The American Green Berets captain, Andrew Eiwa, also fought against us at that time. Do you want to meet him?" I said – of course I do! I thought to myself that this needs to be immortalized. I called my acquaintance from Lithuanian TV and proposed a story: "Two Lithuanians in Afghanistan – one on the Soviet side and one on the American." He found it interesting! I invited Eiwa home, the journalist and TV crew arrived to film it and it aired. This was 10 days before the declaration of independence. And then Eiwa and I went to a restaurant, had a good drink and my cousin asked him: "After the war, the Americans always kept promising to help Lithuania, but never came. What if it will be the same thing now? And the Americans won't come?" And he was repeating that question over and over until Eiwa cut him off calmly and confidently: "We are already here"...

Sapozhnikova: *By your estimates, what was the proportion of those in favor of independence and those against within the Lithuanian population?*

Kasperavičius: My entourage was mostly of those who wanted to improve quality of life while part of the Soviet Union, rather than escaping it. There weresn't a lot of the "advanced" people who stood for independence.

Sapozhnikova: *So they needed an event which would convince the Lithuanians that they must flee the Soviet Union as quickly as possible?*

Kasperavičius: Honestly, they could have seized the television without a single shot. At its base, it was a brilliant provocation from Landsbergis, fanning the flames of panic over the media and forcing Moscow to take some measures to stop that wild, anti-Russian, anti-Soviet, anti-communist propaganda. And the military and KGB fell for it. So the ones in the know already had an idea that Lithuania, Latvia and Estonia will be independent. In that sense, Landsbergis didn't need any sacrifices, he could have just calmly waited for his hour. The victims were needed in order to have Russia leave the USSR, for the Union to completely fall apart. And I think it wasn't Landsbergis who planned all of this, but those sitting in Moscow and preparing to privatize the factories, already knowing what to do after the Soviet powers would be gone.

I think that Lithuania wasn't ready for independence. It was dragged into it.

What Vision?

Sapozhnikova: *How did you become a TV host?*

Kasperavičius: There was a decision in Moscow to send national staff who worked in various central Union agencies to all of the republics, including Lithuania. Usually in military and security: KGB, the defense ministry – so, proven men. The chief of the Baikonur launch pad political department, Naudžiūnas, was sent to Lithuania. He started gathering people to help the local communists with national staff. And I was recommended to him as well. My conflicted state at the time – to go with the flow or against it – was pretty much gone by then. I decided that Landsbergis and I were going on different paths. I was made a consultant at first and then the one in charge of the organizing department of the CPL Central Committee. And when Landbergis had the TV taken away from him, there was a question of who would be the first to go on the air?

I didn't have TV star ambitions. I was told about this by the head of the Central Committee ideological department, Juozas Jermalavičius. She came in and said: "We think you need to be the TV program host."

I remember the January 1991 days like some madness. And the people seemed unreal. I even wondered whether mood-altering weapons were used – but then discarded that theory. You walked as if drunk, even though you drank nothing.

Around midnight you could hear the hum of the car engines, I ventured outside and saw an acquaintance from the civil defense HQ. He was the one to tell me that there already were casualties. As a Soviet army colonel, I didn't believe him when he said that the people were shot by the soldiers, because I knew how Soviet men were brought up. I knew that it just couldn't have happened! And somehow I think, that Butkevičius knew this as well; that is why he told the crowd not to worry and that they won't be shot… And not just me – no one around me believe that the tank crews would run over the people like they said. And now, it is not simple disbelief – I am completely certain of it.

After the TV center was retaken by the military and we entered the TV studio, we found it completely unusable; everything was wrecked to the root. It was all blamed on the Alpha Group and the troopers, even though it was broken by the leaving Lithuanian TV guys – I have a confession of one that they resolved not to leave anything for the enemy and ripped all of the equipment out. It took four days in order to restore everything.

Sapozhnikova: *What did your family think of your TV experience?*

Kasperavičius: It just so happens that they were burying the dead on the day of my first broadcast. I took my brother aside – he was opposed to me, as were all of my relatives, who thought that I was simply crazy – and told them that I would be on TV that day. He almost punched me… I was worried, very worried. Not worried about whether I should read the text or not, however. Because I was 100 percent convinced that it was just.

Sapozhnikova: *Were you recognized on the street?*

Kasperavičius: Yes, every dog on the street knew my face.

The feelings towards me were very mixed though. They started screaming Judas at my back on the second day of broadcast. And called the TV Kaspervision. It is a game of words only Lithuanians get. My name is Kasperavičius and "kas" in Lithuanian is "what" and "per" is "the," adding it up it is a mocking "What the vision?" But the people who were opposed to Lithuania leaving the USSR saw me as a hero. Most, however, treated me neutrally. I traveled Lithuania a lot, met relatives and no one asked any questions.

The Last Letter

Sapozhnikova: *You left Lithuania, because you assumed you would be persecuted?*

Kasperavičius: I left at the night of the Moscow coup, not knowing what was happening. The thing is, I was sent on an education course to Beijing for 10 months. So I was leaving by myself, not hiding from anyone.

Sapozhnikova: *Did you have the feeling that you would never return home?*

Kasperavičius: Many times I remembered how I drove my mom to the countryside for the last time. It was late, I didn't go inside, just hugged her and sat in the car to drive to Vilnius. And in the early morning I went to Moscow. And my heart ached as if I would never see her again. And that is how it turned out: the house burned down, my mother died – all of that without me.

I was always in touch, I knew she had cancer, she was in pain, everyone knew she would die, but didn't know which day. I asked my friends' advice: maybe I could use a fake name and travel to Lithuania for my mother's funeral? I was told that I could try, but if they got me, they wouldn't be able to get me out of there. In one of my books I published my last letter to her:

Hello, mom! This is your son, Edmundas. I am

writing you a letter again. I heard from you last on the 16th of April. You didn't hear me, but told me that you were saying farewell.

I don't want to believe that those were your last words to me. Today I found out that Your condition worsened and I want to say: "I am proud to have a mother like You. I know You were overjoyed when people praised me. I know You were worried when people spoke ill of me. But You always believed that the son You brought up couldn't bring evil to people."

A Life-Long AWOL

Sapozhnikova: *How did you find out that the Lithuanian prosecution was looking for you?*

Kasperavičius: The Lithuanians sent an inquiry to China through law enforcement. It was 1992. And in June 1991, a few months before the coup, two Chinese communists from the Central Committee came to Vilnius to see if Lithuania would secede from the Union. And I, as the chief of the organizing department, who also happened to speak Chinese, was attached to them as support. I drove them around the republic for two days and as a sign of gratitude they gave me their business cards. And upon arriving in China, I called them. They immediately came over, even though both of them were big bosses, and they set up their protection. And they were the ones who told me that there was an inquiry. But the Chinese side just said that there was no such man in the country.

I lived there for five months, then suddenly the Soviet Union is gone. Everyone, except the Russians – Georgians, Kazakhs, Kyrgyz, Lithuanians – were told that Moscow won't pay for their studies anymore. I was forced to leave China on 1 January 1992, but where would I go? I couldn't return to Lithuania. There was nothing for me in Moscow either. And then China decided to help the national minorities – and started giving us 350 yuans for food. You could make a living on that. Everyone remained there to continue their studies. Then everyone went home and I, a Soviet Army colonel, remained abroad, AWOL. I had nowhere to return to. That is how I got stuck in China for a whole 25 years. The past family fell apart and a new one appeared. Now I have a half-Chinese and half-Lithuania daughter Yulite growing up in China as a continuation of my story.

Sapozhnikova: *What part of your life would you like to live through again?*

Kasperavičius: Anything but the years when Russia was being turned into an enemy of Lithuania... Such absurd nonsense!

ROMAS KONSTANTINO JUKNEVIČIUS
100 Percent Lithuanian Retired Soviet Army Colonel

Stolen Victory

"Romas Konstantino Juknevičius," the man with a bushy moustache introduced himself. That name was hard on the ears of the inhabitants of the small Belarussian village in the Vitebsk region, but it was known to all of them.

The apartment was draped in camouflage, which surprised no one nowadays. There was a lake behind the building and a smokehouse near the door. At first glance, this man was just a fisherman.

But then he took out his uniform and started listing: 4 orders and 18 medals. Three awards for Afghanistan alone – the Order of the Red Star, the Afghan Order "For Bravery", the Order of the "Star" 3rd class. Also a medal "For Merits in Combat" and the Order "For USSR Armed Forces Service". And so on...

A retired Soviet Army colonel, a 100-percent Lithuanian Juknevičius was at the top of the list of people who Lithuania aims to try in absentia.

Sapozhnikova: *I am curious as to why you became a military* *man? It was probably not a popular choice among Lithuanians – to join the Soviet Army.*

Juknevičius: We hail from a poor farmer family. There were six kids – five sisters and me. And my father, who finished just three classes of parochial school and was always breaking his back for the estate owners, told me: "Son, if I had five sons and one daughter, then I would order them all to protect the Soviet government. But I have only you, so you must go serve in the army. Go!" That was the kind of patriot he was! I will tell you something else: out of three thousand Lithuanian officers serving in the Soviet army, only a few joined the Sąjūdis side. The overwhelming majority didn't abandoned their pledge.

After boarding school, I joined the Kaliningrad High Military Engineer Academy, which I finished with honors in 1969. And I was sent to the Zabaikalsky Military Command as a vice-commander of a pontoon squadron of the explosives engineer battalion of the 122nd Guard motorized rifle division under the command of the future USSR Minister of Defense, Dmitry Yazov. He exemplified the highest officer honor and dignity to me. Many years later, I was a lieutenant-colonel and arrived to Belarus for the convention of the USSR Armed Forces commanding staff – this was, around 1985 or 1986. I was in the officer cafeteria. Suddenly the general of the army, Yazov, enters. He was in command of the Far East front at the time, along with his HQ head and chief political officer. I stood up, of course, and he suddenly turns to me and says: "I have seen you somewhere before!" I was his lieutenant in 1969. I answer him, "Yes, you were my first division commander." And Yazov continues, "I will even recall your name, it was a Lithuanian one." He had a phenomenal memory. He knew all of the division officers up to the squadron commanders and up. Everyone!

Occupiers, Get Lost!

Sapozhnikova: *I know that you were shuffled around the world a lot – Transbaikalia, Germany, Latvia, Afghanistan. A sizable service* *record to be at home at retirement. So: you returned to Vilnius not long before the Perestroika and the new times rolled in...*

Juknevičius: I dreamt of Lithuania all the time, all of those 25 years of service. And here I am finally assigned the post of the vice-chief of the Vilnius High Party School reserve-officer training department. I had a glorious set-up in Vilnius! General-Major Vladimir Uskhopchik, as head of the city garrison, gave me a four-room apartment. My wife went to work at a store. My youngest daughter went to kindergarten and my oldest – to school. I built a country house. After the Transbaikal bases and rented apartments with iron beds, I thought to myself "This is the life!" I had many friends – factory directors, party committee secretaries. A great job: three officers in the military department and six women. Then unknown, Dalia Grybauskaitė also taught the economics of socialism there, if my memory serves me well. And six months later, when all of the events in Lithuania began, the pressure on the High Party School began. Landsbergis demanded that Gorbachev hand over the building, because they didn't have enough buildings to teach students. Ultimately, there would be a professor setting up seats and students at the doors to imitate doing a lesson just for show... Once I was fed up with it and told them to get lost! And I was instantly slammed in the papers for it. There was also a divide in the High Party School – some for Brazauskas and some for the CPSU platform Communist Party of Lithuania. Russian-speaking teachers mostly allied with Burokevičius with the rector going for Brazauskas. And then Gorbachev betrayed us completely – six months later he terminated the High Party School as a whole. Where could I go? At the time, the Communist Party Central Committee on a CPSU platform had a legal department form, where they started gathering ethnic Lithuanian officers. That was when they called Naudžiūnas, another Baltic Fleet admiral, colonels Kasperavičius and Shurupov, so I was invited to join them – that is how we formed the administrative-legal department. Our function was to maintain connections between the army and the internal troops.

Sapozhnikova: *Is it true that Soviet officers and soldiers were constantly getting attacked?*

Juknevičius: I remember one time Landsbergis organized a protest near Severny Gorodok. It was Summer 1990. Vladimir Uskhopchik called me and said, "Romas, come and see the comedy we will do for the protests going around Vilnius with 'Occupiers, get lost!' posters." I arrive there and see two fire trucks. The protesters approach, scream and shout, and then the fire trucks start hosing them down. Then the gates opened and around 15 soldiers fired blanks at the sky. The protesters started running off. And the people who lived nearby applauded us, cheering us on! The next day, a similar event planned by Landsbergis in Kaunas was cancelled. He got scared.

During my service, I have worked with more than one hundred Lithuanian soldiers. And they all served honorably. I am sure that those who served in the Soviet army recall that time with a smile.

We Were Held Back by Gorbachev

Sapozhnikova: *As a military man, did you think any signs pointed to the fact that something grand was brewing in Vilnius?*

Juknevičius: Of course. Military commissions were blocked, so that the youngsters wouldn't be drafted into the Soviet army, and Lithuanian mothers ran there secretly at night and begged to have their sons enlisted. The situation was heating up due to the constant protests. While on the bus, I have many times overheard talks of how the local authorities bought out bologna and buried it in the sand quarry in order to make the people nervous and discontent. The same was happening in Russia. It was an American scenario. The CIA really had a field day. We, Afghan veterans, got rations at a special store and did feel it, but there was turmoil stirring in Lithuania...

Sapozhnikova: *Was the military preparing for anything? How could you sense that situation would be resolved by force?*

Juknevičius: We took no measure whatsoever, even though there was enough troopers in Lithuania. We were held back by Gorbachev. The troops remained neutral so they wouldn't be able to say "Russian occupiers, get out of Lithuania!" I guess that is why something reached Gorbachev and he gave the order to take the TV center and the TV tower. But first the militiamen and I were carrying the petition for the government to resign. I led the column to the Lithuanian Minister Council. And the leader of Venibe-Edinstvo-Ednost Valery Ivanov carried a similar petition to the Supreme Council.

But there was one traitor there, the division propagandist, who told Landsbergis everything that was happening in the military towns. So they were already waiting for us. The thugs ran up from all corners and started hitting and ripping! I had a pistol with me and I could have dropped, like, five people there, but I didn't shoot – they were just kids… The men fought back as much as they could, two people made it past the crowd and handed in the petition – they were saved by the police, who were protecting the Ministry Council, otherwise the crowd would have torn them apart. I told the boys to retreat, because there was a major fight from all directions. Around twenty people out of the fifty returned to the City executive committee – the rest were driven off in ambulances.

After an hour, there was a new assignment: everyone to the TV and radio center. I had around 80 men with me. We rode in on two buses. There was a sea of people. Everyone was applauding, because they thought it was more thugs for back up. The TV center was taken, surrounded by SWAT members with assault rifle. The tanks were firing blanks, the people were screaming, it was chaos. I ran to a soldier and demanded he get me to an officer. But I was in civilian clothes and the soldier fired a burst over the bus roof! He saw how they applauded us and thought we were thugs as well… I went back and sat to think what to do. The Sąjūdists started shaking the bus, because by then they had figured out that we weren't the thugs they were expecting. We needed to get out or they would flip it over. I asked the soldier to get an officer again! Nobody understands anything, utter chaos, the bus is being flipped over. Then the soldier finally called a major. I tell him to let us through and that we are there to help. They reply that I am being called by the Spetsnaz[1] Internal Troops squad commander, Sergey Fedorov. And he pointed and said, "Look how many thugs are on the roofs!" I gathered the militiamen at the basement and told them that if comes to it, they were to go hand to hand...

Sapozhnikova: *What did you see inside the building?*

Juknevičius: Our special forces officers said: "Comrade colonel, there is a lot of alcohol there – whiskey, cognac and champagne! Also a ton of imported food, like caviar and ham. Everything but the kitchen sink and loads of it!" That means that the officers had to gather the alcohol, so that the soldiers wouldn't drink it and start shooting. So the officers started going around cabinets. We managed to gather two crates of alcohol – me and Fedorov personally broke the bottles, but left the food for the soldiers. Let them eat their trophies. I guess the corrupt journalists were well compensated for their slander on the Soviet Union and Soviet Army... Fedorov kept one bottle of cognac, saying that we should drink it to our victory.

Sapozhnikova: *So you had a sense of victory?*

Juknevičius: Of course!

Sapozhnikova: *A victory that was turned against you the very next morning... When did you realize that they pulled it right out of your hands?*
Juknevičius: Eight months later, when Yeltsin, after the August coup, ordered us to give all of the television to the Sąjūdists. I don't know why they made a museum of him in Ekaterinburg,

because he betrayed us all! He and Gorbachev broke the Soviet Union into pieces! The next morning, when the city was under curfew, everyone hushed down. They started pulling their party tickets out and joining the party anew... We only needed the command and we would have restored order splendidly, and Landsbergis would have fled to USA. When the tanks went through Moscow during the coup, the people were in such high spirits, finally hoping for order! Everyone was tired of this babbling. The collapse of the Soviet Union started with Lithuania. But are revolutions made with shaky hands, like the GKChP? We needed to arrest Yeltsin and try him as a state criminal and everything would have been normal. And the USSR would still remain! We wouldn't have today's oligarchs, who are embezzling Russia's wealth. Russia was brought to its knees, kneeling before the Americans...

Ride Along, Please!

Sapozhnikova: *How did events unfold between 13 January 1991 and August Coup?*

Juknevičius: Television resumed its normal programming, we started doing revelations on who Landsbergis and Sąjūdis were. The people started to slowly realize what the Soviet government gave them, understanding where the money for their houses, factories and roads came from. There were those entranced, but they started coming through and allying with our communist party. We gathered protests of 80-100 thousand men. All of the power was in our hands. And Yeltsin took it all away.

Sapozhnikova: *How soon until the repression machine started in Lithuania?*

Juknevičius: The persecution started after the coup. Instantly, in a flash. A day before that I called my friend Vyacheslav Namestnikov in Moscow, he was the head of DOSAAF (the Voluntary Association for Assistance to Army, Air Force and Navy) and cheerfully told him how Vilnius views the August coup events. I tell him, "Atta boy, lads. Good thinking, Yazov, for bringing in the tanks!" And the general on the other end of the phone goes quiet and tells me to wait, because Yeltsin wasn't arrested yet. Instead the GKChP were arrested. It all fell apart... Yazov, a combat officer, a frontline veteran who had to rouse people for an attack many times and made it up to infantry battalion commander during the war – I can't believe he would chicken out. It was definitely a misstep of the security agencies. We should have grabbed Yeltsin by the family jewels, arrested the instigators from the American funds and that is it, the Soviet Union would still be there!

After the GKChP arrest, the American appointee, Landsbergis, called Yeltsin and asked him to return the television and all of the other sites we had reclaimed. And Yeltsin instantly gave the order to return the TV center, the printing house, DOSAAF and others. Also he disbanded the Vilnius OMON. This untied the hands of all Landsbergis thugs and they immediately surrounded the Central Committee, CPL on the CPSU platform buildings. They started persecuting the staff and arresting them; my family couldn't escape it either. A few days later, the police arrived at my apartment early in the morning. At the time, my little daughters and mother-in-law were home. They ransacked the whole apartment, searched everything, including the toy boxes. They were searching for evidence to link me to the coup preparation. But they found nothing, only managing to give my daughters a fright and almost giving my mother-in-law, a World War 2 veteran, a heart attack.

Sapozhnikova: *How did you leave Vilnius?*

Juknevičius: When the thugs surrounded the CPL Central Committee, Burokevičius, Jermalavičius and the Central Committee bureau were driven out to Severny Gorodok. And I immediately drove to my niece and told her that things were bad, we lost, we were betrayed... Naudžiūnas had a Volga car in the

Central Committee garage, the building was taken over and he lost the car. And I had a new Zhiguli car parked at the back yard. I came there the next day, a sergeant jumps out and tells me to run away faster because the thugs would be there in an hour. I jumped into my car, called my wife, telling her to get my uniform and documents and we went to her father in Kaliningrad. We waited it out there for a while. Sometime later, I was driving to Riga. Stopping at a gas station, I was in the line when a Sajūdist walks up to me and shouts: "What are you doing here, occupier? Here to take our gas?" And I replied to him: "This gas isn't yours, it is Russian, and when you will be free, then you can buy Russian gas."

Had to start life over from scratch. Back when I served and moved from place to place, the soldiers and officers gave me their addresses and said they would be happy to see me as a guest. So I opened my notebook to see who I knew in the Vitebsk region. Sure enough, I had a senior lieutenant in Beshankovichy, who was the commander of an explosives engineer platoon in Afghanistan. We meet, hug and he tells me that his friend, a kolkhoz director, just built three new houses. We tell him the situation and he says that he will take me into his Kolkhoz, letting me stay in an apartment.

I almost had to fight to get my wife out of Lithuania. Colonel Valery Frolov, who became the Vilnius motorized rifle division commander after Uskhopchik, helped my wife load our belongings, giving her two cars and officers. And Lithuania adopted a law, stating that Lithuanian furniture had a three-fold customs fee. But he outsmarted them, he sealed the cars and provided a paper saying it was military cargo. And he gave her two BTRs[2] with machine gunners to escort it to Belarus. They arrive at the border and the Lithuanian customs officer demands they unseal it. Then the officer gives the BTR commander the signal – they open the hatch, shoot blanks into the air... They quickly became much more agreeable, "Ride along, please!"

There Is No Blood On My Hands

Sapozhnikova: *Right now you are telling this story with a smile, but back then, I doubt it was a laughing matter. Was it difficult?*

Juknevičius: It was saddening, of course. I love my people. But there is no blood on my hands. I am not guilty of anything in Lithuania. It was Gorbachev who gave the order to take the TV center.

...It is impossible to describe how it felt to me, an officer, to hear stories of the Soviet Army leaving Lithuania. I wasn't there anymore, I know these stories thanks to what my fellow servicemen told me. The first one goes like this... Six months after the coup, the commander of the 3rd Guard motorized rifle division in Klaipėda, Ivan Cherhykh, and his adjutant were kidnapped, for supposedly sympathizing with the GKChP... The division was put on alert and went to Vilnius, and on its way there it was joined by two motorized rifle squadrons from Telšiai. Can you imagine how badly that could have gone down? Thank god, they came to their senses and released the commander.

The second story was told to me by a warrant officer whom I served with in Afghanistan. When the troop withdrawal started, the division's weapons were loaded onto fleet ships. As soon as they left the shores –suddenly there was an order from Defense Minister Grachev: return and hand over the 15 thousand firearms – grenade launchers, machineguns, assault rifles – to the Lithuanian army. That was Russia arming a country, a future NATO member.

Sapozhnikova: *How did you find out you were on the wanted list?*

Juknevičius: When Burokevičius and Jermalavičius were arrested, it was a big scandal in Belarus. Two KGB officers from Polotsk came to my home and told me: "If any suspicious individuals start closing in on you, immediately call us and we will ride over to handle it." And I replied, "I will handle it myself – just shoot them and be done with it. I am a battle officer!"

Sapozhnikova: *So you never feared anyone all these years?*

Juknevičius: I am not scared even now. Let them just try and show up, any Lithuanian secret services agents – there are those who will protect me in Belarus. First of all, I am a citizen under the protection of our president, Aleksandr Lukashenko, who, even as a Belarus Supreme Council member, fought for the Soviet Union until the last day. Any attempt at my kidnapping will cause a negative international reverberation. Secondly, I am a member of the Belarusian Officers Union and a member of the Afghanistan War Veterans Union. The latter organization includes around 30 thousand members. Many know me and won't leave me if the going gets hot, because we have a real battle-forged brotherhood.

They need to put Landsbergis on trial and not me. The trial currently going on in Vilnius of the participants of the 13 January events is 100 percent a show. The Lithuanian government is accusing us of something we didn't do, specifically the casualties of the 13 January 1991 events. I claim with confidence that our soldiers did not shoot at the unarmed people.

The whole process was organized like the one in Ukraine right now. Blood needed to spill in Vilnius, so they shot their own, the same thing in Kiev, to raise the spirit of the masses. They ban the communist party and so do the others.

Sapozhnikova: *Are you following your homeland's fate? Or do you not care for it?*

Juknevičius: I follow it. Lithuania had 3.5 million residents. A million is already gone. Where did they all go? Sweeping floors in the European Union, working for free. Three years ago, I met a group of young men from Lithuania in our village, they came from Alytus to build a cowshed for a thousand cows for our kolkhoz. When I asked them why they were here, they told me that there was total unemployment in the republic. They were all openly discussing the government that led the country to poverty. Oh what kolkhozes Lithuania had! Millionaires! And now they are gone.

Sapozhnikova: *Do you think this state of affairs will last long?*

Juknevičius: If the people won't rise, then who will raise them? The Communist Party? Banned. Left wing? In the crosshairs. So they will keep living in debt. America isn't funding the Lithuanians just because... Look at how much noise Lithuania makes! They know that the economic and military potential of Russia rises – and they bark, but can't bite.

GENERAL-MAJOR NAUDŽIŪNAS

You Can Order a Coffin – the Soviet Union Has Fallen Apart

Mikhail Gorbachev is famously not on the Lithuanian wanted list. He was spared. But there is still Yazov, but he is an abstract figure to the Lithuanians. So, among USSR's military, the main target for the people's love-hate was next in line after the Marshall – General-Major Naudžiūnas. The most hated because he is one of them.

"So why didn't the USSR have an Estonian cosmonaut?" [Latvian, Georgian, Turkmen – you could put any nationality here]. I have been asked this question in all parts of the country with a suspicious stare, right before it fell apart. It was a statement which supposedly pointed out that the smaller nationalities in the USSR had it rough. Well, this was asked everywhere, but not in Lithuania, because it had two "cosmonauts". Well, nearly cosmonauts: test pilot Rimantas Stankevičius and space forces general Algimantas Naudžiūnas. However, neither of them were directly in space – one tested the Buran shuttle and the other led work on exploitation and test is of space rockets at Baikonur. One died in a test flight and the other buried him...

It is impossible to make Naudžiūnas into the monstrous figure that the Lithuanian history books try to paint him to be. It just doesn't work. He is smiling, sentimental, honest and capable of admitting his mistakes and weaknesses. There probably aren't enough men like him left in Lithuania.

Naudžiūnas: I was born in 1942 in the village of Novaya Sloboda in the Kaišiadorys region, the same place where our Republic's former president Algirdas Brazauskas hailed from. The war had been raging for a year already. But as my grandfather put it, they themselves didn't understand who fought who. First your soldiers came through – at that moment my grandfather nodded at me – and then the Germans. There were no battles in our region, but it was better when your soldiers came. At least they didn't beat anyone... On my mother's side of the family there were poor farmers and on my father's side they were from the middle class, but very greedy. My mother told me that they wouldn't spare any milk for me. My grandfather had a lot of hectares of land – he was a rich man by those times. For some reason my mother never told me anything about my father, only about my uncles. They all, including my father, joined the Forest Brethren. The eldest uncle was killed, my father went missing in action and the youngest uncle was tried and sentenced to 25 years; he returned to Lithuania only in 1974 and lived in the city of Ukmergė. That city also had a rocket company where I was assigned as political officer after graduating from the Academy... I still don't know if that was a coincidence or a test. My mother remarried and gave me to my grandparents and they in turn, sent me to a boarding school, because they just couldn't feed me. At least I ate there three times a day! There were around 300 of us there and we all survived thanks to the Soviet government.

During the summer, I worked at a construction site earning money for clothes and a backpack. For the first times, I carried my textbooks and notebooks in a plywood box which I made myself. After school I had to face the question of what to do with myself? And fate presented me with a gift – a military commission agent came to our school, a senior lieutenant by the name of Dainis and told us about the army. I figured I wouldn't make it into the institute anyway and decided to go to flight school. But I had studied in a village school, they didn't have Russian there, all I could say in Russian was "Hello". They gave us an interpreter and drove us to the Kazan aviation and technological academy. There were four tents of Lithuanians, 25 people in each. We didn't understand anything in Russian, wandering around like sheep, playing basketball 24/7. The first exam – failed, the second one – failed. But I got an excellent grade in math. Four fails and one excellent grade and...I am among the first to be accepted into the academy! Out of 100 people, only 4 Lithuanians were accepted, including me. I finished the academy with only one grade short of an excellent mark. The training was highly competent in Soviet times. I couldn't do anything when I was accepted, and upon graduation I was a multi-discipline specialist: I could work on a lathe, do any sanitary engineering work, drove all manner of transport vehicles (motorcycle, tank, APC) and knew how to plant flowers, clean the equipment and the barracks. We were even taught ballroom dancing! I am very thankful to the armed forces for making a man out of a young freeloader!

When I was already a senior lieutenant and came home on vacation, the elder of the village also returned. His name was Ramoška – the one we had under the Germans. He knew my uncles. He had served time in prison, returned from Vorkuta and decided to see me. He had a very rough and sulky look. I thought he was going to pick a fight. And he suddenly said, "I knew your father, he was a scoundrel! But you did good, lad! You chose the proper path. I respect the Soviet government, because they didn't have me shot. Yes, I did time, but I have done enough to deserve it!" My grandmother heard everything and when he left, told me not to greet him, because he was a right bastard. Then, rather quickly, he died. No one in the village was there to bury him…

Which "Mess" Is Better?

Naudžiūnas: Because I graduated from the academy with first class, I had the right to freely choose my place of service. I chose Vinnytsia, because it had a lot of air units. And I was assigned to completely new equipment. That is how I became a rocket man instead of a pilot.

…In the early 80s the Western rocket divisions were being outfitted with a new type of weapons, the so-called SS-20. I was sent to outfit the units and bases of the strategic rocket forces in Lida, then I was sent to new rocket tests at the Plesetsk cosmodrome, and a year later I was in Baikonur as head of the political department. We conducted tests and launches of the multi-use space shuttle Energia-Buran. Nothing was simple in Baikonur, there were huge projects underway, but socially there were a lot of problems. There weren't enough apartments, schools and kindergartens; there were shortages of provisions. The officers voiced their discomfort, wrote reports of resignation. Once two scientists from Moscow came to us on assignment and I told them all of this and they replied, "Algis, don't worry, we will tell Misha and he will help you." I asked who Misha was and they said it was Mikhail Gorbachev, he was their friend ever since Stavropol.

And something in me started to turn, I had a feeling that we got into trouble with this new General Secretary... However, they kept their word and wrote an internal memo to Mikhail Gorbachev. And then it began, commission after commission. Gorbachev arrived with nine members of the Political Bureau. He instantly got a construction division there and built a new micro district. Prepared a law as well, where every Republic was to build a store on Baikonur and send their goods here. And we started living like kings.

But Gorbachev asked me during a conversation, "What are you doing here?" I was surprised by his question and he continued "You have a mess in Lithuania right now and you are here!" I didn't give it any meaning, but in a short span of time, there was a phone call from Moscow, from the political department asking "Wouldn't you like to continue your service in Lithuania?" I said that of course I would like that! They invited me to the Central Committee to interview me, asking what would I say if I was elected the Secretary of the Lithuanian Central Committee? I said it was no problem – it was my beloved Homeland, after all! In late August 1990 the order came through. And 13 September 1990, I flew to Vilnius.

Come After Dark...

Naudžiūnas: I was given the task of immediately addressing the morale and political situation in the military units, restoring the party organizations in cities and regions. I travel around the republic – city and regional committees are all closed, no one there. Some buildings are already occupied, the documentation thrown out. In one region, they gave me a hint, "We know you are Naudžiūnas, we are proud of you, but please come when it is dark. Fascists have come to power, the people are scared and no one will contact you. We will meet at night and only at the military commission." No party activity was going on, everything was falling apart or destroyed. We were gathering information on events in the Supreme Council, what was the situation on the factories, and quickly realized that foreign specialists were working around the clock in the republic. Soon we had lists of those who instructed Landsbergis and his entourage. We informed Moscow and received no reaction. Time was ticking, so I started asking uncomfortable questions to Kryuchkov, Pyzhkov, Lukyanov and Sheynin, like "Why is my table equipped with high-frequency communication and the same one is set up for Landsbergis? Why does he, just like me, have the right to call all of the Moscow ministers directly? Why are all of the foreign instructors flying in through Moscow and no one is stopping them? Why is the Soviet Union giving Lithuania money, even though it declared that it had left the USSR?

A group from the CPSU Central Committee arrived and said, "Naudžiūnas, you need to make peace with Landsbergis" Me?! I told them that they asked me to make peace with their enemy. "I am here standing up for the Soviet Union and you are saying I should convince those bandits to stay in it? Do you even know who they are? They are animals who will trample not just us, but you as well! Why haven't you, members of the Supreme Council from the Lithuanian Republic, which has made the decision to leave the Soviet Union, been removed from your posts and stripped of you mandates? Why did the CPSU Central Committee not exclude Brazauskas from the party? No, I won't make peace with anyone!" I told them.

Who Broke the Soviet Union Apart?

Sapozhnikova: *Other USSR citizens had this strong feeling, that your countrymen all wanted independence, as one. Many later said that this was a grave mistake, that in actuality, there was a huge number of people in Lithuania who respected the Soviet government and didn't want to leave the USSR. How do you view the stance that Lithuania was forcefully dragged into independence?*

Naudžiūnas: Lithuania joined the USSR on its own, let them read the documents. Actually, under Soviet rule, it blossomed like no other Union republic. Oh, the roads, cozy villages, cities and hamlets we had... The common people didn't want the USSR collapsing, the ones at the top wanted that: the slumbering traitors, who hid after the war, nationalists, who collaborated with foreign agents and high-ranking ministry and agency officials, who actively worked with the Moscow traitors and followed their orders.

The results of the referendums, which were in Latvia, Lithuania and Estonia – and I was the president of the referendum preparation and execution commission – showed 68% of the Baltics' residents voted in favor of preserving the Soviet Union. They made it clear that they wanted more freedom in order to go abroad, said they didn't want to "get Moscow's approval on the recipes of their cakes" and feed all of the Soviet Union. And on the street level, the people lived wonderfully. The quality of life levels in Lithuania were second only to Georgia during that period. Lithuanians had good doctors, engineers and high caliber specialists, every one of my classmates had a house, a car and a country house. After 1991 there were no jobs, the engineers were unneeded, the houses and country houses had to be sold, because you had to pay, pay and pay.

The Soviet Union wasn't broken apart by America, but by people from CPSU Central Committee, KGB, the Foreign Affairs Ministry, Supreme Council and many other agencies. Only the military took a more or less cohesive position, but they understood the situation in their own way.

State of Emergency

Naudžiūnas: Working in the CPL Central Committee, I traveled the Republic, met with the party activists, fellow servicemen, classmates and told then what would happen to Lithuania if it leaves the USSR. I, without any politics or lies, told people that us simple folk will have it rough. No one is waiting for us in the West, we will lose our oil and gas, the kolkhozes will be shut down and the factories will be destroyed, the people will slide into poverty. The youngsters didn't believe it of course, but the older generation started thinking, more and more people started coming to the Central Committee and complaining about the government's lawlessness. The people were scared and concerned, asked worrying questions, told me what the Sąjūdists were doing in the outskirts of the republic... And at one of these meetings I was asked a question: why are they sending everyone to the TV tower on 5 January?

Then I found out after the fact, that the operation to free the TV center and TV tower was initially planned for 5 January 1991. Can't say anything on that: Landsbergis had great spies...

Why was the operation even started? After 11 March 1990, the Sąjūdists claimed all of the mass media outlets in the republic, along with all of the party buildings. They purged the mass media, the organizations, the factories and put ardent nationalists at the head of everything. This government didn't let us in anywhere. Not only that, but they also had a non-stop smear campaign against us through all of the channels, calling us "occupiers" and "rapists". The communists were attacked, threat letters were thrown, saying they would hang us soon. There was a whole wave of disinformation against the Soviet army, the nationalist-minded youth made attacks on army personnel, tried to provoke them and threatened to massacre them. In one division the nationalists welded the front doors shut, threw bottles at the guards and ran off. The military went to the police and those just laughed at them... We reached out to the republican government many times, demanding they stop the attacks on the army and stop slandering us through the media. There was no reaction. At one point the party newspaper *Tarybų Lietuva (Soviet Lithuania)* was published in Belarus and delivered to Lithuania in trucks – so they started provoking and attacking the trucks. One printing shipment – the one talking about American emissaries – was burned completely! We reported to Moscow daily, brought up examples and facts, insisted that the buildings captured by the Sąjūdists be returned to their rightful owners.

In other words: we openly asked Gorbachev to declare a state of emergency. But he was waiting for it to work itself out on its own? But nothing worked out. And he finally decided...

And in the morning of 13 January they called me from the Vilnius city hospital – go there and see who arrived. And so I came. They had normal regular corpses, some from under a tractor, some from a car and the doctor tells me that they have been brought over from all over Lithuania today...

On the next day, three women came to my office, who told me they saw a few policemen go to roof of their five-story building, carrying guns and they shot into the crowd. This and a lot of other information we handed to the Lithuania prosecutor's office. It all should have been in the criminal case files.

Betrayal Happened There

Sapozhnikova: *Do you remember the morning of the first day of the August coup?*

Naudžiūnas: I woke up at 6 am along with my security, turned on the TV and went to do my exercises. I then heard strings.[3] They say it is a coup... I arrive at the Central Committee and people with banners are already gathering there and singing Soviet songs. And then I get a call from Prime Minister Česlovas Juršėnas and he asks me if we are going to shoot him or not.

Then Landsbergis' aide called me, then Kazimira Prunskienė's aide – everyone was asking me what would happen to them. Many said that Landsbergis led them all astray... There were hundreds of journalists in the office, couldn't get by, interview after interview. 20 August, a BBC correspondent asks me if it is true that one of my divisions went on Yeltsin's side? I ran to the other office and called the Deputy President of the Defense Council Oleg Baklanov over a secure line. What is this about a division? And he calls me back – betrayal happened there… By the end of the day, there was no one in the office. Nobody called us and we called no one… And on 22 August, there were crowds of "patriots" with pitchforks, sawn-off shotguns and clubs.

Until the evening of 22 August, we were burning papers at the CPL Central Committee. There wasn't a single document left in a drawer. There were 73 people left in the Central Committee.

Deep into the night, we got three APCs. I gathered everyone and said the following, "Thank you all for not abandoning the Central Committee in a desperate time and for believing in Soviet government. I ask you not to go home for now, because they will be looking for you, and I will send you to the Northern Town." I said farewell to each one personally. And myself, I went to a safe house and lived there for a week and a half. The people listened to my warning, remained safe – no one was arrested.

Mama

Sapozhnikova: *How did you leave Lithuania?*

Naudžiūnas: Around one or two weeks later, when it all calmed down, I asked my friends to give me two Zhiguli cars, requesting women drivers, because a traffic police mindset has a steady rule of not harassing the ladies. I got in the back seat and draped myself in rags. I sat there, napping. There were around 15 people on the border post. The girls immediately asked them on how to get to Minsk. And they were all friendly and smiling, telling them to ride on through. That is how I got out. Easy. There was a tinge of fear, I won't deny that.

They brought me to Minsk and I didn't even have a tie, having left my general uniform, suits and casual clothing in the

Central Committee office. I came to the train station and asked them to help me get to Moscow. "Are you from Lithuania?" they asked and I said that yes, I am a Central Committee secretary and showed my documents. "Oh, a lot of yours already left." And they gave me a ticket on the prosecutor's office bill. I came to Moscow to my Main Space Department and there finally, for the first time in four days, I cried...

I spent three months in a hospital. Then I went to the commander of the military space forces, General Vladimir Ivanov, and I told him to send me to serve somewhere far away, in the woods, so the Lithuanians couldn't get me. And I told him that they had decided to arrest me. The thing was that when I came to Moscow from Minsk, there was a policemen and two Lithuanian intelligence officers outside my home. "Oh don't worry about it. We will leave you in the army," he replied. I came down to the second floor of the HQ and the head of staff gave me an order and said, "You are now fired from the Armed Forces"... The commander apparently decided that it would be cheaper to get rid of me. And he completely didn't care about the fact that I served in the strategic rocket forces and the space forces for 36 years and then went hungry for months, not having money or work...

What could I do? I went to Siberia to my friends from the service; they helped me with work and accommodation. A year later, I returned to Moscow. When everything calmed down more or less, I went to work for a rocket corporation. But when I was back in Siberia, in January 1992 a friend called me and said, "Brace yourself, your mother was found dead in Vilnius. Don't think of going, that is exactly what they want." The apartment door was closed, but the window was open. Mom was lying in a pool of blood near the heater. They said that she had some kind of hole near the temple and apparently she fell on the heater on her own. She was only 69 years old. I still remember her words: "Why did you come to Lithuania, people here hate each other so"...

Sapozhnikova: *So they took not only your homeland, but also your mother from you?*

Naudžiūnas: They took everything from me! Everything! I was morally crushed. I loved my homeland so much, I loved Lithuania so much, I loved the Lithuanian people so much... The first weeks after the hospital, would you believe, I went to the Belarus train depot on a Vilnius train in order to hear people speaking Lithuanian. And every day like that...
I am sad and I hurt.

And the people of Lithuania continue living and believing that the happy and joyous years of the "Soviet occupation" will one day return...

| Chapter Ten |

THE CONSEQUENCES OF ONE EVENT

ANTANAS PETRAUSKAS
General-Major of Justice
the last Prosecutor of the Lithuanian SSR

Two on a Swing

...Another Lithuanian came to the meeting, putting a case file on the table...and a black honorary pistol.

General-Major of Justice Antanas Petrauskas received it from the hands of the Deputy Prosecutor-General – the Chief Military Prosecutor of Russia for distinguished service.

It is important to those slandered, cursed by their homeland and thrown out from their homes: to tell the world that their professional life has gone well even without Lithuania. And in Russia, they are celebrated, while Lithuania, who shunned them, only lost out at least by losing these bright men.

Petrauskas was the last Prosecutor of the Lithuanian SSR. Or it would be better to say that he was one of two, the prosecutor's office at the time had dual powers, just like the Communist party.

All of these 25 years, Antanas Petrauskas was the most coveted target for the Lithuanian prosecution. Who else but him knows the truth about what really happened in Lithuania is January 1991.

Red and White

So who is he, the Lithuanian who became a Russian general? He was born in Lithuania and spent his childhood in Druskininkai. A poor family from the workers. His mother was technically an American citizen, because during the start of the previous century the Lithuanians emigrated in search of a better life almost as massively as they do today. So it happened that Antanas Petrauskas' family on his mother's side were from the first wave of emigration, but after Lithuania gained independence, they returned home. His father took part in World War II, a recipient of the "For Victory over Germany medal" for his work with the Soviet partisans. So his son, who graduated from the air force academy in Latvian Daugavpils and was sent to serve in the rocket forces scientific research base in Kazakhstan, continued in the family line.

Sapozhnikova: *When did you return to Lithuania? And why?*

Petrauskas: While serving in the aviation division on the famous Sary Shagan testing range, I finished the law faculty and transferred into military prosecution. I became the senior investigator on important cases, served as the deputy military prosecutor of 50th rocket army and the prosecutor of the 11th Combined Arms Army in Kaliningrad. When things started going down in the Baltics, I was the military prosecutor of the Riga garrison. And I was recalled from that post to Moscow on 28 March 1990 and made Prosecutor of the Lithuania SSR.

Sapozhnikova: *You came to your homeland on each vacation. As a Lithuanian, did the candles, ribbons and songs of freedom stir any feelings in you?*

Petrauskas: It was all beautiful for sure but... Lithuania, along with Latvia and Estonia were prosperous republics. Industry was booming, roads were being built. There was a shortage of Zhiguli cars in the country back then, but despite that, almost every

Lithuanian in the city had one. Lithuanians are a people who look to the future, so I viewed the Soviet government as something absolutely normal. I came home in my uniform and no one ever told me I was in an "occupation" army. No one ever talked of "occupation", the term just wasn't used.

Sapozhnikova: *Then how did the mindset of the people turn around so fast?*

Petrauskas: Echoes of Stalin's policy. When Lithuania entered the Soviet Union in 1940, a large portion of the officers, clergy and intelligentsia were deported to Siberia. In 1944, the republic was liberated, the front moved further and a second wave of deportations began. A huge role was played by the propaganda from the USA. The Voice of America periodically reminded the people that Lithuania was "occupied" – there was even a government-in-exile in the USA. The famous Donatas Banionis film *Nobody Wanted to Die* clearly showed the power balance of the time, especially in the rural parts of the country, where one power ruled the day and the other had the night. For example, when a man reached the age of 18, the drafting age, that very day, people come to him and tell him that if he goes into the Soviet army, that means you are pro-communist. It happened that families of the ones drafted were shot. What could you do? And the boy would run into the woods. Then they came from the other side and sent his family to Siberia. From one side the white would attack, and the red would attack from the other. The grudge against the Soviet government was dropping around the 70s, but in the late 80s it was brought up again, stirring people up, saying they had been deported undeservedly and illegally. The economy was state-run, but when in Russia you would have to travel from Tula to Moscow just to buy normal bologna, Lithuania's stores were packed with dozens of meats, cheeses and dairy products and speculators were on the rise. "Lithuania has been turned into a pig shed, all of the products going to Moscow…" But no one considered the amount of fuel and compound feed being brought into the Republic.

The Divide in Prosecution

Sapozhnikova: *When you were called into Moscow and given the order to transfer to Vilnius, did you have the option of refusing?*

Petrauskas: They were talking about Lithuania's insubordinate behavior. With the Interior Minister being appointed on the spot, the Republic's prosecutor was exclusively selected by the Union Prosecutor-General. He didn't answer to anyone there, which was right, because otherwise he would have no oversight. The former First Deputy LSSR Prosecutor, Artūras Paulauskas, approved of assigning him as the prosecutor of the Lithuania Republic after it declared independence, even though he was the son of a KGB agent and he served as an instructor for the CPL Central Committee administrative department. Moscow apparently thought that if they replaced the prosecutor and his deputies everything would return to how it was. But sadly at that point all of the other agencies stopped following Moscow's orders, including the Interior Ministry and the Supreme Court. The paradox was that after declaring independence, they were still funded from Moscow.

Sapozhnikova: *When you agreed to the post, did you understand you were entering open confrontation?*

Petrauskas: I couldn't comprehend the wave of nationalism that started in Lithuania, because I was brought up in a different manner. My parents were internationalists and my best friends were Poles, because the Polish border was only 7 km away from home. I saw industry developing in Lithuania and compared it to my relatives in the countryside, who wore wooden shoes in the 20th century. The roofs of houses were mostly straw and the floors were clay. And everything changed in mere years under the Soviet government! So when they told me that I was to transfer to Vilnius, I agreed without a second thought, because I assumed that there would be a series of measures to change the situation in the country.

Sapozhnikova: *How did Lithuania greet you?*

Petrauskas: Everyone was asking where did this Petrauskas come from? Who was he? When I was officially introduced they had all of the regional prosecutors in Vilnius. On the morning of 30 March 1990, I and the First Deputy Prosecutor-General of the USSR, Alexey Vasiliev, went to Lithuanian prosecutor Artūras Paulauskas. Vasiliev read him the order that relieved him of his post as first deputy prosecutor of the Lithuanian SSR, stripped him of his class rank of senior counsellor in justice and said that I would be the acting prosecutor of the LSSR. Vasiliev said the same thing to all of the board. Paulauskas just replied, "Well, we are independent now!"

There was a divide in the prosecution. I understood that it would be meaningless to fight for power, because that would benefit only the criminals. The people who remained on Paulauskas' side approached me when no one saw and told me that they supported me, but they had families to think about. They were already afraid of persecution. And those fears came to pass;I started getting dubious letters and threatening phone calls from the very first day in office. They even called my mother, asking her how could she raise a traitor. My mother nearly had a heart attack...

Me and my Deputy Nikolai Krempovski were offered various high posts in exchange for helping get rid of the Lithuanian SSR prosecutor's office. We kept in contact with thr Prosecutor of Lithuania, Artūras Paulauskas, and he gave the impression of being a normal man, I didn't feel any hostility towards him. When I exited my office and he would be exiting his next door, we would always greet each other. A year after my appointment, the students started a protest saying, "Paulauskas is one of us and Petrauskas is Russian." And Paulauskas spoke at it, saying, "The day of reckoning for Petrauskas will come. Russia is always awakening and he will find no place for himself there. We will try him here, in Lithuania." I call him over the internal phone and asked him "What? Did you start a case on me?" and he started making excuses sheepishly, "No, no, of course not..." This was in March. And in August I found out that they did start a criminal case against me way back...

All Secrets Shall Come to Light

Sapozhnikova: *Did you sense that the pressure among the people would rise to a boiling point in the most tragic of ways?*

Petrauskas: The fact that the situation in the Republic was being built up is certain. The rising prices naturally had the people displeased. The pro-Soviet-minded people were brought before the Supreme Council, Landsbergis asked all who supported him to come. The plans to storm the TV tower and TV and radio committee were secret, but I am sure that Landsbergis knew. Why? There were more than enough traitors, for example, police regiment commander Stancikas went to Landsbergis as soon as independence was declared and said he would work for him now. Passed on any and all information about what was planned. They made lists of who was patrolling what and when, organized food delivery. People were brought in from all over the republic, guard duty was considered as work time.

Sapozhnikova: *Is it true that, after the 13 January events, there were two parallel investigations, Lithuanian and Soviet?*

Petrauskas: That is exactly how it was. I was the one to start the case on signs of mass riots. Literally a week later USSR Prosecutor Nikolai Trubin gathered a group of special case investigators from all over the Union and sent them to Vilnius. I was keeping track of the investigation. And I am aware of what was written in that infamous report from 28 May 1991 and signed by Prosecutor-General Trubin. And I agree completely. It was made from files I held in my own hands.

Sapozhnikova: *So you know the solution to the many secrets of* *that file, the same ones that have been spoken of for 25 years? Who was responsible for the death of Lieutenant Shatskikh? Why did the TV center defender Alvydas Kanapinskas get blown up? And was there a "third party" at the TV tower, talks of which are considered a dirty insinuation in Lithuania today?*

Petrauskas: I have been certain of these things for a long time: Shatskikh was shot from the crowd, he died by accident. He was the last one in the line and when he climbed through the window, the armored plate of his bulletproof vest bent. And at that very moment the shot was taken. It has not been established who was the one to take the shot.

It is also true that they later tried to hide the lieutenant's body. When he was brought to the morgue, the Alpha leader, Mikhail Golovatov, said "I will not leave here until we take the body of my brother in arms." So we started looking for it, but couldn't find it. We received information that it was taken to one hospital, but by the time we got there it was already taken to another. And then we finally found it... Only after that did the Alpha Group under Golovatov's command leave.

And concerning Kanapinskas. If the explosive was thrown at him by the soldiers, then the damage to his body would have been completely different. I assume he had the explosives near his underarm. And when the assault began, he was just careless.

Sapozhnikova: *Did the information of a "third party" at the events arrive at the prosecutions immediately?*

Petrauskas: There were many questions on this. And a group of investigators from Moscow examined the ill-fated shot multiple times – it was made from a Mosin-Nagant rifle, the round was different from the army-use ones. Would Alpha Group go into the assault with a Mosin-Nagant rifle? It is clear that this rifle was left over from the war and was brought out at the right moment. So a third party was definitely at play. As a military man, I was certain that it was planned and Gorbachev knew. Because responsibility for such an operation, with the KGB Spetsnaz flying in, relocation of the troops and using armored vehicles, is not a step the Defense Minister or KGB Chairman would take.

How Did You Save the Case Files?

Sapozhnikova: *I assume, you were at the top of Lithuania's most wanted list after the August coup?*

Petrauskas: They wanted to arrest me as soon as Yazov and Kryuchkov were apprehended in Moscow. A sizable group of prosecutors from all over the Union, headed by Yuli Lyubimov, was in Vilnius at the time to investigate the 13 January events. I came to my colleagues and said, "The events are unfolding in such a way that the situation in Lithuania will change." And they replied, "Oh don't scare us, we were in Fergana, Osh and Tbilisi, we know exactly how things will go!" and the next day they ran to me on their own, saying that we needed to evacuate the case files immediately. At the time, there was a ban on flights, not a single plane could take off, not even a military one. And you couldn't bring the files to Moscow in a tank... We arranged for a special communications car to arrive at the Prosecutor's Office, loaded the case files in and drove all 37 tomes to Moscow. It was in the morning, the Prosecutor's Office was surrounded by lunchtime. Then there was a special operation to get me out of the republic. I wouldn't want to talk about it today, because the people who helped me are still in Lithuania. I owe them my freedom and I hope that I will yet have the chance to thank them personally.

Sapozhnikova: *Did the KGB database leave Lithuania the same way? And was that the reason that the last acting KGB Chairman of the Lithuanian SSR, Stanislav Tsaplin, got in trouble later?*

Petrauskas: I have only the fondest memories of him, as a brave and decisive man. He did a lot for the country. It is no secret that there were agents all over Lithuania – people who had worked with the KGB for the longest time. And there was a database for all of them and when things got heated, Tsaplin took all of the measures to make sure it was shipped out of Lithuania. Can you believe what would have happened to those people if the Lithuanian side got hold of it? And when those files were taking off in a cargo plane from one of the military air bases, there were attempts at stopping it. From Tsaplin himself, I know that at one point he actually pulled out his weapon and said he would shoot everyone who tried to stop him from completing this task. And the plane took off. Later, Tsaplin was murdered in Moscow. The story was shady, no one knew who killed him or why...

And Why Did the Case Files Return to Lithuania?

Sapozhnikova: *You are not among those tried in absentia?*

Petrauskas: I have a different criminal case against me. They couldn't directly tie me to the assault in any way, because the Prosecution wasn't part of the executive branch.

But in September 1991, while I was in the hospital [officers go through a medical examination in order to determine their condition for further service – G.S.], my colleagues arrived and told me that Lithuanian policemen had arrived in Moscow to arrest me. I hurriedly signed out of the hospital. The guys from military prosecution wanted to hide me at someone's country house, but I said no, because I was living at a high security military town at the time and the Lithuanian police couldn't get there...

There was cause for alert. Remember the situation when Latvian policemen arrived in Russia and arrested the former Riga OMON commander, Sergey Parfenov, taking him off for his trial in Riga? There was a lot of buzz: why was a Russian citizen, who was merely doing his duty, sent to be tried by a foreign state? As it turns out later, it was all done with the blessing of the higher ups.

Sapozhnikova: *And how did the 37 tomes of the criminal case, the very same ones that you shipped to Russia, taking risks and thinking it a great feat, end up back in Lithuania?*

Petrauskas: After I was released from the hospital, I came to investigator Yuli Lyubimov and in his office I saw Juozas Gaudutis from the Lithuanian Prosecutor's Office. He was in charge of the 13 January events investigation from the Lithuanian side. The cases I started myself were almost photocopied. "We are transferring the case to the Lithuanian prosecution" explained Lyubimov. Who made that decision? "I don't know, but it was an order directly from Prosecutor-General Trubin." It turned out rather badly: people who supported the Soviet government, who thought that they were testifying to the USSR Prosecution, now had their testimonies handed to the Lithuanians. They started interrogating them and repressing them.

I don't know who gave the command to Trubin. I assume he was not the one to make the call. Because Nikolay would not just hand the case over like that...

***

BOGDAN SUSHCHIK,
Former Deputy Commander of the Self-propelled Artillery Division

Prosecutor-Style Vendetta

"This major who interrogated us, was a right kind of bastard," said Bogdan Sushchik, former Deputy Commander of the Self-propelled Artillery Division, who is now tried in absentia for participating in the 1991 events.

It would be more accurate to say though, 25 years later, he was being tried for giving as honest a testimony as he could, just like the rest. No one assumed that the new "democratic" Russian government would naively and magnanimously give the case files to Lithuania as a sign of eternal friendship, and that Lithuania would turn a blind eye to the accusations of their own testimonies. So Bogdan was reading the indictment act, which contained his words from 25 years ago, twisted in a Jesuit interpretation: "F group of soldiers under the command of B. Sushchik, failing to find the internal corridor and fulfilling an order during a military attack... shot civilians inside and outside the building... the soldiers in question used flashbangs, along with live rounds, as well as close quarters combat – pushing, punching with their fists, feet, an undefined number of strikes to civilians in different parts of their bodies with weapons and other tools for causing bodily harm." Wow!

Bogdan remembered the events of that night well. He would like to forget, but they wouldn't let him.

Sushchik: We were called up a few times, we got into our cars, but then immediately after, we would get the cancellation order, because someone up top couldn't make the decision to go or not. We finally set out. As a deceptive move, we drove around Vilnius for a while, so they couldn't guess where we were headed. It was already dark, January – but many people were standing on the sides of the road and clenching their fists in a Rot-Front gesture, I could swear that on my cross...

The guys from Alpha were behind us, they didn't know our route, just the final destination. But the traffic light cut them off from us – because you see, they were following the traffic laws, resulting in them arriving early and not with us. Maybe that is why they lost one of their guys, because they began their mission without waiting for us, although we were supposed to do everything together. The TV and Radio Committee workers walked out with their hands on their heads. The Alpha guys said, "Lower your hands, you are not under arrest, you just need to go home." And they still walked like we took them prisoner, to make a show.

Sapozhnikova: *Were you questioned in Vilnius?*

Sushchik: No, back in Pskov, about a month after the events. I asked my good squadron commander, Ivan Komarov, on what to say. He told me to say the truth, so I told them the truth. The major who questioned me had a Baltic name, but spoke without even the hint of an accent.

Sapozhnikova: *How did you find out you were on the Lithuanian wanted list?*

Sushchik: I received two letters to my home address. The first notified me that there was a criminal case started against me and the second was a summons: as in, come to Lithuania, the all-European arrest warrant will be suspended for the trial. Well of course I didn't go... I took note of the shining example of retired colonel Yuri Mel getting two years in a Lithuanian prison.

We got state awards for that operation. And when, by officer tradition, we were celebrating it with a drink, my commander told me, "There will be time when we will be ashamed to say what it was exactly that got us these medals." It happened just as he said.

End of the World

At first glance, the list of people tried in Vilnius was put together haphazardly, as if the Lithuanian investigators hastily copied the names from scraps of paper: former Defense Minister and USSR Marshal Dmitry Yazov was right next to regular lieutenants, who were merely guilty of the fact that their commanders followed the orders of some "democrat" in the mad 1991 and obediently handed in the lists of those who were sent into that ill-fated mission. The list of potential defendants is constantly reshuffled, becoming longer or shorter at the whim of the magicians at the Lithuanian Prosecutor's office, pulling names out of their sleeves whenever the wind blows differently.

It isn't even surprising that after official recognition of independence they felt at home in Russia, which fit in well into the national psychology: considering themselves separated, but not shying away from energy resources from Moscow. Considering themselves foreigners, but demanding that all doors be open before them, as if they were in a country of their own.

For example, a November 1991 interview to the *Izvestia* newspaper by Lithuanian prosecutor Jouzas Gaudutis, who headed the group of Lithuanian investigators in Moscow, read as follows:

> The main goal of the group that has been working in Moscow for over three weeks now is to uncover the so-called Moscow trace, determine the extent of the January coup's main organizers in Vilnius.
>
> The Russian and Union prosecutor's offices had built up a good line of communication and mutual help, as is common for professionals. But concerning other "interested" organizations and agencies, that is where the problems showed themselves. As strange as it was, among the three of the strongest agencies – the KGB, Interior Ministry and USSR Defense Ministry – the KGB turned out to be the most open. And thanks to Bakatin's help and his first deputy Oleinikov.
>
> It was most difficult to establish a contact with representatives of the USSR Defense Ministry, which has no small number of people who are responsible for the state coup in Lithuania in one way or another. We approached HQ chief Lobov with a request to question many of the Vilnius events participants, however we received no specific answers.

"We couldn't interrogate general Achalov, nor Alpha," laments Gaudutis. "However we managed to interrogate former KGB USSR Deputy Filipp Bobkob," he gloats... Probably not without the help of Vadim Bakatin, who took that position of KGB Chairman after Kryuchkov's arrest. You can definitely feel that the level of trust between Bakatin and the Lithuanian prosecutors was so high, that Gaudutis casually shares his plans with them: the newly-assigned KGB Chairman promised to help the Lithuanian in apprehending the Communist Party Central Committee Secretary, Mykolas Burokevičius...

But the "cherry on top" personally was not in that, but in a document detailing the extraction of physical evidence from Dmitry Yazov, a report of which was also attached to the file: "Examination was carried out in a service office on building №8/4 on Kuybysheva street, city of Moscow. Signed – investigator S. Valaytis."

Just think about it: an investigator from a country that had considered itself independent for 18 months now! With the approval and knowledge of the Russian government of the time! He did a search of an office of the Marshall and Defense Minister of Russia, a foreign country! It was truly the end of the world...

A One-Sided Game

I have looked for the copies of those ill-fated 37 missing tomes everywhere... The Russian Federation Prosecutor's Office, the Investigation Committee, the State Archive – everyone just raised their hands in dismay. Any trace of the criminal case on the Vilnius events of 13 January 1991 in Russia were gone. Important case investigator Lyubimov, who led the group and made the copies, is long dead. History's last USSR Prosecutor-General, Nikolay Trubin, could have shed some light on this mystery, but in his own words, he has been retired from public life for 24 years now and doesn't give interviews. I managed to talk to him on the phone for just one minute, during which he said two very important phrases. The first, "The report from 28 May 1991 signed by me, may be quoted. It is all truth." It would be prudent to repeat what it said: "The prosecutors have not provided any evidence that confirms the death and wounding of the deceased specifically from the actions of the military and the actual circumstances of the events were concealed... Multiple testimonies show that the majority of the deaths at the TV Center building were in actuality caused not by fire from the military or the tanks running over them, but from the fire dealt by the militias themselves and civilian cars running over and other causes not tied to this incident."

The second phrase by Trubin was roughly like this, "I don't know how the criminal files ended up in Lithuania. I didn't hand them over."

That makes it all the more surprising to later read the Agreement of Mutual Assistance between the USSR Prosecutor's Office and the Lithuanian Republic Prosecutor-General's Office that was signed by him on 26 September 1991, where it blatantly said that, "The USSR Prosecutor's Office completely transfers the case file № 18/5918-91 to the Lithuanian Republic Prosecutor-General's Office. The file consists of 37 tomes, the materials are bound, numbered and catalogued. As per catalogue, along with the file, physical evidence, video and audio cassettes are transferred. The Lithuanian Republic Prosecutor-General's Office takes the responsibility for consolidating the transferred files of case file № 18/5918-91 with the materials of the criminal case file in its possession concerning the same criminal events and to continue the thorough, objective and complete investigation and report those results to the USSR Prosecutor's Office. The Prosecutor-General of the Lithuanian Republic takes responsibility for protecting the citizens from persecution for the contents of their testimonies gathered by the USSR Prosecutor's Office on the transferred case as witnesses and not participating in the detailed events. And the USSR Prosecutor's Office takes responsibility to provide legal assistance to the Lithuanian Republic Prosecutor-General's Office in further investigation of this case."

This document is signed by Artūras Paulauskas on the Lithuanian side, the very same prosecutor who, 25 years ago, addressed the participants of those events calling them to not give testimonies to the Lithuanian SSR Prosecutor's Office under any circumstances. And in Spring 2016, as president of the State Security and Defense Committee of the Lithuanian Seimas, declared that the main threat to Lithuania comes not from Islamic terrorism, but from "states who are unfriendly to us and are all around us", meaning Belarus and Russia.

The promise not to persecute citizens for giving testimonies was ignored by the Lithuanian prosecutors, who were chasing down the witnesses of the unknown snipers shooting from the roofs even after 20 years. The treachery of the situation is that the witnesses testified to the Soviet prosecutors with all of the honesty and trust that they wouldn't accord to their own. And the Lithuanians were the ones using it now.

However, one point of that Agreement, the one that said "The USSR Prosecutor's Office and its successor, the Prosecutor's Office of Russia, shall help the Lithuanian Republic in the investigation by all means" was reinstated two-fold. The childish hyper-inflated honor and decency of The Russian Federation is truly surprising: in those years when Lithuanian president Dalia Grybauskaitė called Russia a "terrorist state", the Russian judges kept inviting former OMON officers and troopers to submit to interrogations at Lithuania's behest. The more stubborn ones received court summons as late as March 2015! And another surprising fact: the list of people that Lithuania wants to try in absentia, has their exact home addresses written down. It would be impossible to get them without Russian assistance. It turns out we provided Lithuania with legal aid in organizing a trial against ourselves...

It would be extremely easy to just blame it all on Trubin now. But the people who know him said that he was a man of the old ways; it is unlikely that he could have given the order to the military to give the case files and list of operation participants. Unless someone pressed him into it. But who? Gorbachev? Yeltsin? It no longer matters.

The most important thing is something else: how Lithuania used those files.

In 1991, the file had 37 tomes. In the following 25 years of intensive "writer-investigative" work they get 19 times larger – into 700 tomes.

The Cases Go On, the Office Keeps Writing...

The Lithuanian prosecution didn't make tracks just in Russia, but also in Belarus, where it acted with even more arrogance, completely ignoring borders. After the extradition of the old Lithuanian communists, the Belarussian State Secretary on Combating Crime and National Defense, G.I. Danilov, was forced to write a report note to President of the Minister Council of the Republic of Belarus V.F. Kebich, saying:

> ...An illegal practice is now in place, where representatives of neighboring states, without the proper approval of the relevant agencies nor filling out the required documentation, arrived at our territory and in violation of the acting laws conducted operative and investigative actions. In many cases the officers of the Republic's Interior Ministry assisted them in any way they could. Thusly, 8 November 1991, the officers of a police station of the Polotsk City Executive Committee apprehended A.R. Smotkin in Polotsk, following a spoken order from Interior Minister V.D. Yegorov, with Smotkin later handed over to representatives of the Lithuanian criminal police to be taken to the Lithuanian Republic.
>
> In 1993, officers of the Lithuanian police inspected cars in the Ashmyany district on numerous occasions... Armed with their service weapons, the group of Lithuanians, counting 8 people, has undertaken numerous investigative actions in the Iwye and Ashmyany districts. They have conducted searches at the home of citizen V.I. Idiatova and citizen V.M.Makarsky. The latter of whiom was beaten, handcuffed and threatened with the use of firearms. Also in 1993, Belarussian citizen P.E. Ermolaev was taken to Lithuanian territory where he was forced to spend 72 hours at the police station.
>
> Judging by the actions of the Lithuanian side, it was well-informed of Burokevičius and Jermalavičius' arrival in Minsk, knew where they were in the city. This points to the fact that Lithuania secret services were tracking them.

...At least now we know where the Lithuanians got their brutal image: Lithuanian bandits brought their traditions to Europe, where around a third of Lithuania's population emigrated over the last 10 years. Lithuanians participate in car theft, robbery, beatings, racketeering – what haven't they done in Ireland and Britain?[1] Crime in Lithuania itself was at a record high during those years. Eye-witness accounts say that prisons were filled to the brim with corrupt customs officers, drug addicts, soldiers and killers, and cells fit to house four people had around sixteen in them. And who should fight crime if prosecutor Paulauskas is completely devoted to his own vendetta? He personally traveled to Russia and Belarus in hopes of catching some wayward Lithuanian communist and wrote letters non-stop, demanding the extradition of his former colleague – head of the "anti-government organization" LSSR Prosecutor's Office, Antanas Petrauskas, with whom he exchanged pleasantries when they sat in the same building.

Deciding a reason for indictment for a professional lawyer is a rather tricky task. So, choking on the lack of creativity, do you know what they finally decided to accuse Petrauskas of? Of committing the grave crime of taking over the Prosecution building... Paulauskas wrote everywhere, to Russia and to Poland, but all for nothing. "Former Lithuanian SSR Prosecutor A.V. Petrauskas is a Russian citizen and can't be handed over to a foreign state," replied the Russian prosecution. And Poland ignored his inquiries altogether.

The Great Confrontation

Because former prosecutor Antanas Petrauskas was unreachable, they decided to hang it all on his deputy, Nikolay Krempovsky.

And I would like to laugh at the case that was started against him ("Gave directions to USSR Interior Ministry soldiers to not allow the workers into the Lithuanian Republic Prosecutor-General Office building, which was taken over and under the protection of the armed forces of a different state – USSR, which hindered normal work and necessitated doing the required work in the Prosecutor's Office on weekends and after 6 pm") but I can't.

These are not jokes, because we are dealing with a police state in its most merciless Bolshevik-like variant: Krempovsky was arrested, set in a pre-trial cell along with the leader, Yedinstvo Valery Ivanov. In one of the prison corridors he met political prisoner Alexander Smotkin, who was quite beaten up. Krempovsky complained about his heart. Ultimately he got five years for "not letting them work on weekends". While under travel restrictions, he went to Belarus to look for work, the borders weren't well protected. But what could he expect from the local Prosecutor-General Vasiliy Shelodonov who, around the same time, handed over the elderly communists to Lithuania earlier? Shelodonov in turn told Lithuania that Krempovsky violated the travel restrictions.

Russia doesn't have anything to be proud of in this story either, although Prosecutor-General Nikolay Trubin tried to help his former subordinate and gave Krempovsky work in the Prosecutor's Office. He lived in a hotel, with his family remaining in Vilnius, there was no chance of getting a home, but that was not the main thing. Here is what was told to me by his best friend and office colleague, police lieutenant-colonel and Deputy President of the Control Commission of the Central Committee of the CPL on CPSU Platform, police colonel Voldemar Nosov. "They came for them from the Lithuanian embassy, with weapons. A small semi-legal country, whose independence was declared in violation of the laws of the time, DARED to arrive at the PROSECUTOR-GENERAL OFFICE of a different state with weapons in order to arrest an acting officer of that state agency. No one, not a single person warned him of this... Kolya accidentally left by the other exit. He was a highly professional lawyer and decided to return to Lithuania saying, 'We didn't do anything, it was them and not us, who broke the law!' I tried talking him out of it."

Soon after his return from Moscow he was arrested and spent three months in prison, he got out with traveling restrictions and went to look for work in Belarus. You know the rest: upon his return Nikolay Krempovsky was to be locked up again. He was waiting for them to come for him. He was worried. Nervous. And before another arrest happened, he died at dinner at his relatives. He was only 50. That is how the story of two Prosecutor's Offices' confrontations came to an end.

Accountable For Everything

Vilnius has a museum to address something that never happened in history – a museum of the Lithuanian people's genocide. Meaning that it is a museum with evidence of how bad it was for the Lithuanians under Soviet rule.

The neighboring Latvia and Estonia were a little wiser, calling their museums "occupation museums", which is also something that didn't happen, but the use of that term ("a state's armed forces occupying a territory that doesn't belong to it") has fewer mistakes, unlike the Lithuanians using the term "genocide" (actions committed with the intent to destroy a national, ethnic, racial or culturally-ethnic group").

The Museum of Genocide is located in the very center of Vilnius, in a building of a former KGB prison. Among the many portraits adorning the walls, there is a stand with photos of those, who, according to the organizers' plan, are responsible for this "genocide." Specifically NKVD and KGB leaders for the over 50 years during which Lithuania was part of the Soviet Union. The last one in this line is General-Major Stanislav Tsaplin, who was acting Lithuania SSR KGB Chairman until late August 1991.

There probably isn't another man in all of Lithuania, who has so many legends told about him even 25 years later.

Formally, he was the Deputy Chairman of the Lithuanian KGB. In actuality, he was the one in charge, because the top brass, his direct superiors, all folded at the most dire of moments. So why did Tsaplin remain? In an interview to the *Izvestia* newspaper given in October 1991, he answered that question like this, "Because it would look like desertion."

The newspapers tried to make him out as Lithuanian Pinochet. Well that was absolute nonsense!

"I was never a Lithuanian Pinochet at least because the events were controlled by people at such a level that they would not even waste their time on me. If someone did have special roles in that story, then the Lithuanian KGB, where I wasn't the first person actually, only had a secondary function," he said.

"Have you ever tried finding out who fired those shots near the TV tower, why there were casualties?" the *Izvestia* journalist tried to get him for an honest talk.

"In the Republic, we were banned from doing any investigative measures – conducting interrogations and the like. Only gathering operative data. We later helped the Union Prosecutor's Office, when they arrived in Lithuania: they weren't shown the bullets and weren't allowed to inspect the bodies, and that is the most important part. Well, we gathered the witnesses, found recordings of the combat vehicle communications, some video recordings. We gave it all to them. The ultimate conclusions are up to the investigation."

But Tsaplin was called to answer for something he didn't participate in, in full force, not even considering what committee he was from.

"Tsaplin came to Moscow from Vilnius, waiting for them to decide his fate. The new KGB leadership still hasn't made up their minds on him: it is conducting an internal investigation, trying to figure out the connection of committee members to the January events in Vilnius. In addition to that, Stanslav Tsaplin will be questioned by investigators from the Lithuanian Prosecutor Office, who are currently in Moscow," the journalist adds in order to give the readers a happy ending.

...It was a time of uncertainty. The country went from fire to ice: a man could feel like a king for smuggling secret documents out of the country and saving people or a crushed pawn when faced with the fact that in his own homeland, he will be interrogated by his ideological enemy. And the interrogation is sanctioned by no one other than his new boss, the USSR KGB Chairman Vadim Bakatin...

Ambush

What awaited Tsaplin upon his return to Moscow? A life in a two-room apartment with the family of his younger daughter. For a long time he didn't have it in him to ask for a bigger living space. Friends would come and exclaim, "My God, I can't believe this is where a general lives. Even our lieutenants don't live in apartments like this…"

Tsaplin would call his acquaintances from dawn till dusk, asking them to hire people from Lithuania. The bills for international calls would be huge. One time he told his family that he needed to disappear immediately and his friends had a safe house set up for him. Did he feel he was hunted? "His Lithuanian friends told him about the plans to take him to Lithuania and have him on trial there. Mom told me that there was an ambush for our father in the apartment building. And he didn't come home or call for a few weeks," his daughter recalled.

No apartment, no glory, no pension – only running on the rickety boards of an old bridge between the previous life and the new one. And then that run stopped in the middle of the way…

On 3 January 1995, General Major Tsaplin was found dead on the thawing ice of river Moscow, at the very middle. The official story is that he died of heart failure. The unofficial one is that he was murdered.

Everyone was shaken, but in different ways. Someone breathed a sigh of relief in Vilnius. Maybe that "someone" sighed in relief in Moscow as well – Tsaplin knew a lot of things. Actually a lot – enough to connect the dots from weapons smuggling to drugs, from Lithuania to Chechnya.

"His death was shocking to me. I was in prison when the Lithuanians mockingly threw me the paper and hissed that Tsaplin was knocked off by the Russians themselves," said political prisoner Alexander Smotkin years later.

In Moscow, they actually suspected the Lithuanian trace. Were there any grounds for that?

"I would be happy if it were the Lithuanian special forces.

We would have something to be proud of. But I don't know who in Lithuania was capable of such stellar feats," said the "gray" cardinal of Lithuania, Audrius Butkevičius, in his cynical manner.

Why did Tsaplin even agree to go to Lithuania right before the Singing Revolution? He told his family that, "I agreed to the most difficult republic, two or three men refused to go there before me, but I said yes." His eldest daughter Rita came over for her mother's birthday in December, mere weeks before the January events. He told her in a sad voice, "They burned a scarecrow in a Soviet soldier uniform. There is terrible anti-Soviet propaganda on TV. The situation is getting worse. Something is going to happen."...

"Early Summer of 1991, he was a guest in my house," recalls the former editor of the *Tarybų Lietuva* newspaper, Stanislava Juonienė. "I have never seen such despair in someone's face. He had just returned from a KGB meeting in Moscow, where he made a report on the situation in Lithuania. And no one, not even Kryuchkov, paid any attention to it! And Stanislav Tsaplin didn't expect such indifference. He was utterly perplexed."...

Aside from Butkevičius, none of my speakers had anything bad to say about Tsaplin. Everyone remembered one thing – how he suffered from not being able to stop a wheel that was already going downhill at full force, knocking all the country down on its way.

From Stanslav Tsaplin's eldest daughter, Margarita:

> I will start from the end. 30 December 1994 I met with my father for the last time. He and my mom came to visit me in Petrozavodsk and we were going to celebrate New Year together, when he suddenly started packing for Moscow. We were used to not asking any questions: if dad said he needed to, then he really needed to. I stood on the train station and waved at the departing train. It is a real holiday only with dad – a warm, happy,

sparkling one. Only next to dad do you feel some unexplained happiness, even if he is busy, silent or angry. Then the train suddenly stopped. Then it started moving and then stopped again. And stood there for a while. We saw each other off many times, but this never happened before, especially not with our trusty Karelia train. And then it started moving again...and stopped again! We started laughing and showing in signs: well the train doesn't want to take dad to Moscow! If only I knew...

If only I knew that four days later I would be standing on the same train station. I would be going to bury my dad.

What attracted people to dad? Probably his unbelievable charm, but more importantly – his unbelievable integrity. I don't know of any of my dad's dishonest actions. He never let anyone down, never refused to help those in need. It was calm and secure around him. And he attracted like-minded dependable and honest people. His integrity also was in how he never sought to gain anything for himself: privileges, ranks, more cozy places to serve. He was put off by the idea itself – to seek a cozier place and have an easy life.

When the hard times started in Lithuania, my dad did everything in his power to help his men. I don't know a lot, but I know two things for sure: my dad managed to evacuate the KGB archives from a surrounded building, those archives contained the fates of people. And second: he helped set up everything for one of his coworkers, who had to leave Lithuania after the 1991 events. Sitting at home on a couch he was making phone calls into cities of the former Soviet Union from dawn to dusk, arranging for housing and work for them, while he himself was out of work and branded a Lithuanian Pinochet.

Things were getting bleak for my father, and friends suggested he hide and sit it out, even found a few safe spots, but dad refused. He was never a coward and didn't feel like he was guilty of something, he was just following orders. He probably just didn't expect that he and many others would be betrayed, and at such a high level. I think he sensed how it would all end, but chose not to hide. It may seem like he was tired of it all and feeling the hopelessness of the situation, he went to face his fate.

Tsaplin's younger daughter, Viktoria:

Mom thought that dad was called to meet one of his subordinates from Lithuania, with a Lithuanian name, she even names the specific person, who called him all day 2 January and tried to get him out of the house all day. And he finally did! But dad's friends said no, of course not, it couldn't be him...

Dad went to the meeting and didn't come back. I know that he went to check on a colleague in the hospital, but that is where the trail goes cold. I get the impression that he was being watched: a car stopped, he was pulled in and they drove off. He was found somewhere behind the park on the ice of the Moscow river, near the ice hole. That place has very desolate, I doubt people just wandered there.

We were told that heart failure was the cause of death. We had a medical report saying he fell from the shore and hit the ice. How could he have rolled off and rolled unto the middle of the lake through all of those bushes and trees? He had a black bruise all over his forehead. And he was wet. An open briefcase was lying next to him. But all of the documents and money were there. He was 58.

Mom was called in for interrogation a few times, but she felt like the case was getting played down and his death was going to be presented as by natural causes. There was a huge number of people at the funeral, I thought to myself – could he really have known so many people? There were at least a few Lithuanians. I saw him in a new light at the funeral. I thought, "My God, turns out I had such a great dad...

Igor, close friend of the family:

Stanislav's wife Zoya called and said I needed to come and identify the body. So I went. Turns out it was really him. And the body definitely had signs of dragging. So he went to a meeting, sent off the agent escorting him, saying he was meeting someone close to him and disappeared afterwards... Someone brought him to the river, pushed him over and dragged him onto the ice. To get to where he was, you would have to go over the edge and walk around 15 meters from the shore. It is not like it was the style of secret services, but... It was disguised as if he accidentally fell. Probably counting on him being under the ice by morning.

Maybe he suspected someone of betrayal or being a double agent back then. Because he frequently said that he trusted only himself and his family.

It was 9 or 40 days[2] after his death, when

his daughter Vika found a message on the apartment's door handle; letters patched together from newspaper clippings spelled the words: "Accountable for everything."

Did he have a loser syndrome upon returning from Lithuania?

Rather a feeling of loss from the country falling apart. He was very worried that they, KGB officers, couldn't do anything to keep it together. He was amazed: how could you hand everything over like that, when you are a leader of a great country? Frequently he asked himself, "How come, when those fellows gathered in Białowieża Forest, Gorbachev didn't call it a conspiracy? It would have been easy: a force would move in, the guys would be arrested and asked, what is it they have written there? How could they divide the Union amongst themselves like that?

But no one did that.

He had his own war, he helped his former subordinates stay afloat and dragged them out from the very lowest of them – from warrant officers, operative workers and tech operatives. He was constantly on the phone and calling everyone. That is why I say that he was a true General – he didn't leave anyone behind.

But he couldn't help those who remained in Lithuania...

***

ALEXANDER OSIPOV
Former Lithuanian KGB Analyst

"We Are Anti-heroes to the Current Lithuania"

We met a few years ago in Vilnius.

This didn't demand anything – Osipov just wanted someone to hear him out. I agreed, because by that time, thank God, I lost the Baltic habit of running way in terror from the "exes."

The letters he asked I deliver to Moscow made me want to cry. It was sad to read them and shameful not to read them. The letters concerned what happened to ex-agents of the Lithuanian SSR KGB after the Soviet Union ceased its existence on their territory. And here is what happened:

> The shutdown of the Lithuanian SSR KGB ended with the firing of several hundred military men without retirement funds.
>
> After the local government passed the law "On Liquidating or Suspending the Cover Activity of Secret Services of Foreign States" the situation got a whole lot worse. Former KGB workers received a 10 year ban from working in any state agencies, banks, administration agencies, strategic sites, in educational facilities, transport companies, security firms, because all companies employing an ex-KGB worker are viewed as cover organizations of foreign states...
>
> Working in private firms also meant letting the employer know about any previous work in the KGB. This firm or company would then be viewed as a possible cover company for foreign (i.e. Russian) special service for 10 years. There were times when someone ex-KGB would open up a business and their company would immediately be on secret service checklists, a cycle of permanent revisions, a set of agent, operative and technical measures for 10 years.
>
> The adoption of the 2001 "On Lustration" law, as well as Lithuania joining NATO, with all of the added hysteria around former KGB agents,

made life completely unbearable. Many of us live below the poverty line and lead a pitiful existence, surviving on odd jobs and help from relatives.

The majority of our former colleagues remained loyal to the pledge they once made, despite the strong pressure, blackmail and threats. There are those among us, who worked more than 10 years and those who fulfilled their international duty in Afghanistan, but didn't quite make it to retirement – we were all in an equally critical position for all of our lives. According to the Lithuanian laws, our military service did not count as any kind of work, so we can't apply even for the minimal pension.

I was ashamed of the answers that came to the authors of these letters from Moscow ("There are no legal grounds for granting your request"), so I decided to ask my speaker about his life. The business trip was coming to an end, the main interviews were recorded, I wanted to compare notes of my findings with the views of a KGB analyst, who would have been professionally addressing these events as they occurred, and by how he spoke, I could tell that he was exceptionally smart; fools didn't make it into Soviet counter-intelligence. His name was Alexander Osipov.

"It Has Been Decided to Give Up the Baltics"

Sapozhnikova: *So, the ex-KGB weren't even offered a chance to help in the construction of this new Lithuanian state, with all of your experience, minds and other achievements?*

Osipov: Of course not. We, as well as the organization itself, were demonized and presented as hell spawn; we are antiheroes to the current Lithuania. Lithuania has over ten laws and other legislative acts which stop us from having a normal life. The situation has not changed one bit over the past 20 years. Moreover, the persecution of former KGB workers is becoming more and more devious. These Jesuit laws completely break any person, even cover people who just finished the KGB Higher School and served only for a few months.

Sapozhnikova: *What is in that blue folder that you brought with you?*

Osipov: Copies of documents form 1991 which were signed by the new Lithuanian government and the USSR KGB leadership, guaranteeing social protection to all former officers, their requalification, job arrangements for them and their families. Out of everything written there, nothing was done. The European Union has specific lustration regulated by law in 11 states, but only Lithuania has these kind of laws aimed directly at staff of the secret services. For example, there is a law where years of work in the KGB are not counted towards retirement, so people don't get pensions when they reach the needed age. What are they guilty of? What are the people who never committed treason and instead remained loyal to the end now guilty of? Why must they suffer?

Sapozhnikova: *Did you try going to court with this?*

Osipov: Of course, the European Court of Human Rights decided in favor of the former KGB workers, but Lithuania is in no hurry to follow through with that decision. Out of the three cases won in European courts, not one is realized.

Sapozhnikova: *Returning to 1991. What signs told you that something grand was going to happen in Vilnius?*

Osipov: The situation was so intense, that it could have ignited in any place. The biggest chaos and pressure came from the protests, which had around 100-200 thousand people. The second instrument was television, which was methodically hammering the point home daily. The new government of independent Lithuania needed just a bit more to tip the scales in their favor. In order to finally unite the Lithuanian people, they needed a little blood. And that blooded needed to be spilled. Which was done rather successfully.

Sapozhnikova: *Did you know about the various foreign specialists and political strategists, like Gene Sharp coming in? Did you track their movements?*

Osipov: Naturally. All of the information was sent to Moscow on a daily basis. Moscow made no decision. Even when we uncovered genuine traitors and treason, when we reported to Moscow, saying that it is necessary to take action, they would just recommend we fire them. And only that.

Sapozhnikova: *Did you understand that the foreign emissaries came to Lithuania for a reason?*

Osipov: We received enough information and had our guesses that all of this didn't happen without outside influence. But it was ultimately made clear in Summer 1989. During one of my assignments to Moscow, after I reported on the situation, one of the KGB leaders told me during a private conversation that we were doing great, but that we should be careful and work in a way where our work wouldn't hurt us. I was surprised and asked him what was the matter. Then he told me that it has been decided to give up the Baltics. All of the events were decided, so all of our work consisted exclusively of observing the situation. And when they say that the Lithuanian SSR KGB directly participated in the January events, that is blatantly untrue.

The Foreign Observers

Sapozhnikova: *How did such a number of foreign journalists end up at the right place and the right time on 13 January 1991?*

Osipov: Representatives of Western media were called in by the new Lithuanian government. There were there for 3-4 days at that point. We noted the mass arrival of a huge amount of press and assumed that something was about to happen. At any moment, because getting 100 thousand people unto the streets and provoking a fight with the Yedinstvo supporters or Burokevičius's communist party would be easy for a professional. And they made an even bigger provocation. With blood.

Sapozhnikova: *Do you have a solid understanding of what actually happened in January 1991?*

Osipov: From the numerous testimonies of the people who were near the TV tower and TV center during those days, the picture is fairly clear. There a dozens of witness testimonies on how they shot from above and the roofs, because it really happened. Are you asking whether we knew that some actions were planned from military? When Alpha arrived, we found out 24 hours before the event. I could feel that something was going to happen. I was particularly unsettled by one conversation.

Before going home, I went to Deputy Chairman Stanislav Tsaplin and he said, "The military are planning something, try not to go anywhere today, and it would be even better if you had witnesses watching you." I went home and made phone calls up until later evening from the house telephone, and woke at the early morning due to the noise, the city was already abuzz. This was around 6 am, I packed my stuff and went to work. All of the Operational HQ found themselves in a situation like this.

Lithuania Needs Heroes

Sapozhnikova: *It wouldn't be difficult for a professional like Tsaplin to guess what the military was planning. But tell me, how did the armed thugs who shot from the roof manage to play into the situation with such surgical precision?*

Osipov: I think only Audrius Butkevičius can answer that question. He knows all of the truth. But we can assume that he had his own sources of intel. And they weren't hiding the fact that they were well informed about the events. This was even in the newspapers: one of the former KGB agents went to the new agency, spoke very openly that he had sources in the military, who reported about the upcoming events. The opposing side found out what was planned and joined the game.

Sapozhnikova: *Butkevičius tried to convince me that Russian nationalists could have been shooting from the rooftops.*

Osipov: I am personally well acquainted with Butkevičius, so I can tell you that he was being dodgy with you. He himself told me that the shooters were former border guards from Alytus, 18 people. And actually during the award ceremony for the heroes of the January events, the defenders of Lithuanian independence, people who truly did the deed and provoked the events were not in the awards list. And they voiced their protest, asking why they were not awarded? [It is also mentioned in Petkevičius' book *Durnių Laivas*, that this delegation came to complain to him as the Seimas Security Committee – G.S.]. Then their main representative was brought before the Seimas' stern glare and told that if he ever dares to even mention that he participated in those events, then his career will be over. Maybe also his life. So it makes sense that they run away from journalists today.

Sapozhnikova: *But if everyone knew everything from the start, why did the people just swallow the lies about those killed by the tower? Why was it not possible to protect Alpha and the army?*

Osipov: No one held their silence. There were even expert reports, statements, the final document signed by Prosecutor-General Trubin wrote it all up – who died and how. No one was hiding anything. However, this situation was made into a cult in Lithuania. Lithuania needed heroes and there was nothing heroic in that event. But the myth was built and they had to support it. And the ideology of the current Lithuanian government hinges on it. You can't bust this myth, because it is a base, without which it will all fall apart. There is no investigation – because it is not beneficial to the Lithuanian government.

Sapozhnikova: *But this can't last forever?*

Osipov: Of course not. But 20 years is not a long time for history. It may take another 20 years, but this case will be investigated in due time, because the situation is far too obvious. But the Lithuanian government still denies the obvious.

The Housing Problem

Sapozhnikova: *Why would Butkevičius tell you about how he put his shooters on the roofs?*

Osipov: That is a whole different story. One time he asked me to testify against Landsbergis, saying that Landsbergis was working for the secret services[3] at the time.

Sapozhnikova: *Was he?*

Osipov: Yes, it is a secret to no one. At the time Butkevičius had a conflict with Landsbergis[4] and he requested my help in investigating the situation. I said I would help with it, because I knew the exact worker, who kept in touch with Landsbergis and can personally confirm that Landsbergis' file is in the auxiliary database. I told this to the commission, which investigated the case. My testimonies are registered, but… The score was 0:0, we couldn't prove that Landsbergis was an agent without his signed agreement to cooperate, so the court just admitted that we slandered him. We parted ways, each with our own interest.

Sapozhnikova: *Is that true that Tsaplin's Vilnius apartment was taken by Butkevičius after he left?*

Osipov: It is true. As soon as the furniture was shipped out, Butkevičius moved in immediately. Tsaplin left on the second day after the events. He didn't run away – there was a warning that there will be repressive measures against him by the Lithuanian government, and it was recommended that he leave Lithuania before that happened. Which he did. And concerning his death, which is still not solved, it is a tragedy not just for his family, but also for me, because he was a friend to me.

Sapozhnikova: *Did his death seem "timely" and strange to you as well?*

Osipov: It is not proven that the Lithuanian secret services had any connection to Tsaplin's death. But if you ask who profited the most from it, then it is obviously the Lithuanian side, because he did a lot to help former KGB workers. He was getting them employed in Russia's territorial agencies, and participated in the fate of these men. He had a remarkable set of information, an Lithuanian archive, which had a lot of documents, which were waiting for their time to be published. In that sense, Tsaplin's death was beneficial to specific circles in Lithuania. But I don't have any proof. The lack of the investigation's results means that this wasn't some common crime. Too many inconsistencies in the case. It is hard to believe that he went to a meeting in the part zone alone, and then walked down, fell and hit himself. He was a smart and careful man. The Lithuanian secret service actually went to "hunt" him over in Russia and Belarus, but we shouldn't demonize them. They still have almost no professionals there to this day.

The Myth Goes On

Sapozhnikova:- *After so many years, have you found the answer to the question of what actually happened to our country in 1991?*
Osipov: We talked about this with Tsaplin, when we were both already out of the KGB, and we came to pretty much the same

conclusions – that there was a betrayal from Gorbachev's side, and we couldn't have changed anything in that situation. However, up to this day, we are frequently blamed for being bad at our job and not preserving the Soviet Union. But if we are guilty of something, then it is for Kryuchkov lacking the courage to arrest Gorbachev and put him on trial.

Sooner or later the reevaluation will happen. But we can't expect anything new while people still live in this myth and they even have bonuses like monthly payments for the participants and heroes of those events. Today, there is a whole class of people in Lithuania, who are considered heroes of the homeland, even though they did nothing. The list of heroes grows with each month, the myth goes on. And to deny it now would mean denying a few thousand people the benefits they have today. Personal pensions and land rights, which were given to the heroes of the January events and protectors of Lithuania's independence would have to return all of that back to the state as an unlawfully received reward. That is why the myth doesn't go away.

Sapozhnikova: *What is the level of fear in the people of Lithuania today? The state continues to persecute those who hold views contradicting the official version?*

Osipov: Even the people who testified in court on what they saw during the January events, that they saw shooters from above, have expressed fear for their future in some way or another. The other dozens of people, including some I know personally, refused to testify in court, fearing persecution. Lithuania, by all accounts, is one of the most unsuccessful states of the European Union. While from outside it may seem like everything is stable, the actual situation is disastrous. The government today outright lies about how the people live wonderfully, that the situation gets better every day. This is not how it is. But the people don't go into the streets to fight for their rights, because they are scared of losing what little they do have.

* * *

Ironically, after talking with Osipov, I was going to meet Audrius Butkevičius. And I suddenly got an idea.

"Can I ask for advice? What question should I ask him in order to rattle him up?" I asked him

Osipov replied, without much thought, "Ask him what he will do, if those 18 border guards suddenly start talking?"

And I did just that.

The reaction was fantastic: the smart and sly Audrius Butkevičius, with whom I have had an endlessly interesting conversation before this, suddenly became aroused. He said I was engaged in nonsense. That I was playing the games of the old communists. Playing political games and insulting the deceased. He even banned me from working as a journalist for a while.

It was a shame to lose friendly relations with an undoubtedly smart, albeit treacherous, speaker. But for the full picture I definitely needed that emotional gem, so I had to take it and listen.

... Alexander Ospiov and I couldn't laugh together at that episode. We didn't see each other anymore. Very quickly after his interview with me Osipov died an untimely death of an unknown disease.

***

VLADISLAV SHVED
Former Second Secretary of the CPL Central Committee, Author

We Dreamed of a Completely Different Lithuania

Why did I decide to return to this topic after a quarter century?

Not just because there is a trial over the participants of the January 1991 events going on in Vilnius right now. And not because it is the 25th anniversary of the USSR collapse, which started specifically in Lithuania. There is the nagging feeling of déjà vu: techniques that were used so many years ago in Vilnius were pulled out of the closet and recently used in Ukraine, almost without alteration. And the smell of death, and the cursing on TV, and the numerous Western consultants – Gene Sharp's theory is once again in demand. Who knows how many times in between it has in fact been applied?

I interviewed another person from that trial-in-absentia list: Vladislav Shved, former Second Secretary of the CPL Central Committee, author of the books *Lithuania vs Russia and Alpha* and *Lithuania's Neonazis vs Russia*.

Sapozhnikova: *I am looking through your books and catch myself thinking that you are not talking about the events of 25 years ago, but of the ones today. Ukrainian ones.*

Shved: You are completely right! I also feel like the same scenario is unfolding in Ukraine as it did in Lithuania in the early 90s, but on a more qualified level.

Sapozhnikova: *Do you mean the shots of unknown snipers on Maidan square? Analogous to how they were shooting from the rooftops around Vilnius TV tower in January 1991?*

Shved: Absolutely correct. And note that it has been repeated in a number of other regions: they shot from the roofs in Egypt and in Iraq. The same pattern there.

Sapozhnikova: *So we are talking about specific tactics?*

Shved: Exactly – and these tactics don't change. It is unthinkable: they made this point when they were able to convince others that the people in Odessa poured flammable liquid onto themselves and set themselves on fire...[5] And in 1991 Lithuania they said: no one could have been shooting except the Soviet soldiers --who were armed with Mosin-Nagant rifles, hunting rifles and small caliber firearms?... It is bullshit! But nobody wants to get into it, because the world dances to the Americans' fiddle. And in Ukraine they did the very thing that they couldn't do in Lithuania: in order to prove the barbaric nature of the Soviet soldiers, there were plans to set the TV tower, printing house and Supreme Council buildings in Vilnius ablaze.

The flames, which would engulf the Supreme Council building were to kill more than 3000 people. The former head of the National Defense Department, Audrius Butkevičius, even proudly declared this in one interview. He was one of the ideologues behind resisting "Soviet", as they said, aggression. Prior to this, 3200 volunteers gathered in the Supreme Council, along with members of parliament, journalists and service crews.

In anticipation of the assault, the entrances were covered with sand bags, and the bathrooms and service rooms were filled with gasoline canisters and other flammable materials. If a fire started, then there would thousands of victims. It would be impossible to evacuate the people as promised. Butkevičius didn't shy away from saying that all of it would be filmed and sent to the governments of the world's leading countries as evidence of the Soviet soldiers' crimes.

The Lithuanian experience in hiding the actual circumstances of the deaths of the January Events were successfully used by Kiev. They hid the bodies from the Kiev Maidan and in Odessa.

Sapozhnikova: *But if the protocols of that old story of the Vilnius TV tower are so obvious – why doesn't anyone pay any attention to them?*

Shved: The Russian government underestimated the situation with the January 1991 events in Vilnius. And the Lithuanian one would not benefit from it. Because their "heroic exit" from the "horrible" Soviet Union, even though during the time Lithuania was in the Union, its population rose by a million people, and the level of its economic development, by CIA expert estimates, was equivalent to Denmark – is the base and foundation that holds it together today.

Tsarist Russia Was Hounded Just as Much as the Current Russia

Sapozhnikova: *I was interested to read in your books, about the many signs of the setup there were in the late 80s – early 90s Lithuania. How much it looks like modern day Ukraine! Is it true that the main Sąjūdis ideologue, Romualdas Ozolas, wrote that, "Russian culture and art is horrible and terrible" and that "the Russian national characteristics are stupidity, laziness, shortsightedness and apathy"? And why was there no reaction?*

Shved: I'll add that Ozolas was a member of the Communist Party Central Committee at the time and during his time, he wrote propaganda books about Soviet Lithuania's achievements. Why did no one react to Ozolas' slander? There was no one there to. The CPL was already under the Sąjūdists control, and Gorbachev in Moscow heeded his promise to free the Baltics, a promise he made to Reagan in Reykjavík and he did all in his power to do so. He thought that the USSR would be accepted into the European house if he did... He was an amateur and didn't know Russian history. Tsarist Russia was hounded just as much as the current Russia!

Sapozhnikova: *Does the fact that Lithuania, after 25 years, reanimated this old story by making a list of "war criminals" containing dozens of Russians, fit into this hounding process? Alpha Group commander, Mikhail Golovatov, was arrested in Austria, trooper Vasily Kotlyarov was arrested in Rome. Reserve Colonel Yuri Mel has been sitting in a Lithuanian prison for two years now. Why did all of this suddenly become relevant now?*

Shved: If you recall, PACE[6] in 2009 adopted a resolution proposed by the Lithuanian politicians equating Stalinism and Nazism. Well, while fulfilling the directives from Washington – and Lithuania is used to following those orders – the Lithuanian parliamentarians decided that they needed to verbally attack

Russia, as Russia wasn't reacting to the Lithuanian protests. So they needed to prove that Russia is the successor of a criminal state. And when these trials in absentia will pass, where former Soviet and now Russian citizens will be tried and found guilty as war criminals, Lithuania will have the right to say that Russia is the successor to a criminal state and must take moral and material responsibility.

Sapozhnikova: *How did you end up on this criminal list?*

Shved: Easy. I was the second Secretary of the CPL on the CPSU Platform.

Sapozhnikova: *So you were added to the "war criminal" list and accused of anti-government activity on purely ideological grounds, as part of collective responsibility, which was common in the USSR under Stalin?*

Shved: I always spoke in favor of the idea that Lithuania has the right to leave the Union, but legally, by hosting a referendum. The Supreme Council of the Lithuanian SSR, which successfully declared independence in March 1991, got less than 40% of the votes.

The separatists tried to speed up the events, because they knew they wouldn't get the needed 2/3 of the referendum vote. That is why they set up the tragedy by the TV tower. The Lithuanians needed to be convinced that the Soviet government is criminal. The January 1991 events were staged in a way to cover it in blood as well. Similarly, the Lithuanian falsifiers set up the Medininkai border post massacre, while USA President George Bush, Sr. was in Moscow. There was also a mission to hang another bloody crime onto the USSR.

How Can Gorbachev Sleep at Night?

Sapozhnikova: *I assume you are familiar with the letter by*

Konstantin Nikulin (Mikhailov) who was sentenced to a life term specifically for Medininkai? For a murder he didn't commit...

> *The political regime of Lithuania is using my case and the 13 January TV tower in Vilnius case as basis for legal, political and criminal law claims against our former state – the USSR, including the CPSU Central Committee policies, which were the chief and highest control department of our country. With that, the following is of utmost importance: the CPSU Central Committee is considered a criminal organization in Lithuania. Before the USSR's dissolution, this organization was led by Mikhail Gorbachev. For some reason, Lithuania has no claims against Mikhail Gorbachev. He isn't even condemned. But a common military man, who was just serving his country and fulfilling his duty can be accused on all accounts, caught in a European arrest warrant and give a prison term. I have a question, it is a rhetorical one, of course: how can Gorbachev sleep at night? He doesn't want to help the soldiers, who served under his command, and are now in peril for his decision?*
>
> *For nine years now I have been unlawfully imprisoned by the Lithuanian Republic, sentenced under article 100 of Lithuania's Criminal Code – "war crimes against humanity" with the aforementioned accusation. I am not the only one like this here – there are many of us. We, who honestly fulfilled our duty and served our homeland – are now tried for being part of the system and all of the system's grievances are hung on us. There is no evidence of my guilt or the guilt of my unit. I am tried for "war crimes against humanity...*

What do you think of that?

Shved: Gorbachev preferred to resign his post as President of the USSR and give up the Union for grabs. May I remind you that by 11 December 1991, the USSR Constitutional Oversight Committee recognized the agreement as illegal. So the President of the USSR had legal grounds to arrest the Białowieża conspirators. In the situation of a military operation to restore the power of the USSR Constitution on the Lithuanian SSR territory in December 1991, Gorbachev acted like a cowardly instigator, saying that he did not sanction the operation. Let me remind you in December 1990, the IV USSR Congress of People's Deputies gave the President of the USSR practically dictator-like power. But this did not give him additional courage. World history has had few examples of such spinelessness, cowardice and betrayal from the head of the country.

Only recently, I was congratulating the famous diplomat Valentin Falin with his 90th birthday – he was a member of the CPSU Central Committee in the early 90s. And do you know what he told me? Turns out, that during the day of 12 January 1991 when he was near Gorbachev's office he overheard through an open door how Gorbachev spoke with USSR Marshal Dmitry Yazov. "No live rounds!" decisively ordered the USSR President to the Minister of Defense, "Only if there will be *a danger to the lives of the soldiers.*"

What is that if not another piece of evidence that the Vilnius events happened by a move from Gorbachev. Of course he knew all about that operation…

Breaking Up? You Should Return the Gifts

Sapozhnikova: *37 tomes of the criminal case on the January Events in Vilnius were given to the Lithuanian side by the USSR Prosecutor-General Office in September 1991 as gesture for a friendly future. That is how friendship and democracy was viewed at the time… There are no warm relations between Russia* *and Lithuania anymore – the present should be returned, logic dictates. And not just that present: I hope everyone remembers that the city of Vilnius was given to the Lithuanians as a sign of eternal friendship between Lithuania and the Soviet Union.*

Shved: Oh if only it just concerned Vilnius! When the Soviet Union was given East Prussia, Lithuania received Klaipėda and part of the Curonian Spit. Lithuania has no documents proving its ownership of Klaipėda or the spit. The city of Vilnius was given to Lithuania by the USSR four times since 1918. Altogether, thanks to the USSR's presents, Lithuania increased its territory by a third. It is a fact! And no gratitude!

Sapozhnikova: *And why do you think Lithuania became this active now specifically?*

Shved: Because today, all of the leading Lithuania elite are former Soviet collaborators, in fact, some of the most ardent ones. For example, the current Lithuanian president, Dalia Grybauskaitė, studied in Leningrad University and was a worker at the Rot-Front factory, which is considered a restricted company under KGB control. There she was a Komsomol member in charge of propaganda. There she joined the CPSU and was noted for her true Communist principles. Returning to Lithuania, yesterday's student suddenly was one of the teachers at the Vilnius High Party School. During the post-Soviet period, Grybauskaitė managed to get into the inner circle of the President of the Supreme Council Russophobe, Vytautas Landsbergis, who was also a Distinguished worker in the arts of the Lithuanian SSR and former informant to NKVD-KGB of the Lithuanian SSR. And now she is into her second term as President of Lithuania!

I would say that Grybauskaitė has the biggest Soviet "baggage," similar to the majority of the modern Lithuanian elite, and she hides it with all of her might. It is no accident that in early 2016, she sent a written refusal to the Lithuanian politician, Zigmas Vaišvila, when he requested her personal data, which was stored in the Russian, or more precisely, the former Soviet archives. According to the law, personal data can't be given out to third parties without the approval of the person in the data. Grybauskaitė understands that after that information is publicized she will have no place in Lithuania. Former Soviet collaborationists, who are currently in power, are trying to completely taint the past black, in order to present their own heroic role as saviors of the people from Soviet slavery...

Sapozhnikova: *I can feel that you have yet to get over this story. Why did you even decide to write these books? Were you driven by personal revenge?*

Shved: Oh Heavens no! I have only the best feelings towards Lithuania, even though I am forced to live in exile for 25 years now. Lithuanian is still the second language in my family. That is not the question. It is just that we all dreamed of a completely different Lithuania...

Why Was Gorbachev Scared to Give the Medal to Viktor Shatskikh's Mother?

...There is something that else that won't give me peace for these 25 years.

Once again it is the morning of 13 January 1991: the journalists ran to the Tallinn press center for information, they were cooped up together like doves. There is still one country for now – the USSR, but everyone was already on their own branch – the Russians on one, the Baltics on the other, the Western ones soaring above all of us. In any case, it was best to stick together: they are expecting Soviet tanks in Tallinn in the coming days, so they were bringing big stones to Toompea, and in the castle halls, where the Supreme Council of Estonia gathers, they were wrapping fire hoses around it. It is cold, hungry and worrying. There is almost no information from Vilnius, and no one believes the TV news from Moscow anymore. And then someone shouted in the acoustics of the hall: a Soviet army sergeant is killed in Vilnius! And the journalists started applauding... Someone even joyfully shouted something like: "One less Soviet bastard!" In the evening they showed the photo of the KGB Spetsnaz lieutenant – Viktor Shatskikh. My God, he was only 21...

I will never forget his name, due to the inconsistencies of the fact of his death and the malicious joy in which it was celebrated. As well as the fact that I kept silent. Of course now I know: I should have stood up and shouted for the whole hall, that they were all idiots, what did it matter a day before or later, I would have still been labeled a communist? But why didn't I stand up... And this question haunted me for 20 years, until I finally found this lieutenant's grave, left flowers at it and met his mother, Valentina Shatskikh.

This interview was conducted Winter 2012. And in February 2015 Valentina Shatskikh passed away.

***

VALENTINA SHATSKIKH
Mother of slain KGB Spetsnaz lieutenant, Victor Shatskikh

My Son Fell into the Abyss

Sapozhnikova: *How did you find out about what happened in Vilnius?*

Shatskikh: I realized it before they told me. Because I have always had the same dream before I got injured or ill. A baby in my hands, I walk through a field to a cliff, as if someone is pushing my elbow and my son calls down into the abyss, but is stopped by a tree.
And that night I had a dream, where he fell into the abyss, not stopping. And when my husband and the Alpha commander at the time, Viktor Karpukhin, I told them that I knew... I only didn't know what exactly happened, but I understood that my

pės ženklas.

KGB Spetsnaz lieutenant Viktor Shatskikh was killed on the night of 13 January 1991 by a shot to the back. The case is still unsolved.

Gorbachev refused to meet with Viktor Shatskikh's mother Valentina.

son was no more. It was sad that government pretended nothing happened, because the coffin was met at the airport only by Karpukhin and my husband. We were later supported by the other Alpha men, and KGB Chairman Vladimir Kryuchkov as well. And Gorbachev said that he had nothing to do with it... Such gall and injustice, if I met him back then, I probably would have killed him with my own hands.

Sapozhnikova: *How old were you when your son died?*

Shatskikh: 42. And my son was 20.

Sapozhnikova: *Please tell me about him. And about you and your husband, How did you meet?*

Shatskikh: We met at the border academy, I taught them ballroom dances there. We got married and we went to Transcaucasia. And there, in Nakhchivan, our son was born. His first steps were in a border post, his first conversations – with soldiers and officers. He grew up with a love of military duty. For a while I had to feed him at the border post, because he refused to eat at home. He was a very energetic boy, capable, talented and responsible from a young age. A year and four months later, his sister was born; he loved her a lot, even though he was very young, rocked her cradle and treated her with great kindness.

Sapozhnikova: *Your son's choice of a military career was determined by the family tradition?*

Shatskikh: Yes. We had a lot of military men in the family. Four Uncles, mother's brothers, and two of my father's brothers fought in the Great Patriotic War and my dad went through the whole war. He had a concussion near Leningrad and died from the concussion in 1946, immediately after I was born.

Who if Not Him?

Sapozhnikova: *Your son went to a military academy right around the years when there was an awful campaign to discredit the Soviet army.*

Shatskikh: He was a maximalist in that sense and was in love with military service. He just couldn't grow up a kid, who wouldn't love military things: his father took him with him to recruit training even when he was in school, taught him to shoot and hand-to-hand combat. Honestly, I was against him going to the military academy initially. But he enrolled, not exactly where he wanted – he dreamed of getting into the Babushkin (Suvorov) Military Academy, in order to be in a parade with his dad. But he had to enroll into the Golitsyn military border academy, because that was the year when the order banning relatives serving in the same detachment came through. They later specified that it included only service, but not education and we proposed our son be transferred to Babushkin Military Academy, but he was already used to his friends and said he would stay in Golitsyno.

And the fact that he loved his work could be seen in his

poems. He started writing them in his 4th year of school. His monument actually has his own words:

> Не знаю, какой охранял я покой,
> Но судьбы для себя не искал я другой
>
> I don't know what peace I was protecting,
> But I was seeking a different fate than this.

Here is another one of his poems:

> Я не хочу смотреть на все, как все, практичными глазами.
> Чужой кумир не нужен мне. Я не за них, но и не с вами.
> Мне говорят – иди за мной? В будешь счастлив вместе с нами.
> Но ведь они ведут домой, К сестре, к отцу и к моей маме,
> А я хочу в пургу, в цунами
>
> I don't want to look on everything, like everyone, with practical eyes.
> I don't need someone else's idol. I am not for them, but not with you.
> I am told – follow me and you will be happy with us.
> But they lead home to my sister, my father, my mother,
> And I want to go into a blizzard, a tsunami.

He was such a busybody... And his school paper was called "I have a stake in everything." And truly so, his whole life, he lived by the principle of "Who if not me?"

> Я непоседа? Ну что ж, пускай смеются надо мною.
> Я не боюсь смешливых рож с пустой, бездумной головою.

Я преклоняться не хочу пред подлостью и всякой гнилью,
И наблюдать спокойно не могу, как преклоняются другие

I am a busybody? Well then, let them laugh at me.
I am not scared of laughable faces with empty thoughtless heads.
I don't want to kneel in front of any treachery or any rot,
And I can't stand to watch as others kneel.

Those are the kind of poems he wrote.

He combined what can't be combined: on one hand, courage, strength, determination, a love of hard work, and on the other – a romantic type. He had a very strong will. After the first battle march in the border academy, they all came back sweaty, exhausted, heads hanging low, and he stood in line and smiled. The commander asked, "Shatskikh, why are you smiling?" And he responded, "Why, should I be crying instead?" He was always smiling. Always raising his mood and everyone around him.

Try Not to Cry at the Cemetery

Sapozhnikova: *Was the word "Alpha" ever spoken in your house?*

Shatskikh: First, my son met the Alpha commander, Viktor Karpukhin. Second, he thought of going into Spetsnaz or reconnaissance, even when he was in the academy. Then the officers from Alpha came to gather workers and he was among the ones chosen. He was one of only three from the academy that were selected. For a long time, no one said anything and he wrote a report about serving in Central Asia. He even had tickets for early August and literally 3-4 days before the flight, he got a letter calling him to his superiors. He returned and said, "Mom, I was take into Alpha."

Sapozhnikova: *Was he happy?*

Shatskikh: That is an understatement! I have not seen him this happy all of his life, until this moment!

Sapozhnikova: *What year was it?*

Shatskikh: 1990. He served in Alpha only for 6 months. He loved Karpukhin and his direct commander Evgeniy Chudesnov. Every time he came back from work, he said, "Mom, you can't imagine how great these people are!"

Sapozhnikova: *Where and why was he going, he didn't tell his mother, of course?*

Shatskikh: No. A few times, when going on an assignment, he just said he was leaving and that was it. But the last time, right before the New Year, he said for some reason, "Mom, you are a strong woman, you know where I serve, and just in case, try not to cry at the cemetery." And I tried to keep strong on the cemetery for him.

Sapozhnikova: *Why did he have that premonition?*

Shatskikh: I don't know. He probably was just a very delicate soul. Whenever he sent me a holiday card, he would always write a poem for me. Played the guitar very well. He was a very talented boy. They all loved him at school and at the academy. I kick myself for not giving him more attention. Like my mom always said "You're fixing other's houses, while your own is open." I worked in a pre-school facility and spent an insane amount of my time with other people's kids.

Sapozhnikova: *Did Viktor have a girlfriend?*

Shatskikh: He did. They didn't have the time to marry. They were going to do it before the New Year, but her father had a heart attack and was in hospital, so they postponed to January. Later she married another officer. She has two daughters. They still visit his grave, along with her husband. Because whenever we come there on Viktor's birthday, there is always a bouquet there.

That Time When an Armored Vest Failed...

Sapozhnikova: *Your husband probably blamed himself for helping his son get into Alpha?*

Shatskikh: He didn't help. My son aced the academy exams, wrote the entry essay in rhyme, for three pages, it is in the Golitsyn academy museum now. His father was also a fan of all things military. We were happy and proud of his song, of course.

Sapozhnikova: *After what happened in Vilnius, there was an information wave. The Lithuanian press wrote that Alpha allegedly shot their own fighter in the back...*

Shatskikh: The newspapers are full of awful lies in general, which made it hurt all the more. He was called a tanker, a trooper, a Soviet Army lieutenant, a KGB agent. And then Kryuchkov officially announced that an Alpha fighter was killed...

Sapozhnikova: *Is it true, that they attempted to downplay the funeral?*

Shatskikh: Yes, it happened almost in secret, just the Alpha lads and our relatives.

Sapozhnikova: *Why is your son's grave to the side of the main alley, where all of the Alpha fighters are? Someone of his colleagues suggested that it was done so the grave couldn't be vandalized by the Lithuanians.*

Shatskikh: No, of course that is rubbish! Because when my son died, I received letters and packages from Lithuanians. A lot of warm words. They expressed their condolences to me, as a mother. They sent treats, Russian and Lithuanian flags, tied together with a ribbon. They wrote letters of sympathy, asking me not to believe if it was said that my son was part of some shady deals... That he and all of his colleagues are honorable men. A mother of one of the killed Lithuanians also wrote me a letter. She said she didn't blame our boys. Another joint letter came from some factory, the people wrote that it was a provocation, wanting to pit Lithuania and Russia against each other. Which they managed to do in the end.

Sapozhnikova: *Are the circumstances of Viktor's death still not known for certain?*

Shatskikh: I read documents that he was shot from the roof. He got a bullet when he jumped into a window, the plates of his armored vest came apart and the bullet went in from above. This is a time when an armored vest failed. Because if the bullet went through him and out, he would have lived. And the armored vest stopped it.

Sapozhnikova: *I mean to say, it is unknown who was shooting...*

Shatskikh: How is it unknown? Ours couldn't have been shooting! And the weapon time, and the way the bullet was retrieved, and how the shot was made, it all points to someone shooting from above.

Sapozhnikova: *Is it important to you who made the shot? Or doesn't it matter anymore – because it won't change anything now?*

Shatskikh: Of course I would like that man to be brought to justice, but I don't feel a need for revenge. I think those who do bad things need to be pitied, and not judged. You envy only the good people.

What Was Gorbachev Afraid Of?

Sapozhnikova: *When and how did you receive the award for your son?*

Shatskikh: It was presented personally by Kryuchkov, in his office. First, he gave the Order of the Red Star, and then we were in his office for an hour or two, just talking; he asked about the family's needs. My husband then asked for team medics to be implemented in Alpha, and I asked for a swimming pool for the kindergarten. He kept all of his promises. Everything was received. Although, they never finished building the swimming pool because the August 1991 events took place. But we already had all of the materials and plans for the project. Construction was planned for September. The kindergarten was left without a swimming pool. They drove the building materials back...

Kryuchkov later said that he addressed Gorbachev, requesting that he would present the award to us, but Gorbachev declined. I don't know what he said exactly, but something along the lines of my son being part of Kryuchkov's organization, so he, Kryuchkov, will be the one presenting it.

Sapozhnikova: *What do you think Gorbachev was scared of?*

Shatskikh: To look us in the eyes. Probably didn't lose all of his dignity. That is what I think. But I would like to meet him at least once and hear what he would tell me. That he didn't know anything and did nothing wrong? Turns out the guys went there on a joy ride? How could the president not know of such an operation?

I Hold No Grudges, Nor Hate for the Lithuanians

Sapozhnikova: *Did you expect destiny to once again turn you to these events after 20 years? Or did it never leave you?...*

Shatskikh: No, I didn't think it would. But I am very happy that we have started discussing this again, because I felt very bad for our lads.

Sapozhnikova: *If you had the ability to say something to all Lithuanians, what would you tell them?*

Shatskikh: That the common people hate war and provocations. The common people always dreamed, dream and will keep dreaming of peace. You know how we lived in the USSR. Me and my husband served in Azerbaijan, and in Armenia, we went on vacation to almost every republic, and we never felt a hateful stare, felt any contempt. I guess it depends on people and not their nationality. I am not referring to governments – governments have been and always will be fighting over briefcases with nuclear buttons or simple briefcases. It is not the Russians', Lithuanians' or Estonians' fault. We were in Estonia once and they fixed our car for free! We stopped with a tent near one hamlet with our kids, and were almost dragged inside and fed dinner. They said, why would we stay in a tent, when there is plenty of room in the house. They didn't know us, they were strangers... Which is why I say that people are all the same. There are good ones and then there are bad ones. Ask any person if he would want a war? No. And I hold no grudge, nor hate for the Lithuanians. Despite that a few Lithuanians died in those events, it was Lithuanians who wrote letters of condolence for me. I am merely sad that we were betrayed by our own. Gorbachev. I am religious woman, so I can't allow myself to say that I curse him. But I would like for him to answer for what he did by the law. I had the idea with my husband, back in 1991-1992, to sue Gorbachev if our lads weren't left alone. Apparently I will actually do it.

* * *

Alas, Valentina Shatskikh didn't do it. Didn't have the time...

Nor did she go to Vilnius to stand where her son was killed. Instead, I did it for her. I looked at the tours they now give here to the young and old, I looked at the roofs, where the shots were made by the unknown assailants. And for some reason I remembered the words Valentina Shatskikh said off the record, and later refused to repeat them on camera:

"Maybe if he died for the kids or freeing hostages, I would feel better. As is, he died in vain…"

I had nothing to say to that…

***

Instead of an Epilogue

**Defendant YURI MEL
taken prisoner during peace times:**

"I was sure that I was serving my country"

Soviet army colonel Yuri Mel, who fired 3 blanks 26 years ago, now has to answer for all of the Soviet Union.

Speech in court on the 13 January 1991 events trials.
Vilnius, 8 February 2016.

Mel: Dear members of the trial! I understand the essence of the accusations brought against me by the court. I plead not guilty to crimes against humanity and war crimes.

I disagree with every point of the prosecution. My participation in the operation to secure the TV tower and firing three blanks from the tank I was controlling, I confirm. I completely support the testimony I gave in pre-trial investigations.

Today I would like to add the following. I, Yuri Nikolaevich Mel, after finishing the Ulyanovsk Guard High Tank Command Academy, was assigned to the 106th Tank Regiment of the 107th Motorized Rifle Division, located in Vilnius in the rank of lieutenant, where I assumed command of a tank platoon. So most of my service on the territory of the Lithuanian Republic I spent in the Pabrad training grounds, within the regiment, where the training vehicle was. I did not go to Vilnius often and did so by request of command or while serving as part of a group or due to service necessities.

After retiring due to health reasons, I have openly and without any attempt to hide, received tourist visas in the Lithuanian Republic general consulate in the city of Kaliningrad, where I stated all of my information. I have crossed the border multiple times in the defined procedure since 2012, until I was arrested on 12 March 2014 while returning home. I was not aware that there was a criminal case against me, otherwise I would not have been here.

"I have received no order to kill"

Military service in the any state's armed forces includes a voluntary waiving of certain civilian freedoms and is founded on strict discipline, heavily regulated by the state pledge, codes and orders of commanders and chiefs. According to the code of the internal service in the USSR Armed Forces, a received order must be completed, refusing the order or not fulfilling it, is punished severely, up to a military tribunal. The Soviet Union military pledge ends with the words "And if I violate this honorable pledge, then may severe penance, contempt and hate of all the people fall upon me." So there is no choice when following orders. The responsibility lies on the one giving an order. This is the foundation of any army, otherwise, it is not army, but a gang. In the described events, I was part of the crew and under orders from the regiment commander, lieutenant-colonel Astakhov, and took part in the operation to secure the TV tower with the goal of ensuring unhindered advancement of the line to the designated object. And myself and my mechanic-driver were replaced in the crew and put in formation right before the advance of the line. This is proven by the amended order of the military unit 78018 № 3 from 9 January 1991, which further proves that there was no premeditated conspiracy. I have received no order to kill, on the contrary, we were constantly warned on multiple occasions, that we were to act with care and that under no circumstanced were the civilians to get harmed, which is mentioned in the case files multiple times. The tank crew, where I was, did not run over anyone or kill anyone. On the regiment commander's orders, we fired two blank shots from the tank gun, with the maximum level of elevation. The blank shot itself was not and is not anything extraordinary, was and is frequently used and will be used to imitate a shot in the future. Pyrotechnical means are not sound, light or any other type of weapon.

"I saw the Minister of Defense only in photographs"

16 January 1991, on the regiment commanders order, as part of the line, we moved out from the unit's base, where we started giving testimonies almost instantly, first to the Main Military Prosecutor's office, then the Soviet Union's and Lithuanian Republic's Prosecutor-General as witnesses. There were no facts stating we were connected to the casualties. I was asked no further questions. Until late 1992, I continued my service

here in Lithuania, not hiding from anyone, living in a hotel of the High Party School, after which I left for my next place of service. I am a soldier, not a politician and I was sure that I was serving my country on the territory of the Soviet Union, until Lithuania was recognized by the USSR Supreme Council on 6 September 1991. My rank was "lieutenant" at that time, and my first position – "platoon commander" – left no decisions up to me and my opinion was of interest to no one. The attempt to present me as part of criminal group is confounding. The prosecution states that most of the defendants are warrant officers and lieutenants, fresh out of the academy – junior officers are suddenly important military and political figures? Anyone at least slightly familiar with the armed forces knows that the Defense Ministry has a very limited circle of advisors. The Defense Minister talks to the commanders through proxies – lieutenants and warrant officers have nothing to do there. This is not in their category of subordination.

According to the report by the division HQ chief, the January 1991 events had 1567 taking part from the Severny Gorodok alone. 25 years later, all servicemen, who freely gave their testimonies in 1991, have been requalified from witnesses to defendants. I would like to reiterate, I was not part of any criminal groups, took part in no conspiracies, I saw the Defense Minister only on a photograph, had no plans and was not part of preparing any plans. I was part of the military staff in my country and did not violate the pledge I gave to that country. We had a direct order to proceed as part of the line, with no additional information and no options of actions.

Communists, forward!

Supporting the court's intention to investigate this case from a criminal standpoint would, I think, be hard to achieve. The events themselves had political meaning, so politicization is inevitable. Accusations against me start with "While being part of the Communist Party of the Soviet Union…"… I would like to reiterate, that I am a citizen of the Russian Federation, where the communist party is not banned. Yes, during the investigate period, I was part of the Communist Party of the Soviet Union, because the state system at the time did not allow a different membership. In Lithuania itself, according to the case files, in 1991 there was approximately 208 thousand communists, and this is after the January events. So the accusation that I was a member of the CPSU at the time, seems strange. My membership in the Communist Party of the Soviet Union is part of the accusation against me, but it doesn't stop others in the Lithuanian Republic from holding high government posts.

Having studied the criminal case files, I have come to the conclusion that during the 13 January 1991 events, certain political forces and people criminally used the army without its knowledge in order to achieve their goals. Undoubtedly, the fact that the army was used to restore order can't be justified. In world practice, the responsibility is carried by the leaders, who gave the order and not the common servicemen. Undoubtedly, all cases of abuse of power and violence against civilians must be investigated and given a legal evaluation. However these actions have nothing in common with crimes against humanity or war crimes.

New Untruth

I am interested in this investigation, like no other. But I see certain problems in utilizing my right to defense. How can I defend myself if the Lithuanian Supreme Court, when examining the case of Algirdas Paleckis, stated that no other interpretation of the events is possible and different opinions are a crime? Analyzing statements by politicians and the country's president on this case, I can sadly state, that negative statements against Russia, of which I am a citizen, present an unprecedented amount of pressure on the court. Can Lithuania's court exercise impartial and unemotional justice? I greatly hope so. In essence, this process is a sort of exam for the country, a test of its dedication to European values and values of true democracy.

In proof of my stance on the legal background of the

described events, I would once again like to state, that on 13 January, when taking part in the operation to secure the TV tower, I was absolutely sure that Lithuania was part of the USSR. The situation was ambiguous, controversial and complex. On one hand, Article 71 of the USSR Constitution mentioned the people's right to separate. Lithuania was one of the republics which de facto declared itself independent. On the other hand – after the declaration of restoring independence, Lithuania and USSR negotiated and on 23 May 1990 the Lithuanian Supreme Council froze negotiations with the Soviet Union on issues regarding the restoration of independence. In 1991, Lithuania was recognized diplomatically by the Soviet Union, the European Community and the United States of America. It is at this point when, in accordance with international law, Lithuania became an independent subject of international law, a sovereign state.

I have always respected and still respect the people of Lithuania, even despite the suffering that I have endured for two years of imprisonment.

The European Human Rights Court decision on the case of Mykolas Burokevičius states that justice can't be used as a weapon for forming recent history, which is still under-researched. The people consciously and subconsciously feel a deep need for vengeance and the threat of it coming to pass, creates a new untruth. However, in my opinion, one cannot live with past grudges and revenge.

***

How They Tried to Stop Me From Writing This Book

The small girl in the middle (photo right) is me, Galina Sapozhnikova. I am wearing a national Lithuanian costume. I was probably in 3rd grade when our Izhevsk School № 27 celebrated the USSR's birthday and I got Lithuania. This means that I needed to go to the library and read everything about Lithuania, sketch and make some kind of semblance of a national costume, bake some kind of Lithuanian treat, learn a poem or song and present it at the school party, commemorating the USSR's establishment. That is how the "prison of nations" looked.

Cruel irony: during her youth, the author of this book read poetry about love for Lithuania on a school celebration.

For the life of me, I can't remember where we got the vests and skirts. Probably borrowed them from the dance club. As it turned out later, we had the blouses on inside out. We glued the cardboard crowns on our own – I remember us cutting them out of colored paper. I still remember the poem of the Lithuanian poetess, Salomėja Nėris: "My small homeland – like a golden drop of thick amber..." Oh how I dreamed of seeing Lithuania back then!

...Somehow now, when in the middle of an empty field, I am being told that I am an "unwanted person" in the Lithuanian Republic because I present a "threat to its security" and am read a decision to ban my entry into the country for 5 years, I think of that small girl, who couldn't imagine that the Baltics would be a cross to bear and a love.

And almost 40 years later, this girl, now a journalist, was deported from Lithuania as a "threat to national security."

A Tail that Wags the Dog

That was a lyrical digression. And now to the point.

They caught up to us on the road, around 60 km from Vilnius, when I and one the book's heroes – Algirdas Paleckis – were on our way to another hero, the former Secretary of the Central Committee of the CPL on CPSU platform, the 85-year-old, Juozas Kuolelis. The car was overtaken by a border guard car, with two men exiting it. Expulsion from a country seems like a rough romantic thing to many. The ones sending people off later say how they risked their lives, catching Russian spies, shooting and taking cover from poisoned umbrellas. And the ones deported share the details of how the angry policemen cuffed them to bars and took them to the airport in a cage. And I really have nothing to tell: I came to Vilnius normally and went on for the interview. If I was a spy, I probably would have noticed the tail, turned off my phone and hid my tracks. However, I am not a spy, I am a journalist, and I don't plan on crawling over the border like a snake. And I don't feel any guilt. All of my publications on Lithuania in recent years were exclusively about the January 1991 events, which Vilnius doesn't want to investigate. I have no negative feelings towards Lithuanians, on the contrary, I find them warm and soulful. And also incredibly brave: I don't know many fighters like the previously jailed communists, Juozas Jermalavičius and Mykolas Burokevičius. Or true Soviet officers Algimantas Naudžiūnas, Romas Juknevičius, Edmundas Kasperavičius and Antanas Petrauskas, who weren't afraid to fight the Sąjūdists, who had the same blood as them, but poisoned by nationalism.

That, probably, is the main lesson of that Vilnius story for me as a journalist. And it is not in fact that 25 years ago, we couldn't solve the simplest puzzle of the "sacred sacrifice" needed for the color revolution in complete adherence to Gene Sharp's theory. It wasn't hurtful: we were outplayed by experienced players, who were already well-versed with the famous 198 points of non-violent regime change, and we were starry-eyed and inexperienced and believed that we would be in for a wonderful life under capitalism, not a half-baked life.

Initially, we included all Lithuanians into the list of those who desperately wanted to leave the USSR. We were elegantly eased into that interpretation throughout the late 80s, leaving us with a guilt complex for the crimes of the USSR in the 20th century, which, at the time, eclipsed the crimes of the Nazis and the Forest Brothers. TV was exclusively showing those who protested, danced and cried, openly mocking those who tried to resist the dismemberment and dissolution of the Soviet Union. And do you know what was the biggest revelation from working on this book, which included dozens of interviews with witnesses and direct participants of these events 25 years ago? That at least half of the population of Lithuania in 1991 were people who benefited from an education and work in the USSR – farmers – became professors and they knew what might happen to their small homeland if it were channeled into aggressive nationalism.

But they were not the ones to win; instead it was the TV picture of candles and national flags.

The tail that wags the dog won. Which apparently was the main point of contention in that tragic night from 12 to 13 January, a quarter century ago.

Plus by a Minus

...It is not too scary, when you are turned around in an empty field and told to return to the airport. It is a lot less pleasant when they publicly burn your portrait during a protest – as it was with a photo of Algirdas Paleckis. Or climb into your apartment at 6 am, as happened in 2015 with anti-fascist Giedrius Grabauskas. That was an actual event and not a made up one: that was the exotic method the Lithuanian police investigators chose for their searches at his house and his allies – just for standing in an anti-NATO protest outside the USA Embassy. So they did a similar search on me. They never told me what it was they were looking for, but they took my Dostoyevsky and Starikov books. So my deportation from the Lithuania fields is a light variant.

"We inform you, that you must leave the Lithuanian Republic. And if you do not leave – you may be arrested and deported," the border guard read me the paper.

And I thought to myself: let it be. I wasn't in Lithuania for the past two years, and won't be there for five more. Life is good, even without Lithuania. And if my deportation will let the world know of the Lithuania "punitive democracy" – then it is all for the good.

Being deported from a county is an Event, if it is exclusive. But when journalists, in the wave of the current Russia-Europe information war madness, get deported each day by the dozen as a caricature of a government tries to show power that it hasn't had in a long while – it becomes a farce.

And that is what I was going to say in this book, which the current Lithuanian government tried to stop with all of their power. But they couldn't do a thing about it.

GLOSSARY OF NAMES

Achalov, V.A. - Soviet military and political figure. Deputy USSR Minister of Defense (1990-1991). General-colonel. Creator and first president of the All-Russian Union of VDV "Paratrooper Union of Russia"

Adiklis, G. – founder of the Lithuanian Republic's criminal police. Arrested A.Smotkin in November 1991 on a false accusation in Belarussian city of Polotsk. Was later convicted by a Lithuanian court for a murdering someone during an interrogation.

Akhromeev, S.F. – Soviet military leader, marshal, Hero of the Soviet Union. Chief of the USSR Armed Forces HQ – first deputy USSR Minister of Defense (1984-1988). Since March 1990 – advisor to the USSR President Gorbachev on military issues. Died mysteriously in the Kremlin in August 1991.

Alukas, A. – former member of the Šalčininkai district council. Was sentenced by the state for the so-called Šalčininkai separatist case.

Antonenko, A. – major of LSSR Police criminal investigations unit. Was the deputy commander of the Vilnius OMON.

Antonov, V. – former Secretary of the Communist Party Committee of the Vilnius Radio and Electronic Test Equipment Research Institute

Asanavičiūtė, L – one of the victims of the January events, was run over by a tank, according to the official version/

Astrauskas, V.S. – Lithuanian state and party figure. President of the LSSR Supreme Council presidium (1987-1990)

Bakatin, V.V. – USSR Interior Minister (1988-1990). The last USSR KGB Chairman (August-December 1991)

Baker, James – USA Secretary of State (1989-1992) White House Chief of Staff under President George H. W. Bush. (1992-1993)

Baklanov, O.D. – Soviet economy and political figure. USSR Minister of General Machine Construction, secretary of the CPSU CC, Hero of Socialist Labour. GKChP member.

Barannikov, V.P. – Soviet and Russian state figure, RSFSR Interior Minister

Glossary of Names 359

(1990-1991). Last USSR Interior Minister. RF Security Minister (1992-1993). General of the army.

Bartoševičius, L. – former CPL CC member, director of the CLP Central Committee publishing

Betingis, K – Lithuanian Republic Prosecutor-General investigator. Led criminal cases against the leaders of the CPL CC on CPSU platform.

Bilans, K – human rights activist, former member of the Šalčininkai district council, Was sentenced by the state in the so-called Šalčininkai separatist case for "antigovernment activity."

Bobkov, F.D. – First Deputy Chairman of the USSR KGB (1985-1991)

Bobylev, A.G. – physics engineer. Commission chairman in organizing the 17 March 1991 Vilnius region referendum. Was arrested on 7 November 1991 and imprisoned for 3 years for "antigovernment activity."

Boldin, V.I. – Soviet party figure, CC CPSU member (1988-1991). Leader of the presidential administration (17.04.1990 – 22.08.1991).

Boltunov, M.E. – colonel, military journalist and writer. Head of the Defense Ministry's referents. (1994-1997). Author of 28 books in Russia and abroad.

Bondarev, Y.V. – Russian writer. Hero of Socialist Labour, winner of the Lenin prize and two USSR state prizes.

Bradauskienė, K. – a witness in the Paleckis case. In court, said she saw people shooting from the roofs into the crowd, near the Vilnius TV tower on 13 January 1991

Brazauskas, A.M. – the First Secretary of the LSSR CP (1988). On Gorbachev's orders, in December 1989 on the 20th Congress of the CPL, took it out of the CPSU, creating a Liberal Democratic party on its platform, becoming its leader. First President of the Lithuanian Republic (1993-1998). Under his personal orders, his former comrades of the LSSR CP, Burokevi?ius and Jermalavi?ius, were kidnapped and taken out of Belarus and sentenced to prison.

Burokevičius, M.M. – professor, doctor of history, former member of the Politburo of the CPSU Central Committee, the First Secretary of the Central Committee of the CPL on CPSU platform (1990-1991). Was sentenced to 12 years of prison on the fake crime of "taking part in the attempted coup and being an accomplice in the January 1991 murders in the Lithuanian SSR."

Bush, G.H.W., Sr – 41st USA president (1989-1993)

Butkevičius, A. – First director of the National Defense Department of Lithuania. Supposed organizer of the casualties of the January events in Vilnius. A user of "color revolutions". Had a hand in creating the script for the Orange Revolution in Ukraine and the Rose Revolution in Georgia.

Butrimovich, I. – secretary of the Sovetsky region Vilnius party committee. Died in an attack by Lithuanian nationalists on the night of 13 January 1991 near the Vilnius TV tower.

Cininas, A. – Vilnius judge. Acquitted the former Vilnius OMON commander Makutynovich and HQ chief Razvodov.

Clinton, B. – 42nd USA president (1993 – 2001).

Danilov, G.I. – Belarussian state secretary on combating crime and national security (1993)
Dmitrov, G.M. – Bulgarian communist. General secretary of the Communist Party of Bulgaria (1948-1949).
Donaldson, J. – acting legal council in the UNESCO secretariat.
Dragun, O.D. – Belarussian police lieutenant-colonel in Polotsk, who handed over militiaman A. R. Smotkin to the Lithuanian government.
Dzagoyev, H. – Soviet Army sergeant who served in Vilnius. One of the ones sentenced on the Shumsk case.
Egorov, V.D. – Belarussian Interior Minister (1990-1994). He sanctioned the turnover of the CPL on CPSU platform secretaries to Lithuania.
Eismuntas, E.A. - the Chairman of the KGB of Lithuania in 1987-1990
Eiwa (Eitavicius), A. – a USA special forces captain. Fought in Afghanistan with the Taliban. Agent of Western secret services.
Falin, V.M. – diplomat, social and political figure, referent to Gromyko and Khrushchev. CPSU CC member (1989-1991). Doctor of history. Winner of USSR state prize.
Fedorov, C. – commander of the Soviet internal troops, participant in the January events.
Frolov, V. – Soviet Army colonel. Commander of the Vilnius 107th motorized rifle division after V.N. Uskhopchik.
Garmus, A. – head of the Republican forensics expert bureau in LSSR in 1991.
Gaudutis, J. – Lithuanian prosecution investigator. Was in charge of the January events investigation.
Gedvilas, M.A. – LSSR state and political figure. Communist since 1934. Interior Minister and later president of the LSSR People's Commissioner's Council (1940-1956). LSSR Education Minister (1957-1973
Gergiev, V. – famous Soviet and Russian conductor. 13 January 2012, his orchestra was harassed by Lithuanian nationalists about his concert in Kaunas.
Golovatov, M.V. – Alpha group commander (1991-1992). Chief of the operation in Vilnius.
Gorbachev, M.S. – CC CPSU General-Secretary. USSR President (1990-1991)
Grachev, P.S. – Russian state and military figure. RF Defense Minister (1992-1996)
Gribanov, N. – CPL CC on CPSU platform. He was arrested as soon as independence was declared, sentenced to a fine.
Gromov, B.V. – Soviet and Russian military and political figure. Deputy USSR Interior Minister (1991).
Gross, A. – PACE representative, who handled human rights questions in the 90s.
Grybauskaite, D. – Lithuanian politician. Former Vilnius High Party School teacher. President of Lithuania since 2009.
Ivanov, V.L. – Soviet and Russian military figure, commander of the military space forces of Russia (1992-1996).
Ivanov, V.V. – president of the Venibe-Edinstvo-Ednost organization, historian, philosopher, political prisoner. Was imprisoned twice by the Lithuanian

court for his beliefs and the book *Lithuanian Prison*.

Jermalavičius, J. – Soviet and Lithuanian political figure. Doctor of history, professor. In 1990-1991 secretary of the CPL CC on the CPSU platform. In January 1994 he was handed over by the Belarussian Interior Ministry to Lithuania. Was sentenced to 8 years of prison for his beliefs and resisting the Sąjūdists during the January events.

Juhnevičius, R. – retired Soviet army colonel, deputy chief of the military department of the Vilnius High Party School (1990-1991). Wanted by the Lithuanian prosecution.

Juonienė, S. – CC CPL on CPSU platform member, former editor of the Taryb? Lietuva (Soviet Lithuania) newspaper, Wanted by the Lithuanian prosecution since 1991.

Juozaitis, A. – Sąjūdis activist.

Jurgelis, J. – Director of the Department of National Defense LR (1993-1998)

Jurolait J. – former member of the Šalčininkai district council. Was sentenced by the state for the so-called Šalčininkai separatist case.

Juršėnas, Č. – Lithuanian politician, state and political figure of the LSSR and the Lithuanian Republic. Seimas president (1993-1996, and April-November 2008).

Kaliačius, E. – first commander of the Vilnius OMON. Joined S?j?dis in 1990 and was the Vilnius police commissioner. Was later fired for abuse of power.

Kanapinskas, A. – Sąjūdis activist, TV tower defender. Died during the January events when an improvised explosive device he made and wanted to throw at the Soviet troops exploded on his person.

Karpukhin, V.F. – Hero of the Soviet Union, commander of Alpha group at the USSR KGB 7th department (1988-1991).

Kasperavičius, E.V. – deputy chief of Civil Defense of the LSSR (1989-1991). After the January events was a TV host for the CPL CC on CPSU platform.

Kebich, V.F. - candidate in economic sciences, Belarussian politician, president of the Belarussian Minister Council (1990-1994).

Komar, I.G. – commander of the Pskov paratrooper division, participated in the January events.

Korzhakov, A.V. – candidate in economic sciences, first chief of the Security detail for the President of the Russian Federation

Kosolapov, R.I. – doctor of philosophy, professor. Author and editor-in-chief of the Kommunist.

Krempovsky, N. - deputy LSSR prosecutor-general. Was sentenced to 5 years of prison on trumped charges. Died in 1996 of a heart attack.

Kryuchkov, V.A. – Soviet state figure, USSR KGB chairman (1988-1991). GKChP member.

Kucherov, I. – professor, doctor of law, advisor at the CPL CC on CPSU platform. One of the figures of the "red professors" case. Arrested and imprisoned in 1994. Died without being sentenced.

Kuolelis, J. – Lithuanian cultural and political figure. secretary of the CPL CC on CPSU platform (1990-1991). In 1999 he was tried by the Lithuanian court and imprisoned for 6 years on charges of preparing a coup.

Kurginyan, S.E. – Soviet and Russian political figure. In 1991 he was sent to Vilnius to investigate the January events. Wrote the Lithuanian Syndrome along with V. Ovchinsky.

Kutsevich, I. - former member of the Šalčininkai district council. Was sentenced by the state for the so-called Šalčininkai separatist case. Acquitted by court.

Kuzmin, F.M. – General-colonel. Commander of the Red Banner Baltic military district (1987-1991).

Lagodny, P. – witness in the Paleckis case.

Landsbergis, V – Lithuanian politician and one of the founders of Sąjūdis former Marxism-Leninism teacher at the Lithuanian conservatory, known Russophobe. President of the Supreme Council of Lithuania (1990-1992).

Laurinkus, M. - USSR people's deputy, one of the Sąjūdis leaders, Director of the State Security Department (1990).

Lazutka V.A. – professor, doctor of philosophy, first secretary of the Vilnius ciry party committee, CPL CC on CPSU platform secretary. Political refugee.

Lekas, J. – witness on the Paleckis case. Saw shooters on the roof on the night of the January events in Vilnius. Was tried for false testimony but acquitted by the Lithuanian Supreme Court.

Lukashenko, A.G. – President of Belarus.

Lyubimov, Y.D. – USSR Prosecution investigator, chief in the commission investigation the January events.

Makutynovich, B. – former commander of the Vilnius OMON. Died in 2015

Maskhadov, A.A. – military and state figure of the unrecognized Chechen Republic of Ichkeria. Was head of artillery in the 107 motorized rifle division in Vilnius in 1990. Fought Russian Federal forces in the 1990s. Was killed in an FSB operation 8 March 2005.

Maslyukov, Y.D. – USSR deputy prime minister (1988-1991).

Matonis, A. – acting Interior Minister in 1991.

Mel, Y.N. – Russian citizen, former officer. Arrested 12 March 2014 on the border. Tried for the January events.

Mickevic, S. – Lithuanian journalist, editor-in-chief of the Soviet Lithuania radio. One of the figures in the "red professors" case. In August 1991 fled the Lithuanian Republic to Russia.

Misukonis, M. – LSSR Interior Minister, later LR Interior Minister (1990-1992).

Mitkova, T.R. – Soviet and Russian journalist, TV host, deputy CEO of the "NTV."

Mlynnik, C. – commander of the Riga OMON since February 1991. Has moved to Russia after the OMON was disbanded.

Modrow, H. – German politician, one of the last GDR leaders.

Moiseev, M.A. – Soviet and Russian military and political figure, head of the USSR Armed Forces HQ, first deputy USSR Defense Minister (1988-1991).

Nagorny, S. – secretary of the Vilnius city committee of the CPL on CPSU platform during the January events.
Nasinovsku, V.E. – deputy secretary of the Defense Council, head of the information-analytical center (1992-1993)
Naudži?nas, A.J. - General-Major, head of the political department of the Baikonur rocket division and Baikonur cosmodrome (1986-1989). Elected into CPL CC numerous times, wanted by Lithuanian prosecution for a coup attempt.
Neris, S. – LSSR national poetess.
Nevzorov, A.G. – Soviet and Russian journalist, reporter, TV host, publicist. Director and producer of noteworthy documentaries.
Nikulin (Mikhailov), K. – former Riga OMON member. Changed name, was in witness protection in Latvia, but then handed over to Lithuania. Sentenced to life in prison in the Medininkai case without any evidence.
Nishanov, R.N. – Soviet diplomat, Soviet and Uzbek state and political figure. President of the Council of Nationalities in the USSR Supreme Council. Advisor to the USSR President.
Oleynikov, A.A. – deputy chairman of the USSR KGB.
Orlov, V.V. – Shumsk case, was sentenced to 3 years of prison for his beliefs.
Osipov, A – former LSSR KGB member.
Ozolas, R – Lithuanian political figure. Sąjūdis founder, Landsbergis ally, Russophobe. Seimas member (1992-2000), died in 2015.
Paleckis, A – Lithuanian politician figure, Socialist People's Front founder. November 2010 said the phrase "as it turns out, our men were shooting our own", which saw him ostracized, tried and sentenced to a 3000 euro fine.
Parfenov, S. – deputy commander of the Riga OMON. 8 September 1991 was arrested by Latvian policemen in Surgut, Russia and taken to Riga. Imprisoned for 3 years.
Patiashvili, D.I. – first secretary of the Georgian Communist Party CC (1985-1989).
Paulauskas, A – former CPL CC member, Sąjūdis activist, Latvian Prosecutor-general (1990-1995), head of the state security committee of the LR Seimas.
Pavlov, V.S. – Soviet state figure. USSR Finance Minister (1989-1991). President of the USSR Minister Council. GKChP member.
Petkevičius, V – Lithuanian writer and political figure, one of the founders and leaders of Sąjūdis. Lithuanian Seimas member (1992-1996). Author of the book *Ship of Fools*.
Petrauskas, A - General-Major of Justice. General-prosecutor of the LSSR until 1991. Wanted by the Lithuanian prosecution.
Pikauskas, O.M. – general-colonel, deputy commander of the USSR paratroopers. Died in 1995.
Plekhanov, Y.C. – Soviet party and state figure, lieutenant-general, head of the USSR KGB 9th department.
Prokofyev, Y.A – Soviet party figure. CPSU CC Politburo member, CPSU

CC member (1990-1991). First secretary of the Moscow city CPSU committee (1989-1990).

Prokopovich, Y. – LSSR police captain. Was sentenced to 4 years of prison for taking unregistered weapons away from S?j?dis members.

Prunskienė, K. – Lithuanian economist and politician, first prime minister of the Lithuanian Republic. Founder of the concept of LSSR economic independence.

Pugo, B.K. – president of party control committee of the CPSU CC (1988-1991), USSR Interior Minister (1987-1991). GKChP member.

Raugalienė, D. – witness in the Paleckis case. Testified in court that she heard shots fired from the roofs of the buildings near the Vilnius TV tower. Was charged with false testimony, but later acquitted.

Rayackas, R. – LSSR Academy of Sciences, Sąjūdis member.

Razvodov, V. – former head of the Vilnius OMON. Charged with war crimes and crimes against humanity, but was acquitted by the Lithuanian court.

Reagan, R. – 40th USA president (1981-1989).

Reznik, S. – former CPL CC worker. Spent 11 months in prison.

Riga OMON – Riga squad of police special forces of the Latvian SSR. Existed from 1988 until 1991.

Rodionov, I.N. – USSR state and military figure, RF Defense Minister (1996-1997).

Roschin, V.M. –Vilnius OMON, wanted by Lithuanian prosecution since 1991 for not allowing the Lithuanian gangs to be armed with police weapons.

Rostropovich, M.L. – famous cellist, pianist and conductor, human rights activist, five-time Grammy winner.

Ryzhkov, N.I. – president of the USSR Minister Council, CPSU CC Politburo member (1985-1991).

Šepetis, L. – CPL CC secretary on ideology in LSSR, one of the creators of S?j?dis.

Shaimiyev, M.Sh. – Soviet and Russian state and political figure. President of Tatarstan (1991-2010).

Sharp, G. – American writer, known worldwide for his books on non-violent struggles against authoritarian regimes.

Shatskikh, V.I. – mother of Alpha group lieutenant Viktor Shatskikh.

Shatskikh, V.V. - Alpha group lieutenant. Killed by a shot in the back when entering the LSSR TV and Radio committee during the January events.

Shebarshin, L.V. – Soviet intelligence figure, lieutenant-general, head of the USSR Foreign Intelligence (1989-1991), acting USSR KGB Chairman 22-23 August 1991.

Shechkus, A.Y. – first secretary of the CPL CC (1940-1974). Hero of Socialist Labour.

Shein, V.V. – former secretary of the LSSR Interior Ministry party committee.

Shenin, O.S. – Soviet party and state figure, Russian politician, Politburo member, CPSU CC secretary (1990-1993) GKChP member.

Shevardnadze, E.A. – Soviet and Georgian political and state figure. USSR

Glossary of Names 365

MFA (1985-1990). Georgian President (1995-2003). Hero of Socialist Labour, Gorbachev's closest ally.

Shibalko, A.G. – police colonel, heard of the Borisov police department (Belarus) (1986-1995).

Shirkovsky, E.I. – Belarussian KGB chairman (1990-1994).

Sholodonov, V.I. – Belarussian Prosecutor-General (1992-1995).

Shorokhov, V. – "red" militiaman, one of the men from the Shumsk case. Spent 2.5 years in a Lithuanain prison for his beliefs.

Shushkevich, S.S. – president of the Belarus Supreme Council (1991-1994).

Shved, Vladislav - Russian publicist and writer, formerly a member of the Lithuanian SSR Supreme Council and second secretary of the Communist Part Central Committee. Currently wanted by the Prosecutor's Office of the Lithuanian Republic, accused of being part of the 13 January 1991 events

Šimkus, S. – rector of the Vilnius High Party School.

Šimulionis, I – one of the victims of the January Events.

Skučas, A – first security chief of the Lithuanian Supreme Council (1991).

Smotkin, A.R. – "red' militiamen, was handed over in November 1991 by the Belarussian SSR to Lithuania and arrested. Sentenced for the Shumsk case for 8 years.

Sobchak, A.A. – Soviet and Russian political figure. First mayor of Saint-Petersburg.

Stakvilavičius, N. – S?j?dis member, first secretary of the Šiauliai city party committee.

Stanchikas, S. – USSR Internal troops colonel, LSSR police regiment commander, joined Landsbergis in 1991.

Stankaitis, J. – journalist, was beaten to death by Sąjūdis supporters.

Stankevich, A. – LSSR Interior Ministry forensics department expert. Later an expert for the Vilnius OMON.

Stankevich, S.B. – Russian politician, one of the leaders of the Moscow People's Front (1988-1989). USSR people's deputy. Political advisor to President Yeltsin (1991-1993).

Stankevičius, R. – test pilot. Tested the Buran space shuttle. Died in Italy, during a training flight.

Suschik, B. – deputy commander of the artillery division, Pskov paratrooper, one of the people tried in absentia on the January events.

Trubin, H.S. – Soviet state figure. Last USSR Prosecutor-General (1990-1992).

Tsaplin, S.A. – LSSR KGB deputy chairman. General-major. Killed in Moscow under uncertain circumstances on 3 January 1995.

Tudorake, V. - State Small Theatre of Vilnius set designer. One of the "protectors" of the Vilnius TV tower in January 1991.

Uskhopchik, V.N. – lieutenant-general (ret). Commander of the Vilnius 107th motorized rifle division since January 1989 in Vilnius.

Vaišvila, Z. – Lithuanian politician, businessman, one of the signatories of the Lithuanian Act of Independence.

Valaitis, S. – Lithuanian Republic prosecution investigator in the 1990s.

Vare, R. – Estonian state figure, one of Gene Sharp's students. Was an Estonian Minister. Currently head of the Estonian Development fund.

Varennikov, V.I. – commander of the Land troops, deputy USSR Defense Minister, member of the USSR Defense Council (1989-1991).

Vasilenko, P. – head of the people militia at the LSSR city party committee in 1991, assumed to have worked with the Lithuanian secret services on the Medininkai case.

Vasiliev, A.V. – Soviet and Russian lawyer. First deputy of the USSR Prosecutor-General (1989-1991).

Vidmantas I. secretary of the Mažeikiai CPL regional party committee, the first political prisoner in Lithuania's new recent history. Thrown into prison for the Šal?ininkai separatist case. Was acquitted after 7 months.

Vilnius OMON – a police special forces unit in the city of Vilnius, LSSR. Created in 1988. Was under USSR Interior Ministry control January-August 1991. Disbanded after the August coup. Commander – B. Makutynkovich.

Visockis, Č. – Lithuanian exile communist. Granted refuge in Belarus by President Lukashenko. Secretary of the CPL CC, one the Šal?ininkai separatist case.

Yakovlev, A.N. – Soviet and Russian political figure, academic of Russian Academy of Science, one of the main Perestroika ideologues. CPSU member from 1944 until 1991, CC CPSU secretary (1986-1990), CC CPSU Politburo member (1987 – 1990).

Yanaev, G.I. – Soviet party and state figure, USSR vice-president (1990-1991), Politburo member, CC CPSU secretary (1990-1991). During the 19-21 August 1991 events was acting USSR President and de facto leader of the coup.

Yankelevich, L. – former member of the Šalčininkai district council. Was sentenced by the state for the so-called Šal?ininkai separatist case.

Yazov, D.T. – USSR Marshal, USSR Defense Minister (1987-1991). One of the people tried in absentia for the January Events.

Yeltsin, B.N. – the president of the Russian Federation (1991-1999).

Zagryadsky, S. – head of the consul department of the Russian embassy to Lithuania (1991-1996).

ENDNOTES

Introduction

1   As the coup in Russian failed, with the temporary power vacuum in the country, the "parade of sovereignties" began: former Soviet Republics declared their independence one after the other and the West recognized them.
2   Latvia and Estonia were a lot harder towards people of other nationalities than Lithuania. Almost all, immediately upon gaining independence, adopted a Citizenship law, where only those of the titular nation would be allowed to get citizenship. Lithuania just gave citizenship to all of the country's residents, Russians included.
3   A political coup in August 1991 by those who were protesting the USSR's destruction. The reason was their dissatisfaction with Mikhail Gorbachev's policies. The coup lasted for three days and failed, only speeding up the Soviet Union's downfall. All of the coup's organizers, GKChP members , were arrested.

Chapter 1

1   The *Ogonek* (Огонёк) journal was USSR's main source of information on the Perestroika, with a print run of many millions. It published the sensational exposures on Stalin and the repressions, making the readers think that everything was the Russians' fault.
2   One of the infamous tricks, used with large crowds of people, when a "sacred sacrifice" was needed for the revolution to start: unknown snipers appear and shoot into the crowd, as they did in Baku in 1990, Moscow in 1993 and Kiev in 2014. See Stephen Lendman, *Flashpoint in Ukraine: How the US Drive for Hegemony Risks World War III*, Clarity Press, 2014, p. 84.
3   During its period of independence from the USSR, Lithuania's population dropped 28%, from 3,700,000 to 2,650,000 people.
4   It was anticipated that Gorbachev's address would explain to the Lithuanian nation the reasons for implementing presidential rule. Insofar as Russian was the USSR's state language, the message would be broadcast in Russian.

5   Marshal is the highest military rank in USSR, only appointed during wartime. Yazov was the last officer of the USSR to get the title of Marshal.
6   Yazov was one of the people behind the failed August Coup and spent 2 years in a prison in Moscow, suspected of treason of his homeland (USSR), but was then cleared of all charges, because his homeland (USSR) no longer existed and so there was no one to betray.
7   Lithuania's accusations are a joke, because, first of all, Lithuania was officially part of the USSR in 1991, secondly, Yazov personally, was never in Lithuania. In other words, the current Lithuanian government was accusing him of attempting to overthrow it back in 1991, when it did not in fact exist.
8   This was Gorbachev's last attempt to keep his grip on the Soviet Union: according to the Union of Sovereign States Charter, the organization would be built upon the principles of a confederation, the republics would have a lot more rights and could act as sovereign states in foreign relations. This compromise did not sit well with those who wanted to save the USSR, so they organized the August Coup in order to stop the signing of the Union agreement.
9   The effort was to preserve these countries as republics of the USSR since it was not in his place to dissolve it, and to preserve the territories of the republics themselves.
10 Russian Soviet Federative Socialist Republic, as in Russia as part of the Soviet Union.

Chapter 2

1   The tank guns indeed fired, but only with dummy shells; a later interviewee speaks of plastic pieces from those.
2   https://www.rferl.org/a/Gene_Sharp_Theoretician_Of_Velvet_Revolution/1889473.html The following websites are but a few of the listings presently available on Gene Sharp:
http://www.gumilev-center.ru/cvetnye-revolyucii/
http://kerb.livejournal.com/174346.html
http://dfedbees.livejournal.com/496331.html
http://propaganda-journal.net/8020.html
https://topwar.ru/12018-kak-oranzhevaya-revolyuciya-spotknulas-na-venesuele.html
http://serfilatov.livejournal.com/tag/%D0%A8%D0%B0%D1%80%D0%BF
http://serfilatov.livejournal.com/1518810.html
http://dokumentika.org/lt/pasaul-zi-ra/dzhin-sharp-razrabotchik-

revoliutsionnich-technologiy-tsvetnich-revoliutsiy
http://vlasti.net/news/118917
https://nstarikov.ru/blog/41943

3   The Forest Brethren were Estonian, Latvian, and Lithuanian partisans who waged a guerrilla war against Soviet rule during, and after, World War II. They were supported by Nazi Germany and took part in punitive operations against the local population and the Jewish population.

4   Direct presidential rule was the consolidation of power by the president during times of the country's instability. In this case, it was assumed that Gorbachev would cancel the laws of the Lithuanian Republic that contradicted the USSR Constitution and threatened to divide the country. But this never happened.

5   Kazimira Prunskienė – a Lithuanian economist and politician, the first Prime Minister of Lithuania since it declared independence unilaterally in March 1990. Lithuania's independence was not recognized by the world until August 1991. She was the Prime Minister for less than a year. She has retired from politics due to health issues.

6   In Autumn of 1993, there was a large internal political conflict in Moscow due to the President and Government clashing, which led to armed clashes. As a result 124 people died, 350 were wounded. "Unknown snipers" were also spotted on the roofs that day.

7   FSK - Federal Counterintelligence Service, FSB - Federal Security Service. Both Russian.

Chapter 3

1   In this context, patriotism refers to the Lithuanian Republic (LSSR) or the USSR in general, while nationalistic refers to the ethnic Lithuanians.
2   Infantry Fighting Vehicle
3   https://en.wikipedia.org/wiki/Soviet_deportations_from_Lithuania
4   https://en.wikipedia.org/wiki/The_Holocaust_in_Lithuania

Chapter 4

1   State Committee of the State of Emergency – the ones behind the failed August Coup in Russia.
2   Parliamentary Assembly of the Council of Europe.
3   The lack of political prisoners is one of the main requirements for joining the EU. This was the reason that Ukraine and Turkey were denied accession in 2017.
4   "Grach" means "Rook" in Russian

Chapter 5

1   Vytautas Landsbergis was the president of the Supreme Council of Lithuania and the leader of the Sąjūdis party. He was not given power by anyone, they took it themselves, appointing him as the leader. The tricked people didn't resist and blindly trusted him. During the tumultuous times in the USSR back then, this was completely doable.

Chapter 6

1   Slang for secret service agent., referencing the former Soviet national security agency (1917-1922).
2   A Ukrainian slur for Russians.

Chapter 7

1   OMON – a Special Purpose Mobility Unit.
2   Nevzorov is one of those people who are always in the opposition. In the late 80s, he was against Gorbachev, in the early 90s he was against Yeltsin's team, then for a while he was against the Church as the institute between people and religion, and now he is a critic of Putin. But as time shows, sometimes he is right in his protest.
3   Vladimir Razvodov, chief of the Vilnius OMON, along with Boleslav Makutynovich (died in 2015) were first cleared of all charges by the Vilnius District Court, but after an appeal came in, he was sentenced in absentia to 12 years for "crimes against humanity" on the "USSR Aggression against Lithuania" case
4   Infantry Fighting Vehicles
5   Officially called the Pridnestrovian Moldavian Republic, it is an unrecognized state in the Transnistria region, formally part of Moldova. It is a multinational (populated by Moldovans, Ukrainians and Russians) state and spoke out in favor of saving the USSR and against aggressive nationalism. It declared its independence after the August Coup. This was the cause of an armed conflict with Moldovan nationalists in 1992, which led to many casualties. The conflict was suppressed thanks to the Russian Army, but it is still "frozen." Moldova doesn't recognize the existence of the Pridnestrovian Moldavian Republic, considering it a Moldovan autonomy.

Chapter 8

1   Soviet Union's Interior Ministry, officially called "The People's Commissariat for Internal Affairs."

Chapter 9

1. Spetsnaz, abbreviation for Войска специáльного назначéния, (Voyska **spets**ialnogo **naz**nacheniya) is an umbrella term for special forces in Russian and is used in numerous post-Soviet states
2. BTR is a Russian Armored Personnel Carrier
3. Because the regular TV broadcast was stopped, and the TV station started showing the Swan Lake ballet to fill the air time.

Chapter 10

1. http://thestar.ie/about-us/tag/lithuanian-mafia-crime-group/
http://www.politics.ie/forum/justice/10361-latvian-lithuanian-crime-ireland.html
https://www.numbeo.com/crime/compare_countries_result.jsp?country1=Lithuania&country2=Ireland
2. Russian wake ceremonies are done 9 days after the death and another one is done 40 days after the death.
3. Meaning KGB. There are many pieces of evidence that Vytautas Landsbergis worked with the Soviet state security services, with the agent code name "Grandpa"
4. Butkevičius' conflict with Langsbergis started at the very first days of the Sąjūdis' founding and was due to their personal ambitions and the fight for power and a place in history as fighters for Lithuania's independence. Neither have shied away from various tactics: Landsbergis publicly accused Butkevičius of scamming people, and Butkevičius accused Landsbergis of working with the KGB.
5. The events of the Maidan in Kiev led to clashes between supporters and opponents of Ukraine's European integration throughout Ukraine. 2 May 2014, during street clashes, the Ukrainian nationalists cornered a group of pro-Russian minded residents of the city of Odessa at the Labour Union House and set it on fire. According to the police, 50 people died. The pro-Ukrainian press sinisterly said that the people locked themselves inside voluntarily and set themselves on fire. See also Stephen Lendman, *Flashpoint in Ukraine: How the US Drive for Hegemony Risks World War III*, Clarity Press, 2014.
6. Parliamentary Assembly of the Council of Europe

INDEX

13 January 1991 Events, Vilnius TV tower incident – 10, 84 (and sooner) – 10, 12-15, 18-20, 24, 26-27, 41-42, 53-54, 70, 74-75. 78. 80-92. 94-99, 102, 111-116, 125-128, 132, 140, 155, 158, 169-170, 176, 184, 199, 208, 217, 227, 242, 250, 262, 267, 276, 280, 292, 305, 322-332, 336-338, 348, 350-355

A

Antonenko, Alexey – 215-225
Antonov, Vladmir – 153-162, 177
August Coup – 9-11, 29, 36-39, 44, 54, 64, 67, 92, 96, 108, 117, 125, 128, 131, 135, 159-160, 178, 201, 222, 226, 262, 276-277, 288, 299

B

Bilotas, Boleslavas – 81-82
Bobylev, Alexander – 226-238, 242, 246
Bradauskienė, Kristina – 81
Brazauskas, Algirdas – 108, 125, 135, 156, 172, 257, 272, 282, 286
Burokevičius Mykolas – 12, 94-95, 112, 122-130, 143-148, 150-151, 154, 161-162, 167, 170-172, 177, 181, 187, 206, 219, 246-247, 258, 272, 277, 279, 304, 308, 323, 352, 355
Butkevicius, Audrius – 14, 25, 27, 41-49, 52-53, 72, 77, 80, 113, 141, 143, 158, 170, 236, 240, 267, 314, 324-328, 330

D

Dzagoyev, Hetag – 228, 232, 239-240, 245, 253

E

Eismuntas, Eduardas – 69-70

G

Garmus, Antanas - 109
Gaudutis, Juozas – 301, 304
Gedvilas, Mečislovas – 127-128
Golovatov, Mikhail – 14-25, 298, 331
Gorbachev, Mikhail – 9-10, 12, 14, 20, 24, 27, 29-41, 45, 47, 51-52, 59, 61-67, 69, 96, 113, 116-117, 125, 127-128, 136, 140-141, 159, 162, 169-171, 177-178, 181-183, 189, 191, 216, 230, 245, 272-274, 276, 279, 281, 284, 288, 298, 307, 318, 327, 331-334, 336, 338, 345-346
Grach, Yan – 114, 118-120
Grybauskaitė, Dalia – 166-168, 188, 272, 307, 335-336

I

Ivanov, Valery – 12, 73, 87, 95-106, 143, 217, 232, 242, 261, 274, 310

J

Jermalavičius, Juozas – 12, 94-95, 112, 122, 136-148, 150-151, 154, 161-162, 187, 247, 266, 277, 279, 308, 355
Juknevičius, Romas Konstantino – 270-281, 355
Juonienė, Stalislava – 174-181, 314

K

Kasperavičius, Edmundas – 261-270, 272, 355
Krempovsky, Nikolay – 309-311
Kryuchkov, Vladimir – 26-27, 32, 35, 37-38, 60-61, 63, 67, 69, 170, 182,

Index

196, 285, 299, 304, 314, 327, 338, 343, 345
Kucherov, Igor – 114-120
Kucherov, Ivan – 94-95, 106-122, 180, 261
Kuolelis, Juozas – 12, 73, 77, 94, 122, 130-136, 145, 354

L

Lagodny, Pavel – 81
Landsbergis, Vytautas – 13-15, 18-20, 27-28, 59, 65, 71, 75-78, 80-81, 84, 112-113, 124, 127, 133, 135, 140-142, 169-171, 206, 211, 217, 220, 266, 272-274, 276-277, 280, 285, 287, 289, 297, 325, 335
Lazutka, Valentin – 157, 161, 163-173
Lekas, Jaunutis – 82, 85.
Lukashenko, Aleksandr – 119, 145, 161, 182, 187-188, 280

M

Makutynovich, Boleslav – 178, 187, 193, 195, 197, 205, 208, 210-211, 219, 237, 252
Maskhadov, Aslan – 27, 171, 203, 212
Medininkai incident (or Medininkai massacre) – 102, 206, 210-211, 218-221, 237-238, 246, 256, 332-333
Mel, Yuri – 15, 205, 207, 209, 211, 213, 215, 217, 219, 221, 223, 303, 331, 347-352
Mļinņiks, Česlavs - 210

N

Naudžiūnas, Algimantas – 266, 272, 278, 281-291
Nevzorov, Alexander – 192-197, 208, 210.

O

OMON - 178, 187, 192-226, 232, 234, 237, 241-242, 252-254, 256, 277, 300, 307
Orlov, Viktor – 228, 232, 239-247, 261
Osipov, Alexander – 318-328

Ostroumov, Georgy – 34-40
Ovchinsky, Vladimir – 59-69

P

Paleckis, Algirdas – 12, 16, 18, 46, 72-80, 82-85, 89, 91, 128, 142, 351, 354, 356
Paulauskas, Artūras – 147, 150, 202, 295-296, 306, 309
Petrauskas, Antanas – 292-301, 309, 355
Pugo, Boris – 26-27, 37, 64, 67, 203

R

Raugalienė, Danguolė – 83-85
Razvodov, Vladimir – 205-214, 223, 234, 252
Roschin, Viktor – 197-205, 223

S

Sąjūdis – 13, 15, 25, 35, 61-62, 64, 67, 75-76, 78, 81-82, 95, 101, 103, 112, 157, 159-161, 163, 165-168, 171, 175, 186, 194, 199, 207-208, 216-217, 237-238, 251, 264, 271, 275-276, 278, 287-288, 331, 355
Sharp, Gene – 25, 41-45, 49-58, 62, 176, 322, 329, 355
Shatskikh, Valentina – 336-347
Shatskikh, Viktor – 12, 21-23, 28, 61, 155, 197, 236, 298, 336-347
Sheyin, Vladimir – 153, 154-162
Shved, Vladislav – 328-336
Šimulionis, Ignas – 16, 109-110
Smotkin, Alexander – 228-229 246-261, 308, 310, 313
Sniečkus, Antanas – 127-128, 215
Sushchik, Bogdan – 301-303

T

Tsaplin, Stanislav – 12, 19, 62, 67, 299-300, 311-318, 323, 325-326
Tudorakė, Valentinas – 86-92

V

Varennikov, Valentin – 27-28, 30, 31,

373

Index

126, 169.
Venibe-Edinstvo-Ednost – 232, 242, 274
Visockis, Česlav – 181-191

Y

Yazov, Dmitry – 25-35, 37-39, 61, 194-196, 271, 277, 281, 299, 303, 305, 334
Yegorov, Vladimir – 147-152, 308
Yeltsin, Boris – 10, 12-13, 18, 30-31, 34-40, 68, 162, 183, 213, 260, 276-277, 289, 307